YALE HISTORICAL PUBLICATIONS

David Horne, Editor
Miscellany 66

*Published under the direction
of the Department of History
with assistance from the income of the
Frederick John Kingsbury Memorial Fund*

AMERICAN IMMIGRATION POLICY, *1924-1952*

BY ROBERT A. DIVINE

NEW HAVEN

YALE UNIVERSITY PRESS, 1957

London: Oxford University Press

To My Mother and My Father

America is God's crucible, the great Melting-Pot, where all the races of Europe are melting and re-forming! Germans and Frenchmen, Irishmen and Englishmen, Jews and Russians—into the crucible with you all! God is making the American.

Israel Zangwill, The Melting Pot

Wide open and unguarded stand our gates,
And through them presses a wild motley throng—
O Liberty, white Goddess! is it well
To leave the gates unguarded?

Thomas Bailey Aldrich, Unguarded Gates

PREFACE

In 1924 the United States embarked on a policy of immigration restriction which has had a far-reaching influence on the social, economic, and cultural patterns of American life. The wisdom and justice of the restrictive policy were warmly debated at the time of its inception, and the controversy has continued to rage with varying degrees of intensity ever since. My purpose here is to trace the course of the restrictive immigration policy through the second quarter of the 20th century. By focusing on the controversy between the supporters and opponents of restriction, I have sought to uncover the basic factors involved in the formulation of this policy. The aim has been neither to praise nor to condemn the policy of restriction, but rather to provide understanding and insight into a major problem of modern American history.

My main concern is the policy of the federal government toward the admission of foreigners who intended to become permanent residents of the United States; no attempt has been made to trace governmental activity toward aliens once they had been granted entry into the country: though questions of deportation and naturalization are significant parts of the over-all immigration problem, they have little bearing on the central issue—the regulation of immigration into the United States. For the same reason governmental policy toward aliens who entered the country temporarily—tourists, diplomats, students, transient laborers—has not been considered. The emphasis thus remains on the evolution of a governmental program designed to control the quantity and quality of aliens who offered themselves as permanent additions to the American population.

The study began as a research paper in a seminar conducted by Ralph Gabriel, and I wish to acknowledge my debt to Mr. Gabriel for his encouragement and sound advice; his patient criticism has removed many of the more glaring faults from this work. I am also grateful to T. K. Wolfe and William Goetzmann for many helpful suggestions, to Archibald Foord for arousing my interest in the study of history, and to my wife for her many contributions. Finally, I wish to express my debt to the University of Texas Research Institute for the financial assistance they have rendered.

R.A.D.

Austin, Texas
January 1957

CONTENTS

1. Introduction: The Development of Restriction

ONE OF THE most remarkable features of 19th-century America was the absence of any clearly defined immigration policy. In an era when the tariff question was a perennial political issue and the barriers were gradually raised against the influx of goods and manufactures, there was no regulation of the movement of humanity into the country. Immigration was allowed to ebb and flow of its own accord, guided mainly by a fluctuating economic barometer in both Europe and America.

But if there was no official policy, there were, very definitely, popular attitudes toward immigration which by the end of the century had developed into traditional ideals. And the most deeply imbedded ideal was that America was a refuge for the oppressed of Europe, a belief that had its beginnings with the Pilgrim fathers and had continued and developed during contact with the Scotch-Irish of the 18th century and the German 48'ers of the 19th. Along with this asylum concept there was a second ideal which had developed more recently—the belief that the United States was a melting pot in which Europeans were transformed into Americans by an almost mystical process. This second conviction was neither so simple nor so deeply rooted as the asylum ideal, and in the course of time became subject to varying interpretations. Until the 1880's, then, laissez-faire characterized American immigration policy, and open arms was the popular attitude. Everywhere there was confidence that immigrants could be easily absorbed into the life of the nation.

Why this lack of a well-defined policy and why such optimistic ideals? Economically the country was young and underdeveloped, with an urgent need for new recruits to assist in the occupation of the West and the building of industry. In an era before vast technological changes substituted the machine for human labor, immigrants were welcome additions to the nation's supply of manpower. The newcomers furnished the labor for development of natural resources, creation of a railroad network, and growth of an industrial system. Equally important, the influx of foreigners was not viewed as a divisive force in the development of the nation because a feeling of intense nationalism had not yet grown up in the United States. Isolated from the bitter rivalries of European nations and militarily secure from attack by strong powers, Americans in the 19th century had little reason to fear that the influx of aliens would destroy national solidarity. Thus the governmental policy and the popular attitudes were in harmony—immigration was treated as a natural process which benefited the nation.

The beginning of a more sharply defined policy toward European immigration came in the 1880's but was in no way a clean break with the prevailing attitudes.[1] In 1882 Congress passed a law excluding convicts, lunatics, idiots, and paupers. This type of legislation had already been adopted by state governments, particularly in New York and Massachusetts, but in 1876 the Supreme Court had ruled such state laws unconstitutional.[2] The underlying principle of this 1882 legislation was that the government could select individual immigrants, but the law was negative in its approach, with no attempt to establish criteria for choosing those who might be most valuable to the country. But this practice of weeding out obvious undesirables continued as the basis of governmental policy until the enactment of restriction in the 20th century. The sole exception was the contract labor law passed in 1885 at the behest of organized labor, a blanket prohibition of employers from recruiting labor in Europe and paying for their passage across the Atlantic.[3]

Soon after the inception of the new federal policy, an increasing demand for immigration restriction arose, reaching a peak in the mid-1890's. There were several factors which contributed to the movement, probably the most important of which was the change in the sources of European immigration at this time. Until the 1880's, immigration had stemmed largely from the countries of northwestern Eu-

1. For a discussion of oriental immigration policy see below, pp. 18–23.
2. Roy Garis, *Immigration Restriction* (New York, 1927), p. 88; Henry Pratt Fairchild, *Immigration* (New York, 1925), pp. 79–83; Jeremiah W. Jenks and W. Jett Lauck, *The Immigration Problem* (New York, 1917), pp. 328–9. The Court held that immigration was part of foreign commerce and therefore beyond the jurisdiction of state action.
3. George M. Stephenson, *A History of American Immigration* (New York, 1926), p. 143.

rope, particularly Great Britain, Germany, and Scandinavia, but by 1890 these immigrants were outnumbered by those from southeastern Europe.[4] These new immigrants from Italy, Poland, and the Austro-Hungarian Empire brought with them cultural patterns and traits which gave rise to an increasing degree of friction between native Americans and the recent arrivals. Coupled with this shift in source was the climate of crisis that existed in the 1890's. Agrarian distress and financial panic intensified the hostility of many Americans toward the new immigrants. Finally, there was a widespread fear that the United States had suddenly reached the limits of its land supply—the passing of the frontier was viewed with alarm by Frederick Jackson Turner and others.[5] Out of this complex there developed a movement to restrict immigration which continued with varying degrees of success until it achieved total victory in 1924.

The agitation for restriction developed on two levels in the 1890's—a purely emotional appeal to nativist sentiments and a more reasoned argument directed toward thoughtful people. The nativist side can best be seen in the activity of the American Protective Association, which grew up in the Middle West in the late 1880's. Playing upon existing prejudices against aliens and Catholics, the APA stirred up much bitter feeling without achieving any of its legislative objectives.[6] At the same time, in the East, prominent intellectuals were leading a movement for restriction. One of the earliest of these restrictionists was General Francis A. Walker, president of Massachusetts Institute of Technology, who stressed the seriousness of the immigration problem in his presidential address to the American Economic Association in 1890.[7] The founding of the American edition of the *Review of Reviews* provided the restrictive movement with an organ which continually emphasized the dangers of free immigration. The restrictionists were well under way by 1894, when John Fiske, Nathaniel Shaler, and Senator Henry Cabot Lodge organized the Immigration Restriction League in Boston.[8] For the first time in American history responsible

4. See statistics in Appendix A.
5. Lee Benson, "The Historical Background of Turner's Frontier Essay," *Agricultural History*, 25 (1951), 72–6.
6. Stephenson, p. 146.
7. Benson, p. 72.
8. Ibid., pp. 74–5; Harvey Wish, *Society and Thought in Modern America* (New York, 1952), p. 268.

men were leading a serious campaign to limit European immigration.

The immediate objective of the opponents of immigration was the passage of a literacy test law which, though ostensibly selective in theory, would prove restrictive in operation. Such a bill was proposed in Congress in 1896 and passed both houses by overwhelming margins. President Cleveland vetoed the bill, however, terming it a "radical departure" from previous policy. The veto was overridden in the House of Representatives, but the support of southern senators sustained it in the upper house.[9] The agitation subsided for a few years with the return of prosperity and the shift in public attention to war and imperialism. The principle of individual selection was reaffirmed in the law of 1903, which added to the excluded list epileptics, beggars, anarchists, and all who believed in the forceful overthrow of the government. An attempt to pass a literacy test provision in 1907 was defeated by the expediency of creating a commission to investigate the immigration question and make recommendations for future legislation.[10]

The Immigration Commission formed in 1907 played a vital role in the evolution of immigration policy in the United States. Composed of nine members—three senators, three representatives, and three presidential appointees—the Commission made an exhaustive survey of the impact of immigration on American life, which was published in forty-two volumes in 1911. The significance of the report lies in the fact that though it was labeled an objective and scientific study of the problem, the bias of the members was evident in its findings. The Commission, with one member dissenting, concluded that restriction of immigration was "demanded by economic, moral, and social considerations" and recommended the enactment of a literacy test.[11] A noteworthy feature of the report was the contrast drawn between the old and the new immigrants. The old immigrants were portrayed as hardy pioneers who had helped develop the United States and had become an integral part of the nation, while the new immigrants were viewed as latecomers who had migrated to cash in on American

9. Stephenson, p. 149; John Higham, *Strangers in the Land: Patterns of American Nativism, 1860–1925* (New Brunswick, 1955), pp. 104–5.

10. Garis, pp. 110–13; Fairchild, p. 389.

11. *Abstracts of Reports of the Immigration Commission* (Washington, 1911), *1*, 48.

prosperity and had failed to assimilate with the older population.[12] As a result of this comparison, the concept of old and new immigrants developed into a stereotype implying a value judgment.

The recommendation of the Immigration Commission in favor of the literacy test renewed the agitation for that measure, and in 1913 Congress responded by passing a literacy test bill; it was vetoed by Taft. In 1915 and again in 1917 Wilson vetoed similar measures, declaring that a literacy test was a test of opportunity and not of character. In his view, the ability to read was no measure of a man's innate capacity, which Wilson felt was the only essential requirement for immigrants. But by 1917 the restrictionists in Congress had greatly increased in number and were able to pass the test over Wilson's veto.[13]

The literacy test marks a transition in the development of American immigration policy. Outwardly it conformed to the tradition of individual selection, adding an educational qualification to the physical, mental, and moral requirements previously established. But in essence it was a restrictive measure aimed at reducing the number of immigrants. Advocates of the test frankly admitted the purpose of the law and believed that it would decrease immigration by 25 per cent.[14] Even more significant was the fact that the law was designed to reduce the flow of immigrants from southeastern Europe, where the illiteracy rate was high. A new principle, group selection, was evident in such discrimination directed against the new immigration, and this concept of judging men by their national and racial affiliations rather than by their individual qualifications was to become the basic principle in the immigration legislation of the postwar period.

On May 29, 1921, President Harding signed the first bill in American history explicitly restricting European immigration. This law established the quota system, by which immigration was confined to 3 per cent of the number of foreign born of each European nationality residing in the United States in 1910. The number of European immigrants was reduced to a maximum of 355,000 a year, 55 per cent from northwestern Europe and 45 per cent from southeastern. In effect the old immigration was permitted at the prewar level while the new immigra-

12. Ibid., pp. 13, 23–4.
13. Stephenson, pp. 153, 166–9.
14. Fairchild, p. 383.

tion was drastically lowered to roughly 20 per cent of the 1914 total.

The 1921 quota law was a rejection of the traditional ideal of America as the asylum for the downtrodden of Europe, an ideal which was discarded because of the climate of crisis which prevailed in Congress at this time. The law was based on the belief that millions of war-torn Europeans were about to descend on the United States—a veritable flood which would completely subvert the traditional American way of life. Only the erection of a legislative barrier could prevent the impending catastrophe. As a result, in 1920 the House of Representatives had even voted to suspend immigration altogether, though the Senate refused to go that far.[15] Finally, the quota law was passed for fourteen months as a stop-gap measure until a permanent policy could be worked out.

The fear of a great influx of immigrants stemmed from a widespread belief that the economic chaos in Europe would lead inevitably to large-scale emigration. Kenneth Roberts, writing a series of articles in the *Saturday Evening Post*, claimed that all Europe was on the move and that the only limiting factor on immigration would be the amount of available steamship space.[16] Consular reports were equally pessimistic, warning of the universal desire of Europeans to escape from the war-ravaged continent.[17] Moreover, the reports from Europe stressed the low character and degraded condition of the prospective immigrants. Consequently, the debate in Congress was filled with allusions to the "alien flood," "barbarian horde," and "foreign tide." The fact that most of these reports came from the countries of southeastern Europe was stressed, reinforcing the stereotype introduced by the Immigration Commission in 1911. As a result, the fear of foreign inundation became a real and immediate one which acted as a catalyst to speed up the coming of restriction.

The "flood" concept combined with three postwar conditions to bring about the passage of the quota law. First of all, it coincided with a depression which had begun late in 1920 and was in full swing at the time the law was passed. With heavy unemployment prevailing, the friends of restriction could well argue that to admit immigrants at

15. Stephenson, p. 176.
16. Kenneth Roberts, "The Rising Irish Tide," *Saturday Evening Post, 192* (February 14, 1920); "Plain Remarks on Immigration for Plain Americans," *193* (February 12, 1921); "The Existence of an Emergency," *193* (April 30, 1921).
17. "Temporary Suspension of Immigration," *House Report No. 1109, 66*th Congress, 3d Session (Washington, 1920), pp. 9–11.

such a time would be to invite economic disaster. The American Federation of Labor, an ancient enemy of immigration, lobbied vigorously for the bill on economic grounds, urging complete suspension of immigration until recovery set in.[18] Meanwhile, the economic interests favorable to immigration were silent, since their traditional arguments on the shortage of manual labor were inapplicable during the depression.[19] In Congress the advocates of the quota system contended that all nations were undergoing a period of economic readjustment following the war and that the United States had to protect itself from Europeans who attempted to transfer the chaos on the continent to the American scene.[20]

The "flood" concept intensified a second postwar view—that the country was suffering from "alien indigestion." Many Progressives had been concerned with the assimilation of aliens into American society in the prewar period, but gradually this concern had been taken over by more nationalistic groups, who advocated a strenuous policy of Americanization.[21] Generally it was urged that immigration be halted for a few years until the colonies of foreign minorities had been broken up and absorbed in the social structure. The melting pot had failed to melt, charged many restrictionists, and there had to be a breathing spell during which aliens were cleansed of their foreign customs and languages and were taught American patterns of thought and speech.[22] It is interesting to note that the majority of Americans did not view this melting pot as a process of cultural fusion by which each immigrant group contributed its share to a national mosaic. Rather it was generally believed to be a smelting process in which the immigrant was stripped of his old-world characteristics and recast in a standard American mold.[23] The American Legion was especially vigorous in propagating this interpretation of the melting pot idea, demanding the

18. "Report of the Legislative Committee," *American Federationist*, 27 (1920), 1114; 28 (1921), 153.

19. *The American Industries*, organ of the National Association of Manufacturers, came out against unregulated immigration. See Vol. *21* (1920), 22.

20. *Congressional Record* (December 10, 1920), pp. 179, 187; (April 20, 1921), p. 513.

21. Higham, pp. 235–50.

22. *Congressional Record* (February 19, 1921), p. 3456; (April 20, 1921), p. 501.

23. Stow Persons, "The Americanization of the Immigrant," in David Bowers, ed., *Foreign Influences in American Life* (Princeton, 1944), pp. 42–3; T. J. Woofter, *Races and Ethnic Groups in American Life* (New York, 1933), p. 210.

cessation of immigration until all foreign elements in the country had been thoroughly Americanized.[24] Many congressmen echoed this thought in their speeches and warned that the approaching flood would result in complete alienization of American society.

Finally, and most important, was the interaction of the fear of inundation with the prevailing feeling of nationalism. The war had aroused intense patriotic sentiments, which continued into the 1920's to become a major force in the triumph of restriction. The demand for "100 per cent Americanism" and the contempt for "hyphenism" were born of the war and were directed at the aliens in America. National unity was deemed necessary for national survival, and the foreign born were charged with retaining a prior loyalty to their native land.[25] The impending flood was compared to invasion by a foreign army, and the prospective immigrants were termed on the floor of the Senate "dangerous and deadly enemies of the country." [26] Furthermore, the feeling of nationalism was directed against alien radicals, and though the inflamed feelings which had burst out during the "red scare" of 1919-20 had died down by 1921, there was a residue of fear over the dangers of foreign Bolsheviks entering the country.[27] Aroused by these nationalistic impulses, many Americans viewed immigration in a new and hostile light.

These, then, were the factors uppermost in the passage of the 1921 quota law. The economic depression, the belief that the nation had reached the saturation point with aliens, and the intense nationalism created by the war all combined to bring about a policy of immigration restriction, behind which were the leading restrictionists and pressure groups—the American Legion and the American Federation of Labor playing particularly important roles. In Congress, Albert Johnson, representative from Washington and chairman of the House Immigration Committee, was the leader, pressing vigorously for the passage of the bill. Arrayed against these forces in 1921 were only the spokesmen for the southeastern European immigrants, mainly Jewish leaders, whose protests were drowned out by the general cry

24. "New Fire under the Melting Pot," *American Legion Weekly*, 2 (January 30, 1920), 10.

25. *Congressional Record* (December 10, 1920), p. 173.

26. Ibid. (February 19, 1921), p. 3449.

27. Ibid. (December 9, 1920), p. 134; (February 19, 1921), p. 3456; (May 3, 1921), p. 963.

for restriction. The silence of business interests was a great loss to the antirestrictionists, and except for a few dissenting voices from the northeastern states the legislation went unopposed in Congress.

The 1921 law, though enacted only as a temporary measure, marked the beginning of a permanent policy of immigration restriction which ran counter to a 19th-century American ideal. The restrictionists, aware of their denial of the asylum concept, justified their position by stating that they were realists who had adjusted to a changed situation. In the 19th century, when immigration consisted of hardy pioneers from northwestern Europe, free immigration was beneficial, but the new immigrants of the 20th century threatened to become a destructive force, they contended. This change in the source of immigration demanded a corresponding change in American policy.[28] The restrictionists labeled those who talked of a traditional ideal of asylum "sentimentalists" who had failed to face up to the realities of a new situation.[29]

It does seem true that the policy of restriction adopted in 1921 was due to changed conditions, but one might well question the contention of the restrictionists that it was the different source of European immigrants that caused the reversal in policy. Fundamentally, it was the transformations in American economic and political development that set the stage for restriction. The growth of the American economy and particularly the technological changes brought about by the industrial revolution had greatly reduced the need for the raw labor furnished by immigrants. A mature industrial system required a moderate number of trained workers, not great masses of manual laborers. Furthermore, the vast changes in America's role in the world had radically altered the popular attitudes toward what constituted the nation. Emerging from the 19th century as a new world power, then achieving a position of leadership during the first World War, the United States was no longer an isolated country with a feeling of complete military security. As citizens of a world power many Americans felt that the changed conditions demanded a much greater degree of unity and conformity within the nation. It was this drive toward

28. Ibid. (April 21, 1921), p. 565; (May 3, 1921), p. 956.
29. This was especially true of *Saturday Evening Post* editorials, "The Great American Myth," *193* (May 7, 1921), 20, and "America Last," *194* (March 4, 1922), 22.

more intense nationalism, produced by the new position of the United States on the international scene, which lay at the heart of the restriction policy.

The 1921 law did not settle the immigration problem but rather marked the beginning of a prolonged and often bitter controversy that raged until Congress enacted a permanent law in 1924. Organizations representing almost every aspect of American life developed views on immigration and voiced them at Congressional hearings. Public sentiments were aroused by inflammatory editorials in the daily press and virulent articles in popular periodicals, with the *Saturday Evening Post* leading the restrictionist crusade. The public debate grew so bitter that many people breathed a sigh of relief when the question was settled in 1924.

The issues involved in this controversy differed considerably from those uppermost in 1921. The fear of postwar inundation had largely receded from the public consciousness, while the return of prosperity had brought forth the industrial and business interests in their traditional roles as supporters of immigration. But by far the most significant difference was the injection of a new aspect: ethnic theory. Borrowing ideas on the importance of race in human society from continental sources and distorting the concepts of English eugenicists, the restrictionists advocated a new theory of nationalism based on racial homogeneity. It was this new argument which carried restriction to its final triumph.

The return of prosperity relegated the economic issues to a secondary role in the passage of the permanent law. Businessmen, led by the powerful National Association of Manufacturers, appeared in force at Congressional hearings to argue that the economy was suffering from a shortage of laborers. Immigration was vital for economic prosperity, they contended, since native Americans refused to perform the unpleasant but basic jobs in industry.[30] Representatives of labor, particularly the AFL, met this argument head on by charging that the employers were motivated solely by a desire to procure cheap

30. "Immigration and Labor," *Hearings before the House Committee on Immigration and Naturalization*, 67th Congress, 3d Session (Washington, 1923), pp. 238, 289, 549, 559, 576. The entire issue of *American Industries* for February 1923 was devoted to this theme.

labor. There was a more than adequate supply of workers in the country, they rebutted, and the only effect of unrestricted immigration would be to degrade American standards of living.[31] Many disinterested observers, such as the sociologist Henry Pratt Fairchild, supported labor's position, holding that the United States had reached a state of mature development in which immigration was no longer economically beneficial.[32] The over-all result of this economic discussion was a deadlock between opposing pressure groups which forced the restrictionists to concentrate their attack on the ethnic aspect of immigration.

Race prejudice had long been common in the United States, but down until the end of the 19th century it was confined largely to the question of color. Prejudice had developed in regard to the Negro, the Indian, and the Asiatic immigrants on the Pacific Coast, but it did not extend to the European immigrants, where no difference in color existed. However, the rising tide of new immigrants from southeastern Europe, with their distinctive cultural and social patterns, gave rise to a new feeling of racism in the 1890's and early 1900's. Relying on the concept of Anglo-Saxon superiority, heretofore considered largely a matter of national character, many "old stock" Americans began applying racist bias to the new immigrants. Such men as Henry Cabot Lodge and Francis A. Walker began praising the Anglo-Saxon race and condemning the lesser breeds of southeastern Europe. Their views were reinforced by the developing band of eugenicists who preached that heredity determined the development of individuals independently of environmental influences. Thus by the first decade of the 20th century there was in existence a growing body of racist ideas which could be applied to the restriction of European immigration.[33]

The man who played the key role in synthesizing these racist concepts and applying them to immigration restriction was Madison Grant, a wealthy New York lawyer. In 1916 Grant published *The Passing of the Great Race*, in which he attempted to elevate racial

31. "Immigration and Labor," House *Hearings* (1923), pp. 367, 461, 468–84; "Selective Immigration Legislation," *Hearings before the Senate Committee on Immigration*, 68th Congress, 1st Session (Washington, 1924), pp. 184–5, 190.

32. Henry Pratt Fairchild, "The End of Race Migrations," *Yale Review*, new ser. *11* (July 1922), 827–33.

33. Higham, pp. 131–57.

prejudice to the status of a scientific theory and apply it to European immigration. He wedded the racist ideas developing in the United States to the more virulent European race theories which stemmed from the books of Count Arthur de Gobineau and Houston Stewart Chamberlain. The main thesis was that races varied greatly in quality and only superior races, such as the Nordic, were capable of producing great civilizations. As a corollary to this theory, de Gobineau and Chamberlain contended that racial purity was essential to human endeavor, ethnic intermixture leading inevitably to the decline and disintegration of a society. Grant applied these ideas to the American experience, seeing in the colonial stock a pure Nordic race which was the foundation of America's greatness. Immigration, according to Grant, had diluted the American population with inferior races which threatened to overwhelm completely the ever-narrowing Nordic element. This unhealthy situation had been intensified by the false concept of the melting pot, which had encouraged the amalgamation of Nordics with non-Nordics. Such racial interbreeding could lead only to inferior species, to a mongrelization of the American population.[34]

Grant's book appeared just before America's entry into the war, and it seems to have received scant notice at this time. It had a powerful influence, however, on a group of writers who took up Grant's ideas in the early 1920's and broadcast them wholesale in books and magazine articles. These books are all written in a tone of crisis which at times borders on hysteria. The belief in the American melting pot was the chief target of the volumes, with the writers referring to ethnic intermixture as race suicide, mongrelization, and miscegenation.[35]

Grant and his disciples were amateur anthropologists who advanced their ideas under the name of science. This pretension was abetted by several prominent social scientists who in part at least accepted the racist theory. Carl Brigham, a Princeton psychologist, from a study of wartime army mental tests concluded that Nordics were far superior

34. Louis L. Snyder, *Race, a History of Modern Ethnic Theories* (New York, 1939), pp. 93–4, 114, 121–2, 140, 147; M. F. Ashley Montague, *Man's Most Dangerous Myth: the Fallacy of Race* (New York, 1945), pp. 21–2; Madison Grant, *The Passing of the Great Race* (New York, 1916), pp. 14–16, 77–81.

35. Charles Gould, *America, a Family Matter*, New York, 1922; Lothrop Stoddard, *The Rising Tide of Color*, New York, 1920; and *The Revolt against Civilization*, New York, 1922.

to Alpines and Mediterraneans in native intelligence. In addition Brigham asserted, "American intelligence is declining, and will proceed with an accelerating rate as the racial mixture becomes more and more extensive." [36] A more eminent psychologist, William MacDougall of Harvard, was critical of extreme racist statements but did assert that races varied in temperament, claiming that the Nordics possessed a vigorous self-assertiveness which enabled them to play a dominating role in history.[37] Finally, Harry Laughlin, a prominent eugenicist and biological expert for the House Immigration Committee, surveyed the social adequacy of immigrants and concluded that "the recent immigrants, on the whole, present a higher percentage of inborn socially inadequate qualities than do the older stocks." [38]

The most complete application of the new racial ideas to immigration was achieved by Gino Speranza, a native-born American of Italian descent. A lawyer by profession, Speranza published a series of articles in *World's Work* in 1923 and 1924 which attracted a great deal of attention and were extremely influential. His basic assertion was that the United States had been founded by a racially and culturally homogeneous group of Anglo-Saxon people, and this colonial stock had flowered into an American race which was fully formed when the tide of new immigrants began to enter the country in the 1890's. It had developed democracy and the traditional American way of life by virtue of its homogeneity, but the new immigration, composed of alien races and cultures, was challenging the spiritual union that was the foundation of the American republic.[39]

At the heart of Speranza's argument was his belief that national unity depended upon racial and cultural homogeneity, in which the ethnic factor was vital. This homogeneity could not be achieved by a process of transformation such as that of the melting pot, for "racial characteristics do not die, especially those subtler qualities of mind

36. Carl Brigham, *A Study of American Intelligence* (Princeton, 1923), pp. 155, 168, 208, 210.

37. William MacDougall, *Is America Safe for Democracy?* (New York, 1921), pp. 123, 146, 173.

38. Harry H. Laughlin, "Analysis of America's Modern Melting Pot," *Hearings before the House Committee on Immigration and Naturalization,* 67th Congress, 3d Session (Washington, 1922), pp. 729–30, 749, 755.

39. Gino Speranza, "The Immigration Peril," *World's Work,* 47 (November 1923), 58–65; (December 1923), 153; (February 1924), 400. These articles were subsequently published as a book, *Race or Nation,* Indianapolis, 1925.

and character which profoundly differentiate the culture and spirit
of one people from another." [40] What Speranza had done in this series
of articles was to combine racist theory with the nationalist fervor of
the postwar period. He forged a new concept, racial nationalism,
which was to be reiterated constantly by the Congressional advocates
of restriction.

The debate in Congress followed the same lines as the general discussion. Economic considerations dropped to a subsidiary position
and the main emphasis was on biological factors. The opponents of
restriction were reconciled to the quota system, but they put up a
vigorous battle to preserve the use of the 1910 census as the base,
rather than to go back thirty-four years to the 1890 census, as the
restrictionists proposed. The use of the 1910 census meant an even
allocation of immigration quotas between northwestern and southeastern European nations, whereas the adoption of the 1890 census
would result in 70 per cent of the quotas going to the northwestern
countries. Thus the debate centered on the distribution of immigration between Nordic and Mediterranean peoples.

The effect of racial theory on the Congressional mind was easily
discernible. In 1921 congressmen had argued that restriction was
necessary because the melting pot had failed, causing a condition of
"alien indigestion." In 1924 the charge was that the melting pot concept was a fallacious and dangerous belief which had created "racial
indigestion." [41] "The trouble grows out of a country composed of
intermingled and mongrelized people. The stability of a country
depends upon the homogeneity of population." [42] Thus employing
characteristic racist terminology, a member of Congress substituted
the ideal of racial purity for the melting pot. The report of the House
Immigration Committee indicated that this was the principal aim of
the supporters of the bill. "It is hoped to guarantee, as best we can
at this late date, racial homogeneity in the United States." [43]

To support their case the restrictionists attempted to show that
racial purity was essential for the preservation of both nationalism and
democracy in the United States. The link between nationalism and

40. Speranza (November 1923), p. 65.
41. *Congressional Record* (April 8, 1924), p. 5848; (April 16, 1924), p. 6461.
42. Ibid. (April 5, 1924), p. 5673.
43. "Restriction of Immigration," *House Report No. 350*, 68th Congress, 1st Session (Washington, 1924), p. 16.

homogeneity was succinctly expressed by a Maine congressman who advocated "one race, one country, one destiny." [44] A Maryland senator envisioned the restrictive bill as a means of achieving a degree of racial purity which would cloak the United States with "an individuality as distinct, as salient, and as inspiring as the individuality of England, or of France, or of Germany, or of any of the great civilized powers of the earth." [45] The supporters of restriction saw an equally valid relationship between racial homogeneity and democracy. Holding that the capacity for self-government was a racial trait, they argued that in order to perpetuate the democratic form of government, the Nordic race which had created it must continue as the dominant element in the population.[46] The House Committee on Immigration voiced this belief as the fundamental justification for restriction. "If, therefore, the principle of individual liberty, guarded by a constitutional government created on this continent nearly a century and a half ago, is to endure, the basic strain of our population must be maintained." [47]

In the formulation of their views of racial homogeneity the restrictionists were aware of the weak spot in their armor—their vulnerability to the charge that they were employing an undemocratic concept, racial discrimination. Many denied that the use of the 1890 census evidenced discrimination against southeastern Europeans, claiming that the results corresponded to the actual ethnic composition of the American population. It was to avoid this charge that the national origins plan was finally adopted.[48] Yet a sizable number of restrictionists admitted that they were discriminating between different peoples; they claimed, however, that they were governed by considerations of national welfare and not by racial prejudice. The argument was essentially that the end justifies the means.[49]

As was the case in 1921, the advocates of restriction far outnumbered the opponents, but the minority fought an intense verbal battle in an attempt to stem the inevitable. At the committee hearings, the most

44. *Congressional Record* (April 8, 1924), p. 5868.
45. Ibid. (April 9, 1924), p. 5956.
46. Ibid. (April 5, 1924), p. 5665; (April 8, 1924), p. 5905; (April 16, 1924), p. 6461.
47. *House Report No. 350* (1924), p. 13.
48. Ibid., p. 16; *Congressional Record* (April 3, 1924), p. 5468; (April 5, 1924), p. 5643.
49. *Congressional Record* (April 5, 1924), p. 5680; (April 16, 1924), p. 6464.

prominent group of witnesses against the bill were representatives of southeastern European immigrants, particularly Jewish leaders.[50] On the floor of Congress, the principal defenders of immigration were legislators from the metropolitan districts which had the heaviest percentage of the foreign born. The leading figure in the minority camp was Adolph Sabath of Illinois, who wrote the minority report of the House Committee on Immigration.

The most powerful argument advanced by the antirestrictionists was the assertion that the bill would breed disunity. By establishing a distinction between the peoples of northwestern and southeastern Europe, Congress was creating arbitrary divisions in the American population in regard to national origin. Sabath held that "it would be the first instance in our modern legislation for writing into our laws the hateful doctrine of inequality between the various component parts of our population." [51] The opponents of restriction contended that by creating first and second class citizenship, the bill would disrupt rather than foster national solidarity.[52]

Closely allied to this contention was the further argument that the proposed legislation embodied methods which conflicted with democratic ideals and principles. The charge of discrimination was continually repeated. Senator Colt of Rhode Island asserted that discrimination was a manifestation of racial antagonism, which he labeled "entirely un-American." [53] On the floor of Congress the opposition grew vehement, charging that the restrictionists were permeated with Ku Klux Klanism, religious bigotry, and racial hate.[54] Senator Underwood of Alabama, a lifelong restrictionist, stated that his opposition to immigration stemmed from economic considerations and that the attempt to introduce racial discrimination into the issue was unAmerican. "In other words," he declared, "instead of standing for the great principles of human rights and human liberty, and freedom of conscience, we are going to tear down our standard and yield our cause to passion and to prejudice." [55]

50. "Selective Immigration Legislation," Senate *Hearings* (1924); "Restriction of Immigration," *Hearings before the House Committee on Immigration and Naturalization*, 68th Congress, 1st Session, Washington, 1924.

51. *House Report No. 350* (1924), Pt. II, p. 4.

52. "Restriction of Immigration," House *Hearings* (1924), p. 362.

53. "Selective Immigration Legislation," Senate *Hearings* (1924), p. 75.

54. *Congressional Record* (April 8, 1924), pp. 5863, 5886.

55. Ibid. (April 16, 1924), pp. 6458–9, 6460.

Despite such vigorous protests, the foes of restriction were over-whelmed on the final votes on the quota bill. The measure was passed by sweeping majorities, 323 to 71 in the House, 62 to 6 in the Senate. A sectional analysis of the vote indicates that the legislation met with the approval of all elements in the United States except minority groups from southeastern Europe. The Anglo-Saxon South and West voted unanimously for restriction, while the Middle West, with a pre-dominantly northwestern European immigrant background, was very nearly united in approval.[56] The only dissent came from the North-east, where immigrants from southeastern Europe were strongly represented in the urban areas. Here there was an almost even divi-sion in the voting, with the difference in opinion reflecting an urban-rural split. Political affiliations had no bearing on the question, with 35 Republicans and 36 Democrats opposing the measure in the House. There can be little question that the restrictive law was a popular measure reflecting a triumph of the Nordic majority in the nation over the minority of Americans of southeastern European descent.

In its final form, the Act of 1924 established a yearly quota totaling 150,000 for the European countries based on the number of foreign born of each nationality residing in the United States in 1890. This system was to be replaced in 1927, however, by the national origins plan, under which the quotas were to be computed on the basis of the national composition of the total American population in 1920 as de-termined by a special executive board. The law did not alter the list of excluded classes or change the literacy test requirement, but it did achieve a great improvement in administrative procedure by placing the American consuls in Europe in charge of examining the immi-grants. Instead of rejections being made in American ports, the consuls issued immigration visas in accord with the exclusion tests and the annual quota. While no positive system of selection was established,

56. Ibid. (April 16, 1924), p. 6257; ibid. (April 18, 1924), p. 6649. The sec-tional breakdown of the two votes is as follows:

Section	House		Senate	
	YES	NO	YES	NO
Northeast	53	56	10	5
Midwest	125	15	13	0
South	115	0	21	0
Far West	30	0	18	1

preferences were granted up to 50 per cent of the quota to skilled agriculturalists and parents of American citizens. From the purely administrative standpoint the law of 1924 was a great improvement over the temporary 1921 act.

But far more significant than its administrative details was the philosophy underlying the quota law. The earlier temporary law had ended the unrestricted flow of immigration and had thus discarded the asylum ideal, replacing it with the concept of America for Americans. The 1924 law reaffirmed this earlier action and went further, for it substituted a belief in racial homogeneity for the other 19th-century ideal, the melting pot. The traditional belief that the European who came across the Atlantic could be remade by the power of the American environment and the democratic system was rejected with the acceptance of racist theory. In this respect, restriction, however realistic its advocates believed it to be, was a pessimistic action which reflected a denial of faith in the American tradition.

Implicit in the quota law was a denial of another time-honored American ideal, the principle of individualism. In previous immigration legislation the standard for judging immigrants had been individual tests of mental, moral, and physical fitness. With the quota system these standards were overthrown in favor of group criteria. Instead of judging men by their character and ability, the new law selected immigrants on the ground of their racial and national affiliations. This application of group criteria to individuals ignored the wide range of individual difference in a nation's population and reduced all the people of a country to a generalized stereotype. In essence, the restrictionists, by their emphasis on homogeneity, argued that national unity could grow only out of rigid conformity and like-mindedness. Yet they failed to realize the violence this form of nationalism did to a concept of democratic society in which men were free to assert their own individuality. The full irony of the situation is brought out by the name the restrictionists gave to the 1924 law— "the second Declaration of Independence." [57]

So far we have discussed American policy in relation to European immigration, thereby ignoring the much smaller but highly significant

57. Senator Reed of Pennsylvania in the *Congressional Record* (February 1, 1927), p. 2683.

movement of oriental peoples into the United States. The policy which evolved in regard to Asiatic immigration was radically different from that applied to European peoples and thus demands separate treatment. The most important factor here was the tendency to apply to the peoples of the Orient racial attitudes which had developed toward the Negro. Largely ignorant of the age and dignity of Eastern civilization, many Americans accepted the difference in skin color as proof that the Asiatics were members of a backward and inferior race.[58] As a result of this racial antipathy, the oriental immigrants met with an almost uniformly hostile reception in the United States, which was reflected in the governmental policy of exclusion.

The first Asiatic immigrants to enter the United States were Chinese, attracted by the gold rush in California after 1849. Though at first these people were warmly received, mainly because they performed menial services otherwise unobtainable, hostility and agitation soon developed. The coming of the Civil War prevented a violent outbreak of anti-Chinese feeling, and after the war the Chinese found a place as workers on the construction of the Central Pacific Railroad. But with the completion of this line in 1869 and the coming of the panic of 1873, a movement against the Chinese began which did not reach a peak until the end of the decade, when the depression reached its lowest point in California. The mainspring of the anti-Chinese crusade was the tendency of the laboring class in California to blame all its troubles on the presence of the Chinese. Politicians found that the surest way to win the labor vote was to speak out against the Chinese, claiming that they were unfairly competing with white men. The anti-Chinese campaign was highly successful, and only the action of the Supreme Court in voiding California exclusion laws prevented a complete triumph.[59]

Stymied by the courts, the Pacific Coast agitators turned to the federal government for help. Their appeal was heeded, and in 1876 a Joint Congressional Committee conducted hearings in San Francisco on the question of Chinese immigration. The report of this committee, which was dominated by its two California members, was a biased denunciation of the Chinese and a call for a policy of exclusion.[60]

58. Mary R. Coolidge, *Chinese Immigration* (New York, 1909), p. 75.
59. Ibid., pp. 21–81.
60. Ibid., pp. 96–108.

Congress attempted to act on the committee's recommendation in 1879, but President Hayes vetoed a highly restrictive bill because it contravened the terms of the Burlingame treaty of 1868 with China, which guaranteed reciprocal free entry to the citizens of both countries. To surmount this difficulty, a new treaty was negotiated with China in 1880 which allowed the American government to regulate or suspend Chinese immigration within reason, but not to prohibit it absolutely. In 1882 President Arthur vetoed a bill suspending Chinese immigration for twenty years, but later the same year he approved a second bill which excluded Chinese for a decade. The Chinese Exclusion Act, as it was called, was renewed in 1892, and again in 1902, when it was extended to all American insular possessions. Finally in 1904 the law was made permanent.[61]

In the enactment of the Chinese exclusion policy, Congress displayed a total disregard for the sensibilities and treaty rights of the Chinese. Their protests were ignored, and in a test case brought before the Supreme Court the Justices ruled that the Chinese treaty rights were invalid because Congress had the power to repeal or modify treaties. It was this decision which led the Chinese ambassador to comment to the Secretary of State, "I was not prepared to learn that there was a way recognized in the law and practice in this country whereby your country could release itself from treaty obligations without the consultation or consent of the other party." [62] This highhanded American policy succeeded only because China was a weak power which could not demand satisfaction. However, no such arbitrary course of action was possible with a second form of Asiatic immigration which began at the end of the century—that of the Japanese. Japan had emerged as a world power by this time, and the result was a resort to diplomacy to settle the immigration problem.[63]

Japanese immigrants began entering the United States in significant numbers in the 1890's, with the movement reaching its peak just after the Russo-Japanese War.[64] Agitation against the Japanese, conditioned

61. Stephenson, pp. 261–2.

62. Ibid., pp. 262–3.

63. A. Whitney Griswold, *The Far Eastern Policy of the United States* (New York, 1938), p. 339.

64. In the 1890's, 27,440 Japanese entered the United States. In the next decade, 54,839 Japanese immigrants were admitted. Yamato Ichihashi, *Japanese in the United States* (Stanford University, 1932), pp. 55–9.

by the earlier Chinese experience, broke out in California as early as 1900. In that year the Japanese government, fearing the development of exclusion sentiments, voluntarily stated that it would refuse passports to Japanese laborers leaving for the mainland of the United States. This did not halt the flow of Japanese, however, since many went to Hawaii and then came on to the Pacific Coast.[65] Resentment flared up again in California in 1905, resulting in the formation of the Japanese and Korean Exclusion League, and a crisis was reached in 1906 when the San Francisco school board issued an order segregating all Chinese, Japanese, and Korean children in the public schools. This action caused the Japanese government to protest to the State Department, and President Roosevelt was forced to intervene. After intensive negotiations with both the San Francisco school board and the Japanese ambassador, the executive department finally worked out an acceptable compromise. The movement of Japanese from Hawaii to the mainland was curtailed by an amendment to the 1907 immigration law then before Congress, while the Japanese government again agreed to withhold passports from Japanese laborers planning to emigrate to the United States.[66] This was the famous Gentlemen's Agreement, and it is worth noting that it was an executive agreement arrived at secretly. In fact, the nature of the agreement was not disclosed until July 1908, when the details appeared in the *Annual Report of the Commissioner-General of Immigration.*[67]

The Gentlemen's Agreement was a tactful solution to an unpleasant problem, but it did not succeed in quieting the agitation in California. While most of the earlier anti-Japanese feeling had stemmed from the labor interests in the cities, the farmers in California now became the chief opponents of the Japanese as the latter turned to agriculture for a livelihood. As a result of this new opposition, the California legislature enacted an Alien Land Law in 1913 which prohibited aliens

65. Ibid., pp. 230–3; Thomas A. Bailey, *Theodore Roosevelt and the Japanese American Crises* (Stanford University, 1934), p. 2.

66. Ibid., pp. 29–167; Raymond Buell, "The Development of Anti-Japanese Agitation in the United States," *Political Science Quarterly*, 38 (December 1922), 609–34. The amendment empowered the President to refuse entry to citizens of foreign countries who had been issued passports to American insular possessions, other foreign countries, or the Canal Zone by their home government. Note that there was no specific mention of Japan.

67. (Washington, 1908), pp. 125–6.

ineligible for citizenship from acquiring real property.[68] This was obvious discrimination against Japanese, since the naturalization laws admitted only whites and Negroes to citizenship.[69] During the next few years increasing hostility to the Japanese developed in California, until in 1923 a California Joint Immigration Committee was formed to press for legislative exclusion of all Japanese immigrants. This board, composed of representatives of the AFL, the American Legion, the Native Sons of the Golden West, and the National Grange, took advantage of the general discussion of immigration policy in 1924 to present the case for exclusion to a Congressional committee.[70]

The renewed California demands for exclusion of Japanese had their effect on a Congress permeated with racist ideas. The House Committee on Immigration borrowed from the California land law by inserting a clause in the 1924 bill barring all aliens ineligible for citizenship. Despite vigorous protests from Secretary of State Hughes, who asked that Japan be given a quota, the House Committee refused to reconsider its action. In the final report on the bill, the committee attacked the Gentlemen's Agreement as a surrender of Congressional prerogative to the Japanese government and defended Japanese exclusion on the grounds of harmonizing immigration and naturalization legislation.[71] The House supported its committee wholeheartedly, the only negative speaker during the debate being Representative Burton of Ohio, whose views were considered those of the administration.[72]

In the Senate there was considerable opposition to the Japanese

68. Raymond Buell, "The Development of Anti-Japanese Agitation in the United States, II," *Political Science Quarterly*, 38 (March 1923), 63–4.

69. "White person" under the naturalization law was commonly interpreted as a member of the Caucasian race. This interpretation was reaffirmed by the Supreme Court in the case of Takao Ozawa vs. United States in November 1922. The decision is quoted in Raymond Buell, "Japanese Immigration," *World Peace Foundation Pamphlets*, 7 (Boston, 1925), 345–6.

70. Buell, "Anti-Japanese Agitation, II," pp. 68–70; "Japanese Immigration Legislation," *Hearings before the Senate Committee on Immigration*, 68th Congress, 1st Session, Washington, 1924.

71. *House Report No. 350* (1924), pp. 5–9. Hughes' letter to the committee is printed in "Correspondence with Executive Departments," *Hearings before the House Committee on Immigration and Naturalization*, 68th Congress, 1st Session (Washington, 1924), pp. 1200–5.

72. Rodman Paul, *The Abrogation of the Gentlemen's Agreement* (Cambridge, 1936), pp. 32–3.

exclusion clause, led by Senator David Reed of Pennsylvania, the author of the national origins plan.[73] In the absence of Hiram Johnson, Senator Shortridge of California was leading the fight for exclusion and was making slight progress when a dramatic turn of events occurred which ensured victory for the exclusionists. On April 10 the Japanese ambassador, Hanihara, handed Secretary Hughes a formal note protesting against possible exclusion and warning that "grave consequences" would follow from such Congressional action. Hughes, hoping that the Japanese protest would influence Congress favorably, sent the letter to Congress, where it was printed in the *Congressional Record* for April 11.[74] Three days later, Senator Henry Cabot Lodge discussed the Japanese note and referred to the "grave consequences" clause as a "veiled threat." The effect on the Senate was electrifying, and all opposition to exclusion collapsed, even Senator Reed reversing his position. The exclusion clause was approved 71 to 4, and despite attempts by President Coolidge to delay the date of its effectiveness in order to abrogate the Gentlemen's Agreement by negotiation, it went into operation on July 1, 1924.[75]

The enactment of Japanese exclusion is a further indication of the spirit of intense nationalism and racial consciousness which dominated the United States in the 1920's. The refusal of Congress to continue the Gentlemen's Agreement was due to a belief that immigration was a domestic matter and that any delegation of regulatory power to a foreign government constituted a violation of American sovereignty. The dominance of racist ideas is clearly demonstrated in the rejection of Hughes' proposal to place Japan under a quota, which would have meant the entry of about 150 Japanese a year. To the implied bias against the peoples of southeastern Europe, Congress added outright discrimination against the Japanese. The tragic consequences of this disregard for the sensibilities of a proud nation was the heightening of the estrangement between Japan and the United States. The Japanese considered the exclusion act an insult and the Tokyo press proclaimed July 1 a day of national mourning.[76] The furor over exclusion soon died down in the United States, but in Japan smoldering resentment became a permanent source of friction.

73. Ibid., p. 38.
74. Pages 6073–4.
75. Paul, pp. 68–81, 91–7.
76. Ichihashi, pp. 315–6; New York *Times* (June 9, 1925), p. 9.

The preceding pages have surveyed American immigration policy as it developed in the late 19th and early 20th centuries. From this summary it is evident that the determination of a governmental program toward immigration is a complicated process into which many widely separated factors enter. Before proceeding with the development of immigration policy in the years following 1924, we may recapitulate briefly the major aspects of the problem of regulation.

First, there is the question of the relation of immigration to the economic welfare of the nation. It was this aspect which was uppermost in the 19th-century discussions of the problem. So long as the American economy was in a youthful stage characterized by rapid expansion, immigration was considered a beneficial process. But as the economy matured and mechanization began to reduce the need for common labor, many Americans became sympathetic to the views of organized labor, which had always looked upon immigration as a movement impeding the crusade for higher wages. In the 20th century economic discussions of immigration have become part of the continuous tug of war between labor and management. Except in periods of depression, this neutralization of the economic issue has resulted in its less important role in the determination of policy.

One reason for the decline of the economic factor has been the rise of social and racial issues. The American people have increasingly come to look upon immigration as a cultural rather than an economic phenomenon. The racial aspects of oriental immigration have always been stressed, but in the case of European immigrants it was the social implications which were first noticed. The exhaustive surveys conducted by the Immigration Commission of 1911 pointed out the effects of immigration on American life, while the concern for social justice present in the Progressive movement attracted attention to the problems of assimilation and Americanization. The emphasis on racial theory after the war transformed this concern for the impact of immigrants on American society into a new and powerful issue which dominated the formulation of the 1924 law.

Closely allied to the social and racial factors in immigration policy is the influence of nationalism. This aspect is again a recent development which did not flower fully until the postwar period. After freely admitting millions of peoples from foreign countries, Americans began to speculate on the effect of this infusion of aliens on national unity.

The result of such reflection was a strong feeling that unchecked immigration could lead only to the alienization of the United States and the destruction of national solidarity. The belief arose that patriotism could grow only out of roots which had been firmly implanted in American soil for generations and could not be instilled in the minds and hearts of newcomers by educational processes.

The final aspect of the immigration problem is its relationship to foreign policy. While the majority of Americans were accustomed to considering immigration as a domestic question over which Congress had complete control, more perceptive individuals realized that immigration was an international process which transcended national boundaries. The Japanese experience showed that the manner in which Congress regulated immigration could have a profound effect on American relations with foreign countries. Since the executive branch is most directly concerned with the conduct of foreign affairs, this situation has led to very strong differences of opinion between the president and Congress over immigration legislation.

These, then, are the four principal elements of immigration which enter into the formulation of policy: the *economic, social* (racial), and *nationalistic* aspects, and considerations of *foreign policy*. At times these factors have been complementary, fitting together neatly, as in 1924, when the restrictionists joined racist theories to the feeling of nationalism in support of the quota law. At other times they seem to have been working against one another, as evidenced by the Japanese exclusion debate, when the racist arguments of Congress ran counter to the foreign policy views of the State Department. But whether in harmony or in conflict, these four are the keys to an understanding of American immigration policy.

2. The National Origins Debate

THE YEARS from 1924 to 1927 were quiet ones from the standpoint of immigration policy. With the passage of the 1924 law many people believed that the question of immigration had been permanently settled. No major bills were presented in Congress on the subject and public discussion was limited to praise of the 1924 act. The prevailing attitude was a feeling of relief with overtones of triumph, best expressed by Henry Pratt Fairchild in *The Melting Pot Mistake*. His theme was that the United States had been on the verge of disaster because of its adherence to the dangerous myth of the melting pot, but the wise repudiation of this concept had saved the nation and had opened up a new era in American history.[1]

This lull was rudely shattered when the national origins controversy broke out in 1927. The 1924 act contained a provision that the 1890 census basis should be replaced after three years by a system of quotas based on the national origins of the American population. Strangely enough, in 1924 Congress had adopted this provision almost as an afterthought, with extremely little discussion or debate. The House had voted against a national origins amendment when it was proposed in that body, but Senator David Reed had succeeded in adding it to the Senate bill.[2] When the conference committee approved the Senate plan, the House, with its attention diverted by the Japanese exclusion issue, accepted the national origins amendment over the isolated protests of a few ardent antirestrictionists.[3] This lack of consideration of the national origins plan was amply compensated for when the new quotas were about to go into effect in 1927. A debate over national origins developed which continued intermittently for more than two years.

The essence of this controversy was the distribution of immigrants from the various European countries. The question of quantity was

1. Henry Pratt Fairchild, *The Melting Pot Mistake*, Boston, 1926.
2. *Congressional Record* (April 12, 1924), pp. 6626–9; (April 16, 1924), p. 6472.
3. Ibid. (May 9, 1924), pp. 8218–49; (May 15, 1924), pp. 8626–52. Only Sabath of Illinois and Dickstein of New York spoke against national origins.

not involved, since there was only a very slight difference in the number of immigrants admitted under the two schemes.[4] But the national origins quotas differed considerably from those calculated on the basis of the 1890 census. While the totals for the countries of south-eastern Europe were not appreciably affected, there were very real changes in the quotas allotted to the northwestern European nations. Great Britain was the largest gainer, receiving nearly 50 per cent of the total under national origins, as opposed to 25 per cent according to the old plan, while the other so-called Nordic countries—Germany, the Irish Free State, Norway, Sweden, and Denmark—suffered drastic reductions.[5] This radical shift in the distribution of immigrants from northwestern Europe was packed with political dynamite and caused a great deal of soul searching in Congress before the question was finally settled in 1929.

The opposition to national origins quite naturally came from people of Irish, German, and Scandinavian descent in the United States. Such organizations as the Steuben Society, the Sons of Norway, and the American Irish Historical Society waged a vigorous campaign of protest, arguing that the change in quotas represented discrimination against their nationalities. In reaction to this campaign, the patriotic societies defended the national origins plan, which they believed was essential for proper immigration restriction. The Sons of the American Revolution and the Junior Order of United American Mechanics led this movement, and though these organizations were small, their influence was considerable. This alignment was quite logical, since the members of the organizations were descendants of colonial stock, which was overwhelmingly British in origin. The national origins dispute might well be considered a struggle between minority pressure groups acting out of essentially selfish motives.

The balance of forces was fairly even, and as a result Congress was faced with a thorny decision which it hesitated to make. After two years of delay, the House appeared willing to repeal the national origins law, but the Senate voted to put the plan into operation. The quotas went into effect on July 1, 1929, thus ending the dispute. Though the sole outcome of the controversy was a two-year postpone-

4. The 1890 census quotas totaled 164,666, the national origins quotas 153,714.
5. See Table I, below, p. 30, for comparison between 1890 and national origins quotas for major European countries.

ment, the bitter debate over national origins was significant because it revealed a weakness in the concept of restriction by national quotas. The restrictionists argued that their plan was essential for fostering national unity. Yet any scheme for choosing immigrants by nationality was bound to result in a feeling of discrimination and resentment by minority groups who wished to see their former countrymen favored. The result of the jockeying for a favored position in the allotment of quotas was a heightening of minority consciousness among the foreign born and a spirit of discord which lessened rather than increased national unity.

To understand the national origins debate it is necessary to examine the statistical process involved in the computation of the quotas. National origins could be determined in two ways. First, a board of experts could attempt to trace the individual genealogies of some 120 million Americans, determine the ethnic background of each individual, and finally arrive at some estimate of the national origins of the American population. Obviously this process would have been virtually impossible and was never seriously considered. The second method was to attempt to determine the weight of each nationality group in the American population by statistical processes. By taking the percentage of each group in the United States in 1790 and then tracing the additions to that number by subsequent immigration, a rough approximation of the national origins of the American people could be achieved. It was this latter method, suggested by Congress in 1924, that was employed.

The Immigration Act of 1924 stated that the secretaries of state, commerce, and labor should perform the task of tabulating the exact quotas and should report their results to the president. The three secretaries delegated this job to a body of six statistical experts from their departments, with Joseph Hill of the Census Bureau acting as chairman.[6] It is important to note that this Quota Board, as it was called, did the actual work, while the three secretaries merely transmitted the results to the president. In approaching their difficult assignment, the members of the Quota Board decided to begin by determining what part of the population was European in origin. After subtracting the

6. "National Origins Provision of the Immigration Act of 1924," *Senate Document No. 190*, 69th Congress, 1st Session (Washington, 1927), p. 2.

Negro, Asiatic, and Indian elements, the Board divided the remainder into two classifications, the native stock (those descended from people in the United States before 1790) and the immigrant stock (those descended from people who had come to the United States after 1790). This division was made on the basis of census figures since 1890, which distinguished between individuals with native and with foreign-born parents, and on a probability basis for the period 1790–1890.[7] After the primary classification the Board proceeded to develop a system for tracing the national origin of each group.

In computing the country of origin of the native stock the experts proceeded on the assumption that the native stock in 1920 had not changed in composition since 1790. This premise enabled the Board to utilize a census publication, A Century of Population Growth, which had been compiled in 1909. This study had classified the 1790 population into nationality groups by examining the surnames reported in the first census. The Quota Board, without further analysis of the 1909 report, then broke down the native stock in 1920 into component national elements in proportion to those believed to exist in 1790.[8]

The determination of the countries of origin of the immigrant stock was a more complex problem. The first step was to subdivide this group into three parts—immigrants, children of immigrants, and later immigrant generations. The ample census statistics which began in 1890 provided direct information on the national origin of immigrants and children of immigrants in 1920. For the later generations the Board assumed that their distribution would correspond to the numbers of immigrants which had come from each European country from 1790 to 1870.[9] Immigration statistics were available for the period from 1820 to 1870, but for the previous thirty years the statisticians relied on estimates. Having thus arrived at figures for the immigration by countries from 1790 to 1870, the Board weighted the earlier immigrants more heavily in their final calculations, since the first arrivals would have more descendants than the latercomers.[10]

7. "Immigration Quotas on the Basis of National Origin," Senate Document No. 65, 70th Congress, 1st Session (Washington, 1928), pp. 5–7. The lack of data on the foreign born in the censuses prior to 1890 was the great stumbling block the Quota Board faced.

8. Ibid., pp. 3, 8.

9. They needed to use this system only down to 1870, since immigrants and children of immigrants after that date were recorded in the 1890 or later censuses.

10. "Immigration Quotas," Senate Document No. 65 (1928), p. 9.

This calculation of the origin of the immigrant stock appears more open to question than the native stock procedure, yet the foes of national origin neglected the immigrant stock computation in their criticisms of the accuracy of the quotas.

The Quota Board completed its preliminary research and reported the results of its effort to the three secretaries in December 1926. This report, which listed the quotas for European countries under both the 1890 census plan and national origins, was the first official tabulation to show the difference in distribution of immigrants under the two schemes.[11] In commenting upon their work, the members of the Quota Board admitted that their calculations were not wholly satisfactory. However, they stated that they believed their results indicated "the national origin of the population of the United States as nearly as may be ascertained within the available data and under existing conditions."[12]

TABLE 1. Comparison of Immigration Quotas under the 1890 Census and the National Origin Plan for Representative European Countries *

Country	1890 Census	1927 Quota Board Report	1928 Quota Board Report	1929 Quota Board Report
Germany	51,227	23,428	24,908	25,957
Great Britain	34,007	73,039	65,894	65,721
Irish Free State	28,567	13,862	17,427	17,853
Italy	3,845	6,091	5,989	5,802
Norway	6,453	2,267	2,403	2,377
Poland	5,982	4,978	6,090	6,524
Russia	2,248	4,781	3,540	2,784
Sweden	9,561	3,259	3,399	3,314

* Compiled from Quota Board Reports, Senate Document No. 190, 69th Congress, 2d Session (1927), p. 5; No. 65, 70th Congress, 1st Session (1928), pp. 4–5; No. 259, 2d Session (1929), p. 4.

So far the determination of national origins quotas had been a statistical problem handled by disinterested experts. But now the quotas entered the realm of politics, where scientific objectivity gave way to expediency. On January 3 the secretaries of state, commerce, and labor submitted the report of their Quota Board to the president. In

11. "National Origins," Senate Document No. 190 (1927), p. 5.
12. Ibid., pp. 3–4.

their letter of transmittal, the executive officers wrote that the report was "self-explanatory, and while it is stated to be a preliminary report, yet it is believed that further investigation will not substantially alter the conclusions arrived at." [13] President Coolidge duly passed these documents on to Congress, but on January 10 he sent a second letter from the secretaries "to replace an inaccurate copy which was inadvertently forwarded to the Senate." [14] This second letter was very different from the first, stating that "in our opinion the statistical and historical information available raises grave doubts as to the whole value of these computations as a basis for the purposes intended." The secretaries then concluded, "We therefore cannot assume responsibility for such conclusions under these circumstances." [15]

There is no direct evidence to show what caused the three secretaries to change their attitude on the national origins computations so radically, but it does seem very possible that the administration, embarrassed over the redistribution of the quotas and fearing the political effect on the German, Irish, and Scandinavian elements, decided to discredit the national origins law and provide Congress with an excuse for its repeal. There is definite evidence that political pressure was brought to bear on President Coolidge. In August 1926 Albert Johnson of Washington, author of the 1924 law, sent Coolidge a telegram urging him to make a public statement against the national origins plan in order to help Republican candidates, including Johnson, in the forthcoming Congressional election. "My opinion," Johnson wired, "is that a pronouncement by you in plenty of time before general elections will save to our party not less than twenty districts in states where German, Irish, and Scandinavian people are disturbed over possible further restriction under National Origins section." [16] Coolidge sent the telegram on to the three secretaries for their attention. In addition, officers of Irish societies in Massachusetts wrote to Coolidge on several occasions during 1926 urging him to take action

13. *Congressional Record* (January 7, 1929), p. 1224. The three secretaries were Frank Kellogg (State), Herbert Hoover (Commerce), and James Davis (Labor).

14. "National Origin Provision of the Immigration Act of 1924," *Senate Document No. 193*, 69th Congress, 2d Session (Washington, 1927), p. 1.

15. Ibid., p. 1.

16. Albert Johnson to Calvin Coolidge (August 25, 1926), Coolidge Papers, File 133, Library of Congress.

against national origins.[17] In early January the New York *Times* reported that Coolidge was very displeased with the report of the Quota Board, fearing that the new quotas would have an adverse influence on voters of northwestern European descent.[18] Thus it seems highly probable that the substitution of letters was not an inadvertent mistake but rather a deliberate political maneuver to enable administration spokesmen in Congress to call for the repeal of the national origins clause of the 1924 act.

The work of the Quota Board continued while Congress debated the national origins issue for the next two years. The experts received valuable assistance from an unexpected quarter in 1927 when the American Council of Learned Societies decided to re-examine the classification of the American population in 1790. Stating that the 1909 study was no better than a "first approximation to the truth," the Council appointed Marcus Hansen, an expert in immigration history, and Howard Barker, a skilled genealogist, to analyze the 1790 census and produce a more accurate classification of the nationality groups.[19] Hansen and Barker went to work in the summer of 1927 and by using a more precise method of determining nationality from surnames revised the 1909 report considerably. The principal fault in the earlier study, they found, was a tendency to place too high a percentage of the population in the English category. Thus their new classification of the 1790 census reduced the English percentage from 82 per cent to 60 per cent.[20]

The report of the Quota Board for 1928 showed substantial revisions in the national origins quotas. The Board stated that the researches of Hansen and Barker confirmed the suspicion that the 1909 study had overestimated the English element and that as a result of the new classification the quota for Great Britain had been reduced by

17. John J. Foley, Secretary, Associated American Irish Societies of Massachusetts, to President Coolidge (May 25, 1926), Coolidge Papers, File 133, Library of Congress. P. J. Dowd, National Treasurer of the Ancient Order of Hibernians in America, to William Whiting, Coolidge's secretary (September 1, 1926), Coolidge Papers, File 133.

18. New York *Times* (January 2, 1927), p. 1; (January 5, 1927), p. 24; (January 11, 1927), p. 21.

19. American Council of Learned Societies, "Report of the Committee on Linguistic and National Stocks in the Population of the United States," in *Annual Report of the American Historical Association, 1931* (Washington, 1932), *1*, 107–8.

20. Ibid., pp. 108, 110–12, 124.

nearly 8,000.[21] On this occasion, the letter of transmittal by the three secretaries was conspicuously neutral in tone, highlighted by the statement, "We wish it clear that neither we individually nor collectively are expressing any opinion on the merits or demerits of this system of arriving at quotas." [22] In their 1929 report the members of the Quota Board wrote that while they had spent considerable time working on the quotas, they had made only very slight revisions. They concluded, "We are of the opinion that further study would not appreciably modify these results." The 1929 quotas were accepted as final and went into effect on July 1 of that year.[23]

The importance of the Quota Board lies in the complexity of its work. The members of the Board were governmental employees with no apparent bias, but the fact that they had to resort to an involved series of statistical computations in order to determine the quotas gave the opponents of national origins a useful argument. The unwarranted meddling of the three secretaries in the evaluation of the work of the Quota Board further confused the issue. The result was a widespread belief in Congress that national origins was a highly impractical scheme which in no way lived up to its advance billing as a scientific plan for immigration restriction.

Though the national origins debate did not fully develop until 1929, sporadic criticisms of the plan occurred from time to time before Congress took up the question. The leading critics were Irish and German spokesmen who labeled the supporters of national origins anglomaniacs and warned that its adoption would lead to the "Anglicization of these United States . . . at a feverish pace." A Massachusetts congressman, representing the Irish element, claimed that the national origins plan would divide the population along racial lines and thus destroy the homogeneity which was the avowed goal of the restrictionists.[24] Such attacks drew quick rejoinders from the defenders of the plan. In 1925 Representative Vaile of Colorado, a leading restrictionist, replied to criticisms by stating, "The national origins

21. "Immigration Quotas," *Senate Document No. 65* (1928), pp. 3–5.
22. Ibid., p. 2.
23. "Immigration Quotas on the Basis of National Origins," *Senate Document No. 259*, 70th Congress, 2d Session (Washington, 1929), p. 3.
24. Roy Garis, "Lest Immigration Restriction Fail," *Saturday Evening Post, 198* (October 10, 1925), 233; *Congressional Record* (May 28, 1926), p. 10,339.

plan is fair to all; it avoids completely all racial discrimination, and it will preserve the blood of the United States in its present proportions." [25]

This early discussion was but a warning of the full storm which broke in January 1927 when the report of the Quota Board was sent to Congress. The doubling of the British quota and the corresponding decrease in the other northwestern European allotments came as a shock to many people. The German, Irish, and Scandinavian elements in the United States responded with a vigorous campaign directed toward the repeal of national origins. Petitions from such organizations as the German-American Citizens League, the Danish Brotherhood of America, and the Sons of Norway came flooding into Congress.[26] The House Immigration Committee held hearings on the issue in January at which representatives of several minority pressure groups made an appearance. The basic argument of the pressure groups, presented both in petitions and at the hearings, was that national origins was a discriminatory measure which would cause deep resentment among the nationalities whose quotas were lowered.[27] There was often an element of hypocrisy in this charge of discrimination, as revealed in a petition from a German group: "It is our firm conviction that the modus employed in figuring these quotas is a gross violation of the admitted intent of the new law to further the immigration of descendants of the Nordic races while lowering the numbers of newcomers of less desirable races." [28]

In response to these attacks on national origins a few prominent restrictionists came forth to defend the plan. At one House hearing John Trevor, a former army intelligence officer and staunch restrictionist, attacked the minority groups and asserted that the immigration question should be decided on the broad basis of national interests rather than on the selfish views of the foreign born.[29] Thirty-four

25. *Congressional Record* (December 16, 1925), pp. 928–30.

26. House Immigration Committee Papers, National Archives, File H.R. 70A-F13; *Congressional Record* (December 9, 1926), p. 103.

27. "National Origins Provision, Immigration Act of 1924," *Hearings before the House Immigration and Naturalization Committee*, 69th Congress, 2d Session (Washington, 1927), pp. 60–1, 69–70; House Immigration Committee Papers, File H.R. 70A-F13.

28. Petition from the German-American Citizens League (January 13, 1927), House Immigration Committee Papers, File H.R. 70A-F13.

29. "National Origins Provision," House *Hearings* (1927), p. 32.

college professors, mainly biologists from Yale, Harvard, and Princeton, memorialized Congress in favor of national origins, stating that the plan preserved the racial status quo of the nation. "Without such basic homogeneity, we firmly believe, no civilization can have its best development." [30] Surprisingly, the patriotic societies did not appear at the hearings to defend national origins, though they did send a joint petition to Congress.[31]

The foreign minority groups were much more effective in exerting pressure on Congress than the supporters of national origins. Albert Johnson, chairman of the House Immigration Committee, stated in a letter to Edward Lewis, a Chicago restrictionist, "The pressure is very great, not only from members of the Committee, but from members of the House generally, who respond to group demand." [32] The House Committee reported out a bill to repeal national origins in early February, basing its decision on the difficulty in determining the quotas. Its report stated that "it seems far better to have immigration quotas for the purposes of restriction fixed in such a manner as to be easily explained and easily understood by all." [33] While undoubtedly the members of the committee were sincere in this statement, it is likely that without the pressure of the minority groups no such action would have been taken.

The Senate Immigration Committee temporized by reporting out a bill for the postponement of national origins for a year.[34] The Chairman, Hiram Johnson of California, stated that a majority of the committee was in favor of repeal but that since a minority vigorously opposed this action, it was deemed best to compromise on postponement.[35] The minority, led by Senator David Reed of Pennsylvania, agreed to a committee report which justified postponement on the ground that the extra year would give the Quota Board time to perfect

30. *Congressional Record* (January 18, 1927), p. 1904.

31. Ibid. (February 1, 1927), p. 2662.

32. Johnson to Lewis (January 27, 1927), House Immigration Committee Papers, File H.R. 70A-F13.

33. "Repeal of 'National Origins' Provisions of Immigration Act of 1924," *House Report No. 2029*, 69th Congress, 2d Session (Washington, 1927), p. 2.

34. "Postponement of 'National Origins' Provisions of the Immigration Act of 1924," *Senate Report No. 2260*, 69th Congress, 1st Session (Washington, 1927), p. 2.

35. *Congressional Record* (February 1, 1927), p. 2677.

this method of calculating the quotas.[36] In order to be in accord with the Senate the House Committee later changed its position and approved the postponement resolution.[37] Thus postponement rather than repeal became the issue before Congress, despite the fact that majorities on the committees in both branches favored the latter course of action.

The Senate disposed of the postponement resolution with dispatch, passing it after a brief debate. In the House, however, the resolution brought forth a bitter debate in which the southern wing insisted upon the immediate introduction of national origins quotas. Albert Johnson introduced the postponement resolution, relying heavily on the substitute letter by the three secretaries to support his position.[38] Johnson also developed the argument that national origins was harmful because it stirred up nationalistic feelings among minority groups. "In fact," he asserted, "the figures under the 'national origins' plan serve to divide the Nordics, practically all of whom should not be divided, for we need a solid front in order to combat the foes of restriction." Instead of changing from one numerical plan to another, Johnson believed that the wisest course of action would be "to provide for the gradual elimination of all immigration." [39]

In reply to this appeal, the southern supporters of national origins, led by John Box of Texas, charged that their opponents were acting in response to pressure from foreign minority groups. Box asserted that the change of letters from the three secretaries was a deliberate political maneuver aimed at discrediting national origins. Decrying the influence of "hyphenate" voters, Box claimed that Johnson had come out against national origins to avert defeat in the 1926 Congressional elections. Several other southern congressmen added to this chant of alien influence, charging that the Republican stand on national origins had been adopted with an eye toward the 1928 elections, with the intent of winning German and Scandinavian support.[40]

When a vote was finally taken, the postponement resolution was passed by a two-thirds majority, 234 to 111.[41] The sectional break-

36. Ibid. (February 1, 1927), p. 2677; Senate Report 2260 (1927), p. 2.
37. Congressional Record (March 2, 1927), p. 5439.
38. Ibid. (March 3, 1927), p. 5648.
39. Ibid., p. 5785.
40. Ibid., pp. 5643–7, 5809.
41. Ibid., p. 5650.

down of the vote is especially interesting, for it shows that 89 of the
negative votes came from the South. Even more significant was the
stand of the midwestern representatives, who voted 104 to 15 for
postponement. The solid alliance of the South and Midwest which
had been the core of the restrictionist movement was temporarily
shattered by the national origins issue. The large Scandinavian and
German elements in the Midwest had caused the representatives from
this section to join with the predominantly antirestrictionist Northeast
on the question.[42] Johnson's fears that the national origins debate
would split asunder the forces backing restriction were borne out
by this first test vote.

Interest in national origins declined after the postponement, but
when Congress met again in the winter of 1928 the pressure from
minority groups resumed with great intensity. The German, Irish,
and Scandinavian organizations led the attack, with the local chapters
of such groups as the Sons of Norway, the Vasa Order of America
(Swedish) and the Steuben Society petitioning Congress.[43] In Detroit
an Anti-National Origins Clause League was formed which attempted
to organize the campaign along more effective lines. This group wrote
to Senator Copeland of New York, an antirestrictionist member of the
Senate Immigration Committee, asking, "What would you say would
be the most effective method of working with your committee?" [44] The
House Immigration Committee received numerous memorials from
midwestern towns, of which the following from Wisconsin is typical:

Changing the basis upon which immigrants are to be permitted to come to this country, as proposed in the immigration
law, would be, in our opinion, unfair and un-American. It is

42. The complete tabulation of this vote by sections was as follows:

Section	Yes	No
Northeast	97	2
Midwest	104	15
South	11	89
Far West	22	5

43. House Immigration Committee Papers, File H.R. 70A-F13; Senate Immigration Committee Papers, File Sen. 70A-J17.
44. Anti-National Origins League to Senator Copeland (January 26, 1928),
Senate Immigration Committee Papers, File Sen. 70A-J19.

well to recognize that people of Scandinavian origin have done
more for building up this state and other western states than
any other foreign people, and changing the quota would deprive these great states of those elements which have contributed so much to their development.[45]

To counter the barrage of petitions against national origins, the
patriotic societies undertook a vigorous campaign of their own. The
most active organization was the Junior Order of United American
Mechanics, which distributed a printed petition form that was used
by many of its local chapters to urge the retention of national origins.
The Congressional immigration committees received several hundred
memorials of this kind.[46] The Sons of the American Revolution, the
Patriotic Order Sons of America, and the Daughters of America were
all prominent in this battle of petitions. In addition, the patriotic
societies made a first step toward coordinating their activities by holding an immigration conference in January of 1928 at Memorial
Continental Hall in Washington.[47] The first postponement had aroused
them; by 1928 their pressure campaign was as active and noisy as that
of the foreign-born groups.

Both sides seemed to agree on one point, that Albert Johnson was
the key figure in the national origins debate. Johnson received a great
many letters from restrictionists who chastised him for his opposition
to national origins. Typical of this pressure was a letter from a Brook-
lyn citizen who wrote, "I cannot conceive that you, sworn to uphold
the Laws and Constitution of the United States, will permit any group
of foreigners to state what the laws of our country shall be." [48] At the
same time Johnson was besieged with letters from his Washington
constituents of Scandinavian and German descent. "If the 'National
Origin' becomes a law," wrote a Tacoma resident, "you are liable to
get that element [Scandinavian] against you in the next election." [49]

45. Petition from residents of Eau Claire, Wisconsin (February 1928), Senate
Immigration Committee Papers, File Sen. 70A-J17.
46. House Immigration Committee Papers, File H.R. 70A-F13; Senate Immigration Committee Papers, File Sen. 70A-J17.
47. Robert Ward, "Immigration," Eugenics, 2 (March 1929), 30.
48. C. S. Doane to Albert Johnson (March 5, 1928), House Immigration Committee Papers, File H.R. 70A-F13.
49. Arvid Rydstrom to Albert Johnson (March 14, 1928), House Immigration
Committee Papers, File H.R. 70A-F13.

Faced with this pressure from both factions, Johnson continued to assert that he opposed national origins because he was afraid it "creates an unnecessary division in the United States among those of ancestors from Northwestern Europe . . . all of whom have been strong in support of the restrictionist movement." [50] Yet the telegram Johnson sent Coolidge in 1926 warning that a failure to repudiate national origins would cost the Republicans many Congressional seats indicates that his position stemmed largely from a realization that the national origins plan was unacceptable to a great many northwestern European voters in his home district.[51]

The Congressional immigration committees again temporized by recommending the postponement of national origins.[52] While no general hearings were held, the Senate committee listened to the testimony of Joseph Hill, Chairman of the Quota Board, who defended the computations but admitted under questioning that another year of study would produce more accurate results.[53] The sharp disagreement inside the Senate committee continued, with both sides compromising on a policy of delay.[54] As a result Congress was once more faced with the question of postponement rather than with the true issue of whether or not to repeal national origins.

The Senate passed a postponement resolution without debate, but in the House both factions criticized the immigration committee for failing to act on the basic issue of proposed repeal. The charge was frequently made that fear of the coming elections had induced the administration to soft-pedal national origins. Representative Kvale of Minnesota, an opponent of national origins, asked congressmen "to face the proposition as men and not dodge aside from it and conceal ourselves under the shelter of an ambiguous vote until the oncoming storm of the presidential election shall have passed." Even more to the point was Representative Box's stinging rebuke, "The foreign blocs have made you afraid to let it go into effect, while the

50. Albert Johnson to B. W. Southworth (February 4, 1928), House Immigration Committee Papers, File H.R. 70A-F13.

51. Johnson to Coolidge (August 25, 1926), Coolidge Papers, File 133.

52. *Congressional Record* (March 19, 1928), p. 4961.

53. "National Origins Provision of the Immigration Law," *Hearing before the Senate Committee on Immigration,* 70th Congress, 1st Session (Washington, 1928), p. 17.

54. *Congressional Record* (March 19, 1928), p. 4961.

patriotic societies and patriotic citizens who believe in restriction have made you afraid to repeal it." After this brief debate, the postponement resolution was passed without a record vote.[55] There can be little doubt that the fear of losing potential votes in the 1928 elections was the principal factor in this artful dodging of the real issue at stake.

During the spring of 1928 the national origins question gradually receded, but it returned to the forefront of public attention in August when the presidential campaign got under way. Though neither the Democrats nor the Republicans mentioned national origins in their party platforms, both nominees took a stand on this question. Or as Senator Reed later said, "both candidates forgot their platforms, shut their eyes to what their parties had done, and went off wooing strange gods." [56]

On August 11 the Republican party nominated Herbert Hoover, who as Secretary of Commerce had taken part in the substitution of letters transmitting the report of the Quota Board for 1927. In his acceptance speech Hoover stated clearly his opposition to national origins, asserting that it was impossible to determine national origins quotas "accurately and without hardship." [57] After this strong criticism of the new plan, Hoover was strangely silent on this question throughout the campaign.[58] In a later debate in Congress several southern Senators charged that Republican orators in the South had denied that Hoover favored repeal of the national origins plan.[59] Thus it would seem that Hoover and his campaign managers tried to win German and Irish votes in the North by opposing the new quotas and at the same time capture the votes of southern restrictionists by favoring the national origins plan in the South.

The Democratic candidate, Al Smith, took an even more ambiguous stand on the national origins question. In his acceptance speech he made no reference to national origins but attacked the existing 1890 census base as "designed to discriminate against certain nationalities." [60] Shortly afterward, at a campaign speech in St. Paul, Smith

55. Ibid. (March 22, 1928), p. 5229; (March 29, 1928), pp. 557–81.
56. Ibid. (June 6, 1929), p. 2413.
57. Ibid. (March 3, 1929), p. 5195.
58. So far as can be seen from the files of the New York *Times* for the campaign period.
59. *Congressional Record* (June 5, 1929), p. 2383; (June 6, 1929), p. 2430.
60. New York *Times* (August 23, 1928), p. 3.

stated that he agreed with Hoover's criticisms of the national origins plan.[61] Smith's criticisms of both national origins and the 1890 census base caused many people to question his sincerity in supporting immigration restriction at all. Most newspapers at the time interpreted Smith's stand as favoring the use of the 1920 census as a base, which would have appealed to southeastern European voters.[62] The Republicans capitalized on Smith's ambiguous position, with vice-presidential candidate Curtis charging that Smith had been opposed to the 1924 law.[63] The Democratic nominee replied to these assaults by reaffirming his support of immigration restriction in speeches in the South, but he still neglected to state which plan he favored as a basis for quotas.[64] Smith's failure to define his views clearly left him open to the charge that he was posing as a restrictionist in the South and a friend to immigration in the Northeast. Moreover, his attack on the 1890 census base created the suspicion that the opposition to national origins was aimed at a sweeping liberalization of the whole policy of restriction.

The close of the presidential campaign ushered in the final stage of the national origins controversy. Encouraged by Hoover's victory, the groups urging repeal seemed confident that the battle was won. During the winter of 1929 the pressure from foreign minority groups lessened considerably. While petitions asking for repeal of the national origins plan continued to flow into the immigration committees, they came in much smaller numbers than in 1928.[65] At the Senate hearing held in February only a handful of witnesses were present to speak against national origins. One witness, a publisher of a German language newspaper, commented on this fact, stating that the German element had assumed that Hoover's election had settled the question.[66] The minority groups undoubtedly felt heartened when both the United States Chamber of Commerce and the AFL came out against

61. Ibid. (September 2, 1928), p. 2.
62. Ibid. (September 5, 1928), p. 26; "The Candidates on Immigration," *Literary Digest*, 98 (September 22, 1928), 16.
63. New York *Times* (November 3, 1928), p. 5.
64. Ibid. (October 13, 1928), p. 6; (October 14, 1928), p. 25.
65. House Immigration Committee Papers, File H.R. 70A-F13; Senate Immigration Committee Papers, File Sen. 71A-J32.
66. "National Origins Provision of the Immigration Law," *Hearings before the Senate Committee on Immigration,* 70th Congress, 2d Session (Washington, 1929), p. 131.

national origins.[67] But neither of these economic organizations had a
vital interest at stake, and their resolutions were merely formal statements to the effect that the present 1890 census basis was satisfactory.
It seemed as though the crusade for repeal had exhausted its energies
just as the controversy reached its climax.

In contrast to the growing inertia of the minority groups, the
patriotic societies, discovering that the key to success was coordinated
effort, organized a thorough campaign of pressure in defense of
national origins. Though continuing to petition Congress, the restrictionists realized that other methods were necessary. On November 28,
1928, representatives of thirty-three patriotic societies met in New
York to found the Immigration Conference Committee, naming John
Trevor as chairman and Demerest Lloyd, a Washington lobbyist, as
his assistant.[68] The purpose of this organization was to coordinate
the activities of the various societies on immigration policy and "to
bring the influence of their many and powerful organizations to bear
upon Senators and Representatives when it was deemed necessary." [69]
To achieve their aims, the societies organized a permanent subcommittee in Washington "to consider ways and means of meeting any situation connected with immigration legislation which may come before
Congress." [70] This formidable array of pressure groups was greatly
strengthened when the American Legion passed a resolution late in
1928 favoring the national origins plan.[71]

The effectiveness of concerted effort was demonstrated at the Senate
hearings held in February. Demerest Lloyd handled the restrictionist
case, presenting the various members of patriotic societies to the committee and rebutting the testimony of opposition witnesses.[72] The
principal argument advanced was familiar—that national origins was
necessary to preserve the racial homogeneity of the American people.
To counter the charge of discrimination, the secretary-general of the

67. United States Chamber of Commerce, *Resolutions Adopted at the Seven-
teenth Annual Meeting, May 3, 1929* (Washington, 1929), p. 13; New York *Times*
(March 10, 1929), p. 3.

68. Robert Ward, "Immigration," *Eugenics, 2* (March 1929), 50.

69. *The Minute Man, 23* (April 1929), 543. This was the official magazine of
the Sons of the American Revolution.

70. Ward, p. 30.

71. *Summary of the Proceedings of the Tenth Annual Convention of the American Legion* (San Antonio, 1928), p. 36.

72. "National Origins," Senate *Hearings* (1929), pp. 30–6.

Sons of the American Revolution asserted, "The temporary 1890 'foreign-born' census harshly discriminates against the native-born descendants of those distinguished patriots which it is the function of our society to commemorate."[73] The defenders of national origins pointed out that the movement for repeal stemmed from the foreign born. Charging that the aliens in the United States had evaded military service during the war, the American Legion lobbyist concluded, "The issue can be brought squarely between patriotism and slackerism—shall slackerism be represented in selecting our immigrants over patriotism?"[74] Apparently such intensely nationalistic appeals were effective, since at the conclusion of the hearings the Senate Committee on Immigration voted seven to four to pigeonhole all bills aimed at postponing or repealing national origins.[75]

The patriotic societies continued to exert pressure while the national origins measure was debated in Congress. The chairman of the Sons of the American Revolution immigration committee found it necessary to issue a call to the officers of all local chapters "to use their influence with their Congressmen and Senators."[76] In March, when a vote on the issue was about to be taken, the Immigration Conference Committee inserted advertisements in the Washington newspapers calling on the legislators to uphold national origins.[77] Having met with success during the winter, the patriotic groups revamped their organization in April, including about twenty more kindred societies and changing the name to the American Coalition. This new body adopted the slogan "Keep America American" and stated that its main purpose was to offset the attempts of "alien hyphenate groups" to weaken the immigration laws.[78] The American Coalition was the final embodiment of the movement to coordinate the activities of the patriotic societies in defense of national origins, and as such proved to be eminently successful.

The final debate on the national origins plan took place in Congress during the winter and spring of 1929. The House considered the ques-

73. Ibid., p. 126.
74. Ibid., p. 76.
75. *Minute Man*, 23, 544.
76. Ibid., 24 (July 1929), 101.
77. *Congressional Record* (March 3, 1929), p. 5200.
78. *The American Coalition* (pamphlet, 1929); *Minute Man*, 24, 101.

tion during its lame duck session in February 1929 and finally passed another postponement resolution. The Senate failed to consider this measure before Congress adjourned but took up the issue in a slightly different form at a special session called by President Hoover in the spring. Despite the time lag, both debates were on the principle of national origins and can be examined together.

Four arguments were advanced and constantly reiterated in the debate. Of the two put forward by the proponents of repeal, the question of the accuracy of the national origins quotas was the simplest and most direct. The supporters of the existing quota plan argued that the new quotas were based largely on the highly questionable practice of classifying nationality by surnames contained in the 1790 census returns. They contended that such a method was sheer guesswork and urged the continuance of the less complex 1890 census plan. The advocates of the national origins plan replied that statistical experts had approved their plan, citing the testimony of Hill at the Senate hearings to the effect that the national origins plan was as accurate as the existing method. They pointed out that the 1790 census played a very small part in the total calculations and concluded that the opinion of experts repudiated the attacks of congressmen unskilled in statistical analysis.[79] On this point the restrictionists seem to have been justified. The determination of national origins was a complex and difficult operation, but it was accomplished by six highly trained and disinterested men who were convinced that their results were accurate.[80] It would appear that the critics of the plan had erroneously equated complexity with inaccuracy in order to discredit a quota system they opposed for other reasons.

Much more significant is the other major criticism advanced by the opponents of national origins. They contended that because the changes in the quotas favored Great Britain at the expense of the other countries of northwestern Europe, the plan was unfair and discriminatory. Senator Gerald Nye, leader of the opposition in the Senate, asserted that national origins "penalizes the races which have con-

79. *Congressional Record* (February 14, 1929), p. 3482; (March 3, 1929), pp. 5192–3, 5196–7; (June 5, 1929), p. 2381.

80. The committee of the American Council of Learned Societies gave its full approval of the surname analysis used on the 1790 census returns. *Annual Report of the American Historical Association, 1931, 1,* 125.

tributed the finest that is in us in America today." At times this argument degenerated into a comparison between Scandinavian and English immigrants, with the assertion being made in the Senate that the Scandinavian immigrants were superior. A favorite theme was that the plan was really a "British-origin law." "The operation of the national-origins clause is an affirmative statement by the Congress of the United States that the continuity of our government is dependent upon England. Such a declaration of subservience should be abhorrent to all who consider themselves Americans." [81] This appeal to nationalism by a congressman of Irish descent is typical of the minority group consciousness which dominated the debate.

The sincerity of the argument that the national origins plan was unfair because it discriminated against Germans, Irish, and Scandinavians is suspect in the light of attacks on the character of the peoples of southeastern Europe. The midwestern opponents of national origins seized upon the fact that the new quotas resulted in very slight increases in the allotments of such countries as Italy and Poland. They labeled the southeastern Europeans undesirable immigrants who displaced superior types from northwestern Europe under the national origins plan. These invidious comparisons between immigrants of different countries contradicted the concept of racial equality inherent in any charge of discrimination. Perhaps the best indication of the racial animosities which lay behind the whole debate is afforded by this comment from Senator Glenn of Illinois: "We are all talking about our admiration for these various nations and how we respect all of them; and yet back in our minds, in our real and deliberate judgment, we know that there are people who will be admitted under either plan that we would much prefer not to have here at all." [82]

In reply to this charge of racial discrimination, the supporters of national origins developed the third argument used in the debate—that the assault on national origins was led by minority groups who had their own selfish interests at heart rather than any consideration

81. *Congressional Record* (February 14, 1929), pp. 3475, 3477; (March 3, 1929), pp. 5200–1; (June 5, 1929), p. 2383; (June 13, 1929), pp. 2777–9. Representative McCormack of Massachusetts made this statement.

82. Ibid. (April 29, 1929), p. 634; (June 6, 1929), p. 2428; (June 13, 1929), pp. 2773–5.

of what was best for the nation. Senator Reed maintained that the national origins plan was an attempt to preserve the racial composition of the United States and was not intended as a slur on any race. But Reed and his fellow restrictionists evidently believed that the best defense was a strong offense, for they concentrated their efforts on discrediting their opponents. Stating that the minority groups were concerned solely with gaining exorbitant quotas for their own nationalities, Senator Reed called for the suspension of all immigration "until such time as the people of this land learn to think as Americans and not as hyphenated citizens of some European country." Many congressmen felt that the very fact that the patriotic societies supported national origins in opposition to the foreign-born groups was sufficient reason to vote for the new plan. Congressman Box expressed this idea most dramatically when he exclaimed, "If the long, loud roll of ayes repudiates the position of the American Legion on this question and proves that the pro-German and alien forces are the stronger, it will constitute a sad tattoo, a retreat, temporary, I hope, of heroes and patriots." [83]

In support of their position the restrictionists put forth the final argument—that the attack on national origins was really an attack on the principle of restriction. They seized on the fact that strong anti-restrictionists such as Sabath of Illinois were against national origins and cited this as proof that restriction itself was at stake. Senator Heflin of Alabama asserted that the agitation for repeal was "a strong and powerful organized effort to break down restricted immigration into the United States." In the House, Jenkins of Ohio envisioned the repeal of national origins as an entering wedge which would lead to the destruction of the 1924 legislation.[84]

The midwestern opponents of national origins rebutted this charge, citing their own voting records in 1924. Senator Nye stated that he agreed with the principle of preserving the existing racial balance in the United States but felt this goal was accomplished by the 1890 census. A shrewder reply was made by Representative Newton of Massachusetts, who claimed that national origins was detrimental be-

83. Ibid. (March 3, 1929), pp. 5195, 5199; (April 29, 1929), p. 637; (May 25, 1929), p. 1900; (June 6, 1929), p. 2422.
84. Ibid. (December 6, 1928), p. 141; (March 3, 1929), pp. 5190, 5195; (June 7, 1929), p. 2502.

cause it split the restrictionist group, forcing many of northwestern European descent into the antirestrictionist camp.[85] The alignment of forces in the debate bears out this observation, which Albert Johnson had advanced back in 1927. The opposition to national origins was founded on a strange alliance between restrictionists from the Midwest who favored German, Irish, and Scandinavian immigration and antirestrictionists from the Northeast who wanted larger quotas for southeastern Europe. The latter group hoped to discredit the principle of restriction by encouraging the battle between the Nordics. Thus the strange paradox of the champions of southeastern European immigration supporting the 1890 census plan, which had been deliberately designed to discriminate against immigrants from eastern and southern Europe.

The debate in Congress ended in the spring of 1929 with a final decision in favor of retention of the national origins plan. The House, where sentiment against it was strongest, passed a postponement resolution just before the adjournment of Coolidge's last Congress in March. The vote was very close, 192 to 152.[86] Again the southern representatives formed the core of the opposition, contributing nearly two-thirds of the negative votes. But 80 per cent of the northeastern congressmen, 75 per cent of the midwestern, and 71 per cent of the far western supported the postponement resolution. The large block of midwestern votes was the decisive factor in this temporary defeat for national origins.[87] Though postponement passed the House, that body failed to work quickly enough to secure Senate action. The resolution was presented to the Senate on March 3, and Senate supporters of national origins were able to prevent Senate action in the final days of that session.[88]

85. Ibid. (March 2, 1929), pp. 5126–7; (March 3, 1929), p. 5192; (April 29, 1929), p. 634; (June 3, 1929), p. 2240.

86. Ibid. (March 3, 1929), p. 5202.

87. The sectional breakdown was as follows:

Section	For	Against
Northeast	80	20
Midwest	89	27
South	3	97
Far West	20	8

88. *Congressional Record* (March 4, 1929), pp. 5222–3.

The situation at the end of the session was extremely embarrassing for the newly inaugurated president, Herbert Hoover. He was on record against national origins, yet the law required him to proclaim the new quotas before April 1. After the Attorney-General ruled that this action was mandatory, Hoover officially announced the national origin quotas which would take effect on July 1.[89] In a press conference the same day, he stated his views. "While I am strongly in favor of restricted and selected immigration, I have opposed the national origins basis. I therefore naturally dislike the duty of issuing and installing the new bases but the President of the United States must be the first to obey the law." [90]

The three months between the date of proclamation and the date of effectiveness of the new quotas afforded the administration one last chance to repeal national origins. Hoover called for a special session of Congress in April and included a request for the repeal of national origins in his program.[91] Sure of House approval, the administration leaders concentrated on the Senate. However, Senator Reed of Pennsylvania, refusing to cooperate, succeeded in getting the Senate Immigration Committee to table the repeal bill.[92] In a desperate effort to get the question of national origins before the Senate, Senator Nye of North Dakota introduced a resolution to discharge the Senate Immigration Committee from further consideration of the repeal bill. The Nye resolution was the subject of the final debate in the Senate.[93] On June 13 the Senate voted 43 to 37 against this resolution, thereby ending the controversy in favor of national origins. In this final vote the midwestern senators stood firm in their opposition, but their colleagues from the Northeast joined with the southern senators to maintain the national origins plan.[94]

89. *Interpreter Releases, 6* (March 25, 1929), 54.
90. William S. Myers, ed., *The State Papers and Other Public Writings of Herbert Hoover* (New York, 1934), *1*, 21.
91. William S. Myers and Walter H. Newton, *The Hoover Administration, a Documented Narrative* (New York, 1936), p. 380.
92. New York *Times* (April 24, 1929), p. 11.
93. *Congressional Record* (April 23, 1929), p. 343.
94. The sectional breakdown was as follows:

Section	For	Against
Northeast	7	10
Midwest	18	3
South	1	22
Far West	11	8

The decision to retain the national origin quotas was a victory for the patriotic societies. A majority of the American people appeared to be unconcerned over how the quotas were distributed as long as the principle of restriction was maintained. Only special groups, the patriotic societies on the one hand and foreign minority organizations on the other, had a vital interest in this question. Though small, both were able to organize pressure campaigns which exerted a great deal of influence on members of Congress. The minority groups took the original initiative in this action, but by 1929 the patriotic societies had learned how to coordinate their efforts successfully. The relentless pressure that these advocates of restriction were able to apply at the climax of the debate proved to be the determining factor in the retention of national origins.

If one analyzes the national origins debate from the standpoint of the four aspects of immigration policy outlined in the first chapter, it is clear that nationalism and ethnic considerations were the two main factors involved. The economic aspect did not enter into the controversy because there was no question of changing the number of immigrants. Nor did foreign policy intrude, since there was no attempt to single out immigrants from any one country for obviously unfair treatment. Uppermost in the minds of both the supporters and critics of national origins were the two factors which had predominated in the passage of the 1924 law. The belief that racial homogeneity was essential for the national unity of the American people remained the basic principle of American immigration policy.

The concept of racial nationalism continued to hold wide currency in the late 1920's. Two of the principal advocates of this theory, Madison Grant and Lothrop Stoddard, reiterated their views in this period, writing that the secret of national unity was a likemindedness which depended on similarity in temperament and blood.[95] The best expression of the philosophy behind restriction was a book by a Chicago lawyer, Edward Lewis, entitled *America, Nation or Confusion*. In contrast to the writings of the more extreme racists, this work was a temperate and carefully reasoned justification of the quota system. Lewis contended that "nations come of slow growth and long travail, that they depend on like-mindedness and that if

95. Madison Grant, "America for the Americans," *The Forum*, 74 (September 1925), 350–1; Lothrop Stoddard, *Reforging America* (New York, 1927), p. 227.

the United States becomes a hodge-podge of a score of races, no one of which is dominant, it will lose its unity and become like Metternich's idea of Italy, a geographical expression." [96]

The striking feature of the national origins debate was the wide agreement between the opposing sides on the basic principle of racial, or at least of cultural, nationalism. The minority pressure groups and the midwestern congressmen stated their belief in the necessity of preserving the racial and cultural homogeneity of the American people. They differed from the patriotic societies and the southern congressmen only on the question of the means to this end, contending that the 1890 census quotas would result in a more homogeneous immigration than the national origins allotments. The absence of a basic conflict on any vital principle helps explain the petty bickering which characterized the debate. It was essentially a "fight between the Nordics" over the preferential quotas which had been won in 1924.

The true significance of the national origins debate is the inherent weakness it revealed in the principle of group selection. By emphasizing the nationality of immigrants, the new quota system stirred up antagonisms among the various foreign elements in the United States. Each minority group wanted a large quota for its own nationality, and therefore a process of competitive bidding for favoritism ensued which led to disharmony rather than national unity. The nationalities which lost out at this public auction became bitter and resentful, feeling that they were being discriminated against. Aimed at fostering national unity by creating a homogeneous population, the selection of immigrants by nationalities tended to stimulate minority group consciousness, the very antithesis of the avowed goal.

It is easy to criticize the quota system, yet one must ask what alternative there was to this policy. The only other method of regulating immigration that had been proposed was a system of individual selection by objective tests. This idea was favored by the critics of the quota system. In Congress, Senators Reed of Missouri and Allen of Kansas had urged a policy of choosing immigrants by their individual qualities rather than by their nationality. [97] Many social scien-

96. Edward S. Lewis, *America, Nation or Confusion* (New York, 1928), pp. 14–15.

97. *Congressional Record* (February 1, 1927), pp. 2680–1; (June 13, 1929), p. 2780.

tists favored individual selection, claiming that tests of moral, physical, mental, and economic fitness would greatly improve the quality of immigration.[98] Fine as this concept was in theory, the restrictionists were able to discredit it on practical grounds. Edward Lewis pointed out that while idealists were fond of advancing the concept of individual selection, they had made no concrete proposals as to what type of tests should be given, nor had they considered the difficulties in administering such examinations to the hundreds of thousands of Europeans who applied for visas annually.[99] There seemed to be no satisfactory reply to this criticism, and as a result individual selection was never seriously considered as an alternative to the quota system.

Whatever the objections against the principle of group selection, there can be no doubt that the national origins scheme provided a sounder basis for quotas than the 1890 census plan. The goal of both methods was to select immigrants in proportion to the ethnic composition of the United States. The 1890 census plan had been adopted because it roughly approximated this objective, but it was far from satisfactory as a precise standard. On the other hand, national origin quotas had been specifically designed to meet the goal of homogeneity, and they were as accurate as was humanly possible in view of the incompleteness of the available data. The whole controversy was unfortunate in view of the animosities it aroused, but in the last analysis —always accepting the basic premise of group selection—one must conclude that Congress made the better choice in retaining the national origins plan.

98. Clifford Kirkpatrick, *Intelligence and Immigration* (Philadelphia, 1925), pp. 105–15; Ales Hrdlicka, "The Choice of Future Americans," *Outlook, 164* (January 15, 1930), 99; J. J. Spengler, "Is the Present American Immigration Policy Sound?" *Scientific Monthly, 30* (March 1930), 233–4.

99. Lewis, pp. 76–85.

3. The Western Hemisphere and the Philippines

WHILE CONGRESS was engaged in determining a permanent policy for European immigration in the late 1920's, two new problems had developed which became the focus of attention in the early years of the next decade. Under the provisions of the Act of 1924 both the countries of the Western Hemisphere and the Philippine Islands were exempted from immigration restrictions. The drastic limitations on European immigration greatly increased the demand for laborers from these areas, particularly in the agricultural Southwest. Mexican laborers began entering the United States in large numbers in 1924, while Filipino immigration reached significant proportions a few years later. This increase in immigrants from Mexico and the Philippines caused a growing demand for effective restriction of non-European immigration. Bills proposing quotas for the Western Hemisphere and exclusion of Filipinos were introduced in Congress and became the subject of debate in 1930. The restrictionists, having successfully defended the national origins system, now concentrated their efforts on plugging the holes in the immigration laws.

The exemption of Canada and the Latin American countries from the quota provisions was not an oversight on the part of Congress. When the 1924 act was being debated in Congress, Senators Willis of Ohio and Harris of Georgia offered amendments to include the countries of the Western Hemisphere under the quota system. Their proposal was decisively rejected by a vote of 60 to 12.[1] In the debate the majority clearly showed that they believed traditional American policy toward Latin America demanded favorable treatment of these countries in immigration policy. Senator Reed, the leading restrictionist in the Senate, appealed to the ideal of Pan-Americanism as justification for exempting Canada and Latin America.[2] Since immigration was almost negligible from Central and South America, the debate focused on the question of Mexican immigrants. The supporters of

1. *Congressional Record* (April 18, 1924), pp. 6620–1, 6634.
2. Ibid., pp. 6623–4.

the amendment repeatedly warned of the danger of leaving the back door open, but they failed to convince their colleagues with prophecies of a great influx of peons.[3]

The fears of a flood of Mexicans entering the United States were not borne out in the latter half of the 1920's. The peak year was 1924, when 89,336 came in, but after this high point Mexican immigration fell to about 50,000 annually, a figure only slightly higher than the average for the period 1919–24.[4] But with the sharp drop in European immigration, the Mexican proportion of the total immigration greatly increased, and the restrictionists found this a cause for alarm. Furthermore, it was generally acknowledged that the official statistics in no way reflected the actual number of immigrants entering from Mexico, since many crossed the border illegally to escape payment of the head tax and visa fees, which totaled eighteen dollars.[5] Thus the belief grew that Mexican immigration was extremely large and out of proportion to the numbers coming from Europe.

From this situation there developed a demand for the restriction of Western Hemisphere immigration, and particularly that from Mexico, a demand which reached its zenith in 1930. The groups behind this movement were familiar ones—patriotic societies, eugenicist organizations, and labor unions. Stressing the need for consistency in immigration policy, the restrictionists found a convenient slogan in the phrase "close the back door." However, this campaign to complete the immigration barrier around the United States ran into strong and well-organized opposition from the economic interests of the Southwest. Farmers, cattlemen, sugar manufacturers, and railroad executives from this region had found Mexico a valuable source of common labor for their enterprises. Asserting that the stoppage of

3. Ibid., pp. 6621, 6630.

4. *Annual Report of the Commissioner-General of Immigration, 1930* (Washington, 1930), p. 206. The sharp drop in 1925 can be accounted for by a $10 visa fee established by the 1924 act.

5. Manuel Gamio, *Mexican Immigration to the United States* (Chicago, 1930), p. 9. However, American statistics did not show accurately the number of Mexicans who returned to Mexico, since most of these did not record their departure with the immigration service. Mexican statistics on this point, probably somewhat inflated, showed that in 1924, 105,834 returned to Mexico from the United States. The unreliability of official statistics makes it very difficult to gauge the actual flow of permanent Mexican immigrants to the United States, but it does seem evident that the restrictionists exaggerated the number considerably.

Mexican immigration would mean nothing less than economic disaster for the Southwest, these employers bitterly contested the efforts of the restrictionists to place a quota on Mexico. In addition, the State Department, which was interested in fostering better relations with Latin America, declared its unequivocal opposition to any measure that would restrict immigration from the countries of the Western Hemisphere. A long and bitter dispute resulted, which was aired before Congressional committees for several years and finally reached the floor of Congress in 1930.

It should be emphasized again that restrictionists were primarily concerned with Mexican immigration. Though about 75,000 Canadians entered the United States annually, a greater influx than that from Mexico, there was little demand for a reduction of this number.[6] Nor was immigration from Central and South America a vital issue, since it totaled less than 5,000 annually.[7] However, the restrictionists, in attempting to devise a plan to limit Mexican immigration, were in a dilemma. If they advocated a quota for all Western Hemisphere countries, as they did at first, they were faced with opposition from northern border states which were sympathetic to Canada and from the many advocates of Pan-Americanism. On the other hand, if they supported a quota for Mexico alone, as they later did, they were open to the charge of flagrant discrimination against a neighboring country. This difficulty in devising an acceptable plan for the limitation of Mexican immigration, together with the strong opposition of southwestern economic interests and the State Department, made the task of "closing the back door" a much more formidable one than any the restrictionists had yet undertaken.

The movement for the limitation of Mexican immigration began in 1926 when Representative John Box of Texas, an ardent restrictionist and member of the House Immigration Committee, introduced a bill to apply the quota provisions to the countries of the Western Hemisphere. For four years the problem of Mexican immigration was discussed at hearings before the House and Senate immigration committees. These bodies heard testimony that filled several thousands of pages in a war of words that seemed to have no forseeable end. The

6. *Annual Report of the Commissioner-General of Immigration, 1930*, p. 206.
7. Ibid., p. 206.

opposing sides failed to agree on even the most elementary facts, and the result of the skirmishing was a deadlock on the basic issue. The question of Mexican immigration did not arise on the floor of Congress during this period, partly because of the absorption of Congressional interest in the national origins problem and partly because of the bitter disagreement which prevailed on the Mexican issue.

A variety of pressure groups appeared at the Congressional hearings to argue for and against a limitation on Mexican immigration. The principal advocates of a quota were the labor interests, primarily the AFL, and the patriotic societies, along with some eugenicist organizations. The labor representatives argued on economic grounds, calling the Mexicans cheap laborers who deprived Americans of jobs, while the patriotic societies and the eugenicists employed racist concepts to justify a Mexican quota. To oppose the restrictionist demands a host of representatives of economic interests appeared at the hearings. Farmers from the Southwest who used Mexican labor for harvesting, railroad officials, sugar beet manufacturers, even livestock and mining representatives, presented the case for Mexican immigration on economic grounds. Even more significant, representatives of the State Department, led by Secretary of State Kellogg, warned the committee that any measure restricting immigration from the Western Hemisphere would contradict the nation's Pan-American policy. Never before had a restrictionist proposal met such stubborn opposition.

The economic argument against Mexican immigration was quite simple and straightforward. The Mexicans, charged the representatives of organized labor, displaced Americans from jobs in the Southwest because of their willingness to work for extremely low wages.[8] According to Box, the immigrants from across the Rio Grande were accustomed to wages and living conditions which would enable them "to drive American labor to the deepest poverty and ultimately to

8. "Seasonal Agricultural Laborers From Mexico," *Hearings before the House Committee on Immigration and Naturalization,* 69th Congress, 1st Session (Washington, 1926), p. 324; "Immigration from Countries of the Western Hemisphere," *Hearings before the House Committee on Immigration and Naturalization,* 70th Congress, 1st Session (Washington, 1928), pp. 689–90; "Restriction of Western Hemisphere Immigration," *Hearings before the Senate Committee on Immigration,* 70th Congress, 1st Session (Washington, 1928), pp. 6–8; "Western Hemisphere Immigration," *Hearings before the House Committee on Immigration and Naturalization,* 71st Congress, 2d Session (Washington, 1930), pp. 347–51.

extermination." [9] When employers contended that there was no competition involved (since there was a shortage of common labor in the Southwest), the restrictionists replied that any shortage could be remedied by the payment of decent wages.[10] In the eyes of the Texas Commissioner of Labor, "The simple and sordid truth is that employers of labor prefer to recruit Mexican labor because they can be induced to work for starvation wages." [11]

Closely related to the cheap labor argument was the position taken by the restrictionists on the social aspects of Mexican immigration. The use of Mexicans might reduce the costs of labor for industry, many witnesses asserted, but in the long run they proved expensive to society. The cost to the taxpayers in terms of crime, charity, and disease far outweighed any short-term benefits that accrued to employers.[12] This viewpoint was concisely summarized by a Texan who charged, "The influx of Mexican peons is already taxing our schools beyond their capacity; it is lowering our educational standing; it is creating an unhealthy political condition, and will ultimately result in the most serious consequences." [13] From every aspect, the Mexican immigrant was described as a social leper who would contaminate the American way of life.

The third argument advanced by the advocates of Mexican restriction was the ethnic one, and there can be little doubt that in their minds it was the most important consideration. In 1925 the House Immigration Committee published a report by Robert Foerster, a Princeton economist, in which he pointed out that over 90 per cent of the Latin American population was of Indian blood. Foerster concluded that these people were racially inferior to white stock and recommended severe limitation of Latin American immigration.[14] Three years later Harry Laughlin, the eugenicist who served as biological expert to the House Committee from 1921 to 1924, testified to the

9. "Immigration from Western Hemisphere," House *Hearings* (1928), p. 782.

10. "Seasonal Agricultural Laborers," House *Hearings* (1926), p. 301; "Western Hemisphere Immigration," House *Hearings* (1930), p. 368.

11. "Immigration from Western Hemisphere," House *Hearings* (1928), p. 724.

12. Ibid., pp. 16, 55; "Western Hemisphere Immigration," House *Hearings* (1930), p. 384.

13. "Immigration from Western Hemisphere," House *Hearings* (1928), p. 739.

14. "Immigration from Latin America, the West Indies, and Canada," *Hearings before the House Committee on Immigration and Naturalization,* 68th Congress, 2d Session (Washington, 1925), pp. 304–37.

same effect on the racial qualities of the Mexican immigrants. Stating that race should be the basic standard for judging immigrants, Laughlin urged that Western Hemisphere immigration be restricted to whites.[15] Members of patriotic societies also brought up racist arguments at the hearings, comparing the influx of cheap Mexican labor to Negro slaves.[16] The most violent racial prejudices on this question were displayed by Representative Box of Texas, the sponsor of the restrictive measure. In an address to a group of patriotic societies at Memorial Continental Hall in Washington in 1928, Box labeled the Mexican immigrants "illiterate, unclean, peonized masses" who stemmed from "a mixture of Mediterranean-blooded Spanish peasants with low-grade Indians who did not fight to extinction but submitted and multiplied as serfs."[17] Speaking before the House Immigration Committee, Box warned that the influx of Mexicans "creates the most insidious and general mixture of white, Indian, and negro blood strains ever produced in America."[18]

The narrow bigotry so evident in Box's statements indicates the basic motivation behind the drive for Mexican restriction. While undoubtedly organized labor was concerned with the effect of Mexican immigration on the wage scale, the drive for restriction represented primarily the desire to keep out what many considered an undesirable ethnic group. The economic and social arguments tended to be window dressing to cover up the basic reason for restriction. The ethnic ideas developed at these hearings differed somewhat from earlier ones, since the more sophisticated argument of the preservation of racial homogeneity in the United States was neglected in favor of outright racial prejudice.

In contrast to the restrictionist emphasis on racial arguments, the opponents of Western Hemisphere quotas stressed economic factors. The economy of the Southwest, they asserted, depended upon farming, livestock, and transportation industries which required a large number of hand workers. Since many of these jobs were both difficult and unpleasant, native American workers refused to perform them. However, Mexican immigrants had no such qualms, and they had

15. "Immigration from Western Hemisphere," House *Hearings* (1928), pp. 711, 716.
16. Ibid., pp. 15–16, 679–80.
17. *Congressional Record* (February 9, 1928), pp. 2817–18.
18. "Western Hemisphere Immigration," House *Hearings* (1930), p. 75.

proved themselves capable and reliable laborers. Witness after witness reiterated this theme, asserting that rather than competing with American workers, the Mexicans did the menial labor which was vital to the agriculture and industry of the Southwest. "Stoop work" in the.beet and vegetable fields, the grubbing of land, and section work on the railroads were described as tedious and backbreaking tasks which were degrading to the native American worker. The Mexican laborers, by accepting these undesirable tasks, enabled agriculture and industry to flourish, thereby creating attractive opportunities for American workers in the higher job levels.[19] Furthermore, the opponents of Mexican immigration quotas claimed that the prosperity of the Southwest was at stake. The fact that only Mexicans could perform the necessary common labor meant that enterprises which required hand labor would be destroyed by the restriction of Mexican immigration. This viewpoint was graphically presented by a Californian who stated, "We are opposed to this bill; absolutely opposed to this bill, because it will reduce the production; it will stop half of the farming on the other side of the Missouri River—it will ruin that farming, because we cannot operate." [20]

In replying to the social and racial charges made by the restrictionists, the witnesses favoring Mexican immigration admitted their partial validity but asserted that in this case the economic factor far outweighed sociological considerations. The opposition witnesses were split on the question of the social desirability of Mexican immigrants. Some held that Mexicans were a social asset, far superior to the Chinese and Japanese laborers on the Pacific Coast. A sugar company executive called them "a God-fearing, family-loving, law-abiding set of people," while a Texas farmer thought that they offered "excellent material for American citizenship." [21] Others were less optimistic, acknowledging the racial inferiority of the Mexicans but claiming

19. "Seasonal Agricultural Laborers," House *Hearings* (1926), pp. 21, 62–5, 155–6, 225; "Immigration from Western Hemisphere," House *Hearings* (1928), pp. 99–101, 187, 253, 388–91, 403–8, 418; "Restriction of Western Hemisphere Immigration," Senate *Hearings* (1928), pp. 88–9.

20. "Seasonal Agricultural Laborers," House *Hearings* (1926), p. 206; "Immigration from Western Hemisphere," House *Hearings* (1928), pp. 160, 191; "Restriction of Western Hemisphere Immigration," Senate *Hearings* (1928), p. 26.

21. "Seasonal Agricultural Laborers," House *Hearings* (1926), pp. 45, 110, 243; "Immigration from Western Hemisphere," House *Hearings* (1928), pp. 185, 412.

that no social problem resulted, since they came in as temporary seasonal laborers and not as permanent immigrants. Representative John Nance Garner of Texas, the future vice-president, stated, "In our country they [Mexicans] do not cause any trouble, unless they stay there a long time and become Americanized." [22]

In the course of the testimony on this aspect of Mexican immigration, the representatives of economic interests showed the basic reason for their support of Mexican immigration. The testimony revealed that the employers preferred Mexican workers because they were docile, unaggressive people who would do as they were told. "We find the Mexicans a very peaceful, timid people." "They seem to know their place." "They can be imposed on; the sheriff can go out and make them do anything." "They will work, and they are not 8-hour men; they are the kind that when you want them they will work all day or night and the next day without ever making a kick." [23] These comments from witnesses at the hearings indicate that despite their repeated denials the employers of the Southwest favored unlimited Mexican immigration because it provided them with a source of cheap labor which could be exploited to the fullest possible extent. The true objective of the southwestern farmers and businessmen is laid bare in the following exchange between Representative Box and a sugar-beet farmer:

> MR. BOX: I may not be able to state it in terms which would be fair according to your view; but what you really want is what two or three other gentlemen have indicated here, a class of people who have not the ability to rise, who have not the initiative, who are children, who do not want to own land, who

22. "Seasonal Agricultural Laborers," House *Hearings* (1926), pp. 105, 190; "Immigration from Western Hemisphere," House *Hearings* (1928), p. 61. The assertion that the Mexicans came only as temporary migrant laborers is highly dubious. There were no accurate figures on the increase of the Mexican population in the United States until the results of the 1930 census were published after the hearings were concluded. For the first time, Mexicans were classified as a separate element, and the census revealed that there were 1,422,533 Mexicans in the United States, an increase of 100 per cent over the estimated number of 700,000 in 1920. *Interpreter Releases,* 8 (August 18, 1931), 176.

23. "Immigration from Western Hemisphere," House *Hearings* (1928), p. 426; "Seasonal Agricultural Laborers," House *Hearings* (1926), p. 190; "Restriction of Western Hemisphere Immigration," Senate *Hearings* (1928), p. 30.

can be directed by men in the upper stratum of society. That is
what you want, isn't it?

MR. WHITEHEAD: I believe that is about it.[24]

The forces opposing Mexican restriction were considerably strengthened by the vigorous stand taken by Secretary of State Kellogg against
legislation which would place any of the Western Hemisphere countries under a quota. The position taken by Kellogg was in line with
the efforts being made by the State Department to improve relations
with Latin America. The United States, by 1930, had renounced the
doctrine of intervention in Latin American affairs, and during this
period Ambassador Dwight Morrow had concluded a settlement of
vexatious disputes with Mexico.[25] In 1927 Kellogg advised Coolidge
to take a strong stand against a Western Hemisphere quota.[26] The
following year Kellogg sent a second memorandum to the president.
"It seems to me inconceivable," Kellogg stated, "that for the sake of
preventing a relatively insignificant migration from Mexico, the unde-
sirability of which is at least questionable, we should endanger our
good relations with Canada and all of Latin America." [27] Thus by
1928 the State Department had developed strong views on the question of Western Hemisphere immigration which were to have a decisive influence on future policy.

Kellogg appeared before the Senate Immigration Committee in
1928 to argue against the proposed legislation for Western Hemisphere
quotas. Warning that such action "would adversely affect the present
good relations of the United States with Latin America and Canada,"
he cited confidential consular reports which stated that the imposition
of quotas would be interpreted by the countries concerned as an
unfriendly gesture by the United States.[28] "Not only would this be
very regrettable from a point of view of international policy but it
would be apt to have an adverse effect upon the prosperity of American business interest in those countries." [29] Pointing out that 60 per

24. "Seasonal Agricultural Laborers," House *Hearings* (1926), p. 112.
25. Samuel Flagg Bemis, *The Latin American Policy of the United States* (New
York, 1943), pp. 217–18, 220–1.
26. Kellogg to Coolidge (July 21, 1927), Coolidge Papers, File 133.
27. Ibid. (February 13, 1928), Coolidge Papers, File 133.
28. "Restriction of Western Hemisphere Immigration," Senate *Hearings* (1928),
pp. 156, 161.
29. Ibid., p. 162.

cent of the total American overseas capital investment and 34 per cent of the total American foreign trade was with these countries, Kellogg warned that the economic well-being of the nation would be vitally endangered by the proposed action.[30]

When the committee hearings closed in 1930, very little had been achieved. The voluminous printed record, filling over 2,000 pages, revealed the wide disagreement between the opposing sides but contained little that would help legislators to form judicious conclusions on the question of Mexican immigration. The verbal strife had generated a great deal of heat but very little light. Most evident were the petty and narrow motives which inspired the antagonists. The supporters of restriction, posing as defenders of the American laborer and protectors of American society, seemed to be moved primarily by racial prejudice. Their opponents, ostensibly acting to prevent a serious dislocation in the nation's economy, appeared to be motivated by economic self-interest. Thus the Congressional hearings, which were held to acquaint congressmen with the basic nature of the problem they faced, turned into a bitter contest between forces of bigotry and greed which did little credit to the democratic processes.

In view of the violent discussion of the Mexican immigration issue at the hearings, it is rather surprising to find almost complete silence on this question on the floor of Congress. The House Committee failed to report any bills dealing with Mexican restriction until 1930. In 1928 the Senate Immigration Committee reported favorably on a bill to place Mexico under a quota, but no action or debate resulted.[31] Meanwhile the restrictionists were airing their views in the nation's magazines in an effort to stir up a greater demand for Western Hemisphere quotas. Kenneth Roberts, the historical novelist who had been very active in advocating the quota system from 1920 to 1924, wrote a series of articles for the *Saturday Evening Post* in which he portrayed Mexican immigrants in a very unfavorable light.[32] Roberts warned that the

30. Ibid., pp. 163, 165–6, 168.
31. "Subject Certain Immigrants, Born in Countries of the Western Hemisphere, to the Quota under the Immigration Law," *Senate Report No. 1343*, 70th Congress, 2d Session (Washington, 1928), p. 1.
32. Kenneth Roberts, "Wet and Other Mexicans," *Saturday Evening Post, 200* (February 4, 1928); "Mexicans or Ruin," *200* (February 18, 1928); "The Docile Mexicans," *200* (March 10, 1928).

farmers of the Southwest might benefit from the influx of Mexicans, but only "at the expense of saddling all future Americans with a dismal and distressing race problem." [33] The advocates of restriction continually stressed the racial aspects. Charles Goethe, writing in *Eugenics*, called the Mexican immigrants "hybrids from an Amerind stock with a menacingly prolific birth rate," while Albert Bushnell Hart, the historian, feared that the influx would "build up a new element of the American population, mostly Indian, who will plague future generations very much as the South has suffered from the presence of unassimilable negroes." [34] The increasing number of periodical articles indicated that the sentiment for Mexican immigration had reached the point where Congress could no longer avoid the issue. [35]

It was this situation which caused the State Department to seek an alternative to the quota system in order to reduce Mexican immigration. In January 1929 the Department sent special instructions to the American consuls in Mexico ordering them to apply more stringently the standards set by law for admission to the United States. [36] The contract labor provision and the literacy test were the two principal means used for rejecting applications for visas. A third method of rejection was a clause in the 1917 law which denied admission to anyone who was "likely to become a public charge." The vagueness of this phrase left a great deal to the consul's discretion and enabled him to operate an effective squeeze play on the prospective immigrant. When an applicant was asked about his financial status, if he replied he had a job waiting for him in the United States, he was ruled out on the contract labor provision, while if he answered that he had no job in sight, he was rejected as likely to become a public charge. [37]

33. Roberts, "The Docile Mexicans," p. 165.

34. C. M. Goethe, "The Influx of Mexican Amerinds," *Eugenics*, 2 (January 1929), 9; Albert B. Hart, "National Origins," *Current History*, 30 (June 1929), 481.

35. Other articles calling for restriction of Mexican immigration include Richard Childe, "Our Open Back Doors," *American Legion Monthly*, 5 (October 1928); editorial, "Protection for Unskilled Labor," *Saturday Evening Post*, 200 (January 7, 1928); and Roy Garis, "Mexicanization of American Business," *Saturday Evening Post*, 202 (February 8, 1930).

36. New York *Times* (January 16, 1929), p. 9; *Interpreter Releases*, 6 (September 18, 1929), 148.

37. "Western Hemisphere Immigration," House *Hearings* (1930), p. 28; United States Department of State, *Immigration Work of the Department of State* (Washington, 1935), p. 12; *Interpreter Releases*, 6 (September 18, 1929), 150–1.

The new administrative orders issued by the Department of State proved highly effective. Within a few months Mexican immigration dropped to considerably less than half its former level: during the first full year it was in operation—the fiscal year ending in June 1930 —Mexican immigration totaled only 12,703, as compared to 40,154 in 1929.[38] In 1930 the Department of State announced the success of its new policy in a press release. Stating that Mexican immigration was no longer a problem, the Department announced that "proper enforcement of existing immigration laws can and will be maintained in the future, in Mexico as in other countries, so as to prevent effectively the recurrence of conditions existing a few years ago, when the recorded admissions of Mexican laborers were very high." [39]

It was evident that the State Department viewed this new policy not as a temporary expedient but as a permanent solution to the problem of Mexican immigration. It quickly informed Congress of the new administrative policy, but this method of limitation failed to satisfy the restrictionists. Senator Harris of Georgia introduced a bill to place all Western Hemisphere countries except Canada under restrictive quotas, and by April 1930 the first extensive debate on the subject had begun in the Senate. The old arguments over the economic, social, and racial effects of Mexican immigration were aired once more. Several senators, including Hiram Johnson of California and Thomas Heflin of Alabama, objected to the racial characteristics of the Mexican immigrants, referring to them as "a mixed breed, low-type, docile people," while a group of western senators pleaded for the continuance of Mexican immigration to save the farmers of the Southwest from ruin.[40] However, even the western senators admitted the need for some form of limitation of Mexican immigration, and the debate centered on the method of achieving restriction. Whether to limit the influx from Mexico by quotas or by strict administrative enforcement of present law became the crux of the argument.

Senators Hiram Bingham of Connecticut and Carl Hayden of Arizona presented the case against Latin American quotas. Bingham hammered away at the Pan-American argument, pointing out that it

38. *Interpreter Releases, 6* (September 18, 1929), 151; *Annual Report of the Commissioner-General of Immigration, 1930* (Washington, 1930), pp. 206–7.
39. United States Department of State, *Press Releases, 2* (June 14, 1930), 304–5.
40. *Congressional Record* (April 11, 1930), p. 6941; (April 15, 1930), pp. 7218–20; (April 22, 1930), pp. 7417, 7422.

was traditional American policy to treat the sister republics of the New World more favorably than the countries of Europe. "I believe that passage of this bill would strike a blow at Pan-Americanism from which it would be very difficult to recover," he contended. To drive home his point, Bingham warned of the harmful economic consequences of a policy which lessened the bonds of good feeling between the United States and Latin America. Senator Hayden then showed that there was no longer a need for such drastic action. In a seven-hour speech, he described the effectiveness of the State Department's policy of administrative enforcement, bulwarking his argument with detailed statistics on the decrease in Mexican immigration in 1930. A presidential proclamation commending the officials of the State Department for their action was all that was needed to complete this wise policy which achieved restriction while preserving the principle of Pan-Americanism, concluded Hayden.[41]

The advocates of the quota replied to this argument by charging that immigration was a domestic question to be determined solely by internal considerations. Senator Harris, sponsor of the bill, went so far as to deny the principle of Pan-Americanism, claiming that the present quota policy discriminated against European countries. Hiram Johnson argued that it would be foolish to consider the views of a foreign country in determining immigration policy, since every country objected to restriction on the emigration of its citizens. Probably the strongest rebuttal to the Pan-American argument was made by Senator Heflin. "If we ever weaken or waver on the question of our absolute right to do what we deem best regarding immigration to the United States, we are undone as a people—we are lost. The right and power, undisturbed by any foreign influence, to do what we feel is best for our country regarding immigration constitute the thing necessary to preserve free government in America."[42] Inherent in this assertion is the intense nationalism which was the mainspring of the restrictionist movement.

When the time for action came on the Harris bill, its opponents attempted to block the bill by amending it to death. Senator Hayden

41. Ibid. (April 10, 1930), p. 6845; (April 11, 1930), pp. 6922–3; (April 16, 1930), pp. 7111–41.
42. Ibid. (April 10, 1930), p. 6843; (April 11, 1930), p. 6942; (April 21, 1930), p. 7325.

proposed an amendment to extend the quotas to Canada as well as Latin America, hoping that this would make the bill obnoxious to senators from the northern border states, but this move was defeated. However, several contradictory amendments were adopted which produced such confusion that the Senate recommitted the bill by a vote of 34 to 30. The advocates of Western Hemisphere restriction, realizing that much of the opposition was directed at the placing of quotas on all Latin American countries, brought the bill back to the floor, where Senator Harris proposed an amendment to apply the quota to Mexico alone. After final debate this was agreed to on May 13 by a vote of 56 to 11, and without further discussion the bill was passed.[43] A sectional analysis of the vote on the crucial amendment shows that the southern senators voted unanimously for this measure, with the eastern and midwestern legislators supporting it strongly, while there was an almost even division among the senators from the Far West.[44] Once more the solidly restrictionist South was leading Congress toward a more drastic immigration policy.

In the lower house, meanwhile, the Immigration Committee had prepared a very cumbersome bill to restrict all Western Hemisphere immigration, but when the Senate acted on the Harris bill, the House committee dropped its measure and quickly approved the bill to place a quota on Mexico alone.[45] Representatives of the State Department appeared at a brief hearing on the legislation, warning that to single out Mexico for discriminatory treatment would have serious repercussions on American relations with Mexico.[46] The committee rejected

43. Ibid. (April 23, 1930), pp. 7531–3; (April 25, 1930), pp. 7711–12; (May 13, 1930), pp. 8841–4.

44. The sectional breakdown on the amendment to place the quota on Mexico alone was as follows:

Section	For	Against
Northeast	8	2
Midwest	13	5
South	19	0
Far West	11	9

45. "Restriction of Immigration from the Republic of Mexico," *House Report No. 1594*, 71st Congress, 2d Session, Washington, 1930.

46. "Immigration from Mexico," *Hearings before the House Committee on Immigration and Naturalization*, 71st Congress, 2d Session (Washington, 1930), pp. 1–7.

the views of the State Department by asserting that immigration was a domestic problem on which international considerations had no bearing. "Congress, exclusively charged with the great responsibility of protecting the country from the menace of infiltration by alien people whose numbers, economic standards, social and racial qualities threaten serious injury to the country, should meet that responsibility with American welfare as a paramount consideration." [47]

Thus the House committee, driven by intense nationalism and jealousy over executive encroachment on its prerogatives, fully supported the action of the Senate. But the administration, facing strong pressure from both the Mexican government and American business interests in Mexico, stepped in to block the restrictionist program,[48] and by exerting influence on the all-powerful Rules Committee was able to frustrate the restrictionists. With the current meeting of Congress drawing to a close, Chairman Albert Johnson of the Immigration Committee was unable to procure a rule for the Harris bill.[49] The session ended in June without any discussion or action on a Mexican quota in the House of Representatives. Though there were strong indications that President Hoover would have vetoed the Harris bill if it had passed the House, skillful parliamentary maneuvering prevented the issue from reaching this final climax.[50]

The issue of Mexican immigration marks the first permanent defeat the restrictionists had encountered. From the passage of the literacy test in 1917 down to the retention of national origins in 1929, the pressure groups which advocated the erection of barriers against the flow of immigrants into the United States had succeeded in embodying their views in legislation. They very nearly triumphed again on the Mexican question, but the enduring principle of Pan-Americanism proved too strong.

The more vehement supporters of Mexican restriction were embittered by their defeat. One ardent eugenicist labeled the failure of Congress to act as "astounding," while John Trevor, president of

47. *House Report No. 1594* (1930), p. 1.
48. New York *Times* (May 21, 1930), p. 11; (May 26, 1930), p. 2; (May 28, 1930), p. 9.
49. Francis H. Kinnicutt, "Immigration," *Eugenics*, 3 (July 1930), 279; John Trevor, "Immigration Legislation," 3 (October 1930), 372.
50. Trevor, p. 374; New York *Times* (April 26, 1930), p. 5.

the American Coalition, asserted that "Congress has never to such a degree flouted the national interest." [51] The AFL was more temperate in its judgment, regretting the defeat of the quota bill but approving of the State Department policy.[52] Though the restrictionists continued to press for a Mexican quota, the issue never again became important. Strict administrative enforcement became the established policy of the United States toward Mexican immigration.

In assessing the struggle over Western Hemisphere quotas, it is evident that the four factors previously involved in immigration policy were again present. The advocates of quotas were motivated primarily by the closely intertwined considerations of race and nationalism. Fearing the social, racial, and political impact of the Mexican laborers on American society, they pressed for severe limitation in the face of economic and diplomatic objections. The western farmers and businessmen were unable to stop this restrictionist drive because they could not conceal the economic self-interest which lay at the heart of their opposition. The vital factor in defeating the restrictionist cause was the opposition of the State Department. Appealing to the traditional ideal of Pan-Americanism, a principle which was to develop into the Good Neighbor policy in the next few years, the officials of the State Department presented a powerful case against Western Hemisphere restriction. Though unable to win over a majority of the Senate, they did convince the more responsible leaders of the House of Representatives of the dangers of quota restrictions for neighboring countries. Thus it was that considerations of foreign policy, based on a long-standing ideal, prevailed over the previously dominant ideas of race and nationalism to halt the restrictionist surge.

There can be little question that the final solution of the Mexican immigration problem was a wise and statesmanlike one. The influx of Mexicans in large numbers into the Southwest was an unhealthy situation which had harmful effects on both the Mexican immigrants and the American residents. Manuel Gamio, an American sociologist of Mexican birth, surveyed the problem in a study published in 1930 and concluded that the failure of the Mexicans to assimilate into American society made Mexican immigration undesirable for both

51. Kinnicutt, p. 279; Trevor, p. 372.
52. *Report of the Proceedings of the 50th Annual Convention of the American Federation of Labor, 1930*, p. 325.

peoples.[53] By formulating a policy of administrative restriction which reduced the flow of Mexican immigrants and yet did not publicly brand the Mexicans as undesirable, the Hoover administration pioneered in a new form of immigration policy. The strong point of this policy was its flexibility, providing an effective remedy to a special situation without creating ill feeling. Restriction by administrative action was a valuable addition to American immigration policy; it was to assume much greater significance in the 1930's.

As the issue of Mexican immigration began to recede from public consciousness, the problem of Filipino immigrants arose to take its place. Entering Hawaii in small numbers after the turn of the century, Filipino laborers did not begin coming to the American mainland until the 1920's. The movement was small; by 1930 there were only 60,000 Filipinos on the mainland, mostly in California, with 75,000 more in Hawaii.[54] The Pacific coast states had experienced two waves of Asiatic immigration, however, and soon a demand arose for the exclusion of Filipinos to head off a third "oriental invasion." This agitation—beginning in 1927 and stemming primarily from the California Joint Immigration Committee, the pressure group instrumental in gaining Japanese exclusion—was intensified by the onset of the depression in 1929. By the next year Filipino exclusion was very much a live issue before Congress.

The problem of immigration from the Philippine Islands was complex because of the peculiar status of the Filipinos. Unlike the inhabitants of Puerto Rico, they were not citizens of the United States but rather nationals who lived under the American flag. Though an oriental people, they were exempted from the clause in the 1924 act which excluded individuals ineligible for citizenship.[55] Thus they were in a twilight zone somewhere between citizens and aliens, and were usually thought of as wards of the United States. How to control their migration to the American mainland posed an even more difficult problem than Mexican immigration had. To declare them aliens from

53. Gamio, Mexican Immigration, pp. 177, 181–5.
54. Bruno Lasker, Filipino Immigration (Chicago, 1931), p. 324.
55. "Restriction of Immigration," House Report No. 2405, 71st Congress, 3d Session (Washington, 1931), p. 5.

the standpoint of the immigration laws and thereby place them under the exclusion clause, as many restrictionists advocated, was manifestly unjust, since this would be a violation of the trust the United States had assumed when it annexed the Philippine Islands in 1898. The other alternative was to give the Filipinos their independence and then exclude them as alien Asiatics. This second line of action became more and more attractive as a movement for Philippine independence stemming from very different sources gained momentum in the early 1930's.[56]

The first attempts to deal with Filipino exclusion were along the lines of outright exclusion. In 1928 Representative Richard Welch of California introduced a bill to remove the exemption of the Philippine Islands from the Asiatic exclusion provisions of the 1924 law. Welch was strongly supported by local West Coast labor unions, and later the same year the AFL adopted a resolution approving the proposed legislation.[57] The restrictionist campaign was greatly aided in 1929 when outbreaks of spinal meningitis which were traced to Filipino immigrants occurred in California and Washington seaports. Acting on the recommendation of the Public Health Service, President Hoover issued an executive order on June 21, 1929, forbidding the entry of Filipinos into the United States until the epidemic ceased.[58] But by 1930 the demand for Filipino exclusion had become national in scope, and the House Immigration Committee decided to hold public hearings on the Welch bill.

56. The movement for Philippine independence came from farm groups in the United States who were interested in placing tariffs on Philippine products, particularly sugar, copra, and hemp. They found willing allies among the Filipino political leaders. No attempt will be made in this study to analyze the general movement for Philippine independence—it will be discussed only from the aspect of Filipino immigration, which was a subordinate theme in the drive for independence. Grayson Kirk, *Philippine Independence* (New York, 1936) and Garel Grunder and William Livezey, *The Philippines and the United States* (Norman, Oklahoma, 1951) contain detailed accounts of the independence movement.

57. Lasker, p. 34; *Report of Proceedings of the 48th Annual Convention of the American Federation of Labor, 1928* (Washington, 1928), p. 217.

58. "Quota Preferences for Certain Immigrants," *Hearings before the House Committee on Immigration and Naturalization,* 71st Congress, 2d Session (Washington, 1930), pp. 57–8; "Exclusion of Immigration from the Philippine Islands," *Hearings before the House Committee on Immigration and Naturalization,* 71st Congress, 2d Session (Washington, 1930), p. 90.

There was an even balance between the pressure groups appearing at the hearings in 1930 to argue the pros and cons of Filipino exclusion. The patriotic societies and organized labor appeared in their familiar roles as advocates of restriction, with the leadership coming from the California Joint Immigration Committee. This organization was an executive board composed of representatives of the California branches of the AFL, the National Grange, and the American Legion, together with the regional patriotic society, the Native Sons of the Golden West. The secretary of this last group, V. S. McClatchy, a member of an influential California family which published the Sacramento *Bee,* was the chief spokesman for the exclusionists. The opposition consisted of Filipino political leaders, representatives of the War Department (which administered the Philippine Islands), and Hawaiian sugar planters, who relied heavily on Filipino laborers. Most effective were the Filipino representatives, particularly Manuel Roxas, speaker of the Philippine legislature, who was in the United States as a member of a special Philippine Commission seeking to promote the independence movement.

The argument which the restrictionists presented was very similar to the one given against Mexican immigration, but with a difference in emphasis. Instead of condemning an existing situation, the advocates of exclusion, in view of the small scale of Filipino immigration, concentrated on the potential dangers stemming from an unrestricted influx from the Philippine Islands. The labor lobbyists gave their familiar views on the menace of cheap labor, but under questioning admitted that the competition they feared was not yet an actuality. The chief stress was laid on ethnic factors. "This mongrel stream is small, but when it is considered how rapidly it multiplies and grows it is clear that the tide must be stemmed before it gets beyond control." This statement by a member of the American Coalition concisely sums up the restrictionist case. Further elaborations were made by McClatchy, who showed little reticence in displaying his racial prejudices. Pointing out that the Filipinos could never be assimilated into American society, McClatchy warned that continued Filipino immigration could lead only to a situation similar to the racial hodge-podge that existed in Hawaii. "We are trying to maintain a white country in California for our own interests and for the interests of the nation," he asserted. McClatchy concluded by defending his intolerance. "In my judgment this racial prejudice is really nature's safeguard against miscegenation." [59]

In defending Filipino immigration, the opponents of restriction relied principally on a moral argument. Representatives of the Hawaiian Sugar Planters Association and the Pacific American Steamship Association spoke on the economic aspects, but the bulk of the testimony came from the Filipino leaders who advocated the right of United States subjects to free movement in all areas under the American flag. They stated that the Filipino immigration was of a temporary character. The Filipinos, taught that the United States is a great country, came to the mainland to study and learn American methods in order to return home to improve conditions in the Philippines, they asserted. Manuel Roxas was the most vigorous Filipino representative, claiming that "while the benefits derived from the presence of Filipinos in the United States are not vital to us, the right itself freely to come here is priceless in our eyes." Roxas presented the core of the Filipino argument in a ringing denunciation of the Welch proposal. "I say unhesitatingly that the action contemplated in this bill has no precedent in the annals of colonization since the birth of time. No country, however imperialistic, however commercialistic its policy in its dealings with its colonies, has ever prohibited the citizens of its colonies from migrating to the mother country." [60] This powerful appeal to the traditional American spirit of fair play and sympathy for the underdog placed a major obstacle in the path of the exclusionist campaign.

The strong moral argument advanced by the Filipino politicians evidently swayed the strongly restrictionist House Immigration Committee, for the exclusion bill was not reported. Representative Welch spoke on the floor of Congress in March on the need for exclusion, warning that the Pacific coast states, which he termed the outposts of Western civilization, were once more imperiled by an Asiatic invasion. For Welch, the moral right of the United States to protect its racial integrity far outweighed any duty we owed the Filipinos as our wards. Camilio Osias, resident commissioner from the Philippines in Congress, found Welch's speech an excellent opportunity to plead for independence. Labeling the exclusion of colonial dependents an un-

59. "Philippine Exclusion," House *Hearings* (1930), pp. 30, 46, 86, 178, 187.
60. Ibid., pp. 110, 116, 126, 168, 171–2, 190–204, 207–8.

American act, Osias asserted, "If we are to be treated as a foreign people for purposes of immigration, we must first be given the category of a free and independent nation." The close relationship between Philippine independence and immigration had also become evident in the Senate, where in January, Senator Millard Tydings of Maryland had portrayed the Filipino influx in bleak terms and then had urged independence as a solution.[61]

However, the advocates of exclusion were reluctant to embrace independence to achieve their ends except as a final alternative. In April, when the Harris bill to limit Western Hemisphere immigration was being debated, Senator Shortridge of California introduced an amendment to exclude Filipinos for five years. This maneuver brought on the first full-scale debate of the Philippine immigration issue in Congress. Shortridge, who had been the sponsor of the Japanese exclusion clause in 1924, emphasized the ethnic aspects, barely mentioning the economic competition of the Filipinos. "It is my firm conviction," he asserted, "that to preserve our form of government we must maintain our racial type, the dominant and controlling race within the United States, to guide and direct its destiny." Shortridge agreed with Welch that considerations of colonial policy were of secondary importance, stating "I conceive it to be our duty to consider first the liberty, the independence, the prosperity, and the happiness of our own people." [62]

There was a good deal of support for the Shortridge amendment among the western senators, but it met with vigorous opposition from other quarters. Hiram Bingham of Connecticut, chairman of the Senate Committee on Territorial and Insular Affairs, opposed exclusion as a violation of American guardianship over the Philippines. Senators Hawes of Missouri and Norris of Nebraska, advocates of Philippine independence, reiterated the trusteeship argument, calling the proposal "dishonorable" and "amoral." Both urged the granting of independence to the Philippines as the proper solution of the immigration problem. On a roll call vote, the amendment was defeated 41 to 23.[63] An analysis shows only the far western senators supporting the meas-

61. *Congressional Record* (January 29, 1930), pp. 2589–90; (March 25, 1930), pp. 6107–8, 6110–11.

62. Ibid. (April 22, 1930), p. 7425; (April 23, 1930), pp. 7510–11.

63. Ibid. (April 22, 1930), p. 7426; (April 23, 1930), pp. 7521–2, 7526–7, 7529.

ure, the southern legislators being almost evenly split and the eastern and midwestern senators overwhelmingly opposed.[64] This vote was not wholly conclusive, since many senators objected to dealing with Filipino immigration in the form of an amendment to other matters, but it does indicate that the majority of senators were unwilling to take arbitrary action against Filipino immigrants.

The failure of the restrictionists to pass legislation limiting Filipino immigration marked the end of the campaign for exclusion short of independence. The Filipino political leaders now came forward with a compromise which they offered to the labor wing of the restriction-ist bloc. The members of the Philippine Independence Commission, reporting in 1933 to the Philippine legislature, stated that in 1932, realizing it would be dangerous "to antagonize organized labor," they had "decided to take a practical view of the immigration question and, in this manner, reached an understanding with the leaders of the American Federation of Labor and their supporters in Congress." [65] The understanding was as follows: "In case Congress should enact a law fixing a date for independence, the Filipino representatives would accept a provision restricting Filipino immigration to the United States during the transition period, provided that the restriction was based not on racial but on economic grounds." [66] Having blocked out-right exclusion, the Filipino leaders were now able to harness the restrictionist forces they had frustrated and employ them in further-ance of Philippine independence. This casts some doubts on the sin-cerity of the arguments against exclusion that the Filipinos had ad-vanced at the hearings. However, it should be noted that the Filipinos made no alliance with the racists who advocated restriction and that they stipulated very clearly that immigration limitation should be by quota and not by racial exclusion.

64. The sectional breakdown was as follows:

Section	Yes	No
Northeast	1	12
Midwest	4	14
South	7	8
Far West	11	7

65. Reprinted from the Manila *Sunday Tribune* (July 30, 1933), in the *Congressional Record* (March 22, 1934), p. 5150.
66. *Congressional Record* (March 22, 1934), p. 5151.

Meanwhile the movement for Philippine independence was gathering momentum. The Senate Committee on Territorial and Insular Affairs in 1930 reported favorably on an independence bill, which, however, did not come to fruition.[67] In 1932 committees in both houses approved independence measures.[68] Originally neither bill contained immigration provisions, but at the urging of Representative Welch, who presented a petition to the House Committee on Insular Affairs from the entire California Congressional delegation, a quota of fifty for the Philippines during the period of transition to independence was written into the House legislation.[69] At the hearings the Filipino leaders acquiesced in this provision and Manuel Roxas stated further, "in submitting our plea for independence we say that after independence is granted to us, should America decide to exclude us from her territory, that is her privilege." The Secretary of War, Patrick Hurley, opposed Philippine independence and suggested that the immigration problem could be solved by quota.[70] The Senate committee report disposed of this proposal by stating, "It would be politically immoral to retain the Filipino people in their present status as wards and at the same time impose upon them discriminating and unfair restrictions and inhibitions." [71]

The Philippine independence bill passed the House in April 1932 with barely a mention of its immigration features.[72] In the Senate, however, Hiram Johnson of California proposed an amendment to limit the use of the quota to persons eligible for citizenship. This would have had the effect of excluding all Filipinos, which Johnson justified on the grounds of maintaining a consistent Asiatic immigration policy. There were strenuous objections, particularly from Senator Hawes, one of the authors of the bill, who charged that the amend-

67. "Philippine Independence," *Senate Report No. 781,* 71st Congress, 2d Session, Washington, 1930.

68. "Philippine Independence," *Senate Report No. 354,* 72d Congress, 1st Session, Washington, 1932; "Philippine Independence," *House Report No. 806,* 72d Congress, 1st Session, Washington, 1932.

69. *House Report No. 806* (1932), p. 16; "Independence for the Philippine Islands," *Hearings before the House Committee on Insular Affairs,* 72d Congress, 1st Session (Washington, 1932), p. 379.

70. "Independence for the Philippine Islands," House *Hearings* (1932), pp. 80, 386.

71. *Senate Report No. 354* (1932), p. 2.

72. *Congressional Record* (April 4, 1932), p. 7411.

ment "would draw the race line against them [the Filipinos] and be objectionable to them and just at a period when we are about to do a gracious act by giving them their independence." The amendment was then accepted without a roll call vote.[73] After the Senate passed the bill in December, a conference committee rejected Johnson's amendment but compromised by inserting a clause stipulating that upon the final separation of the Philippines from the United States, the oriental exclusion provisions of the 1924 act would apply to Filipinos.[74]

In January of 1933 President Hoover vetoed the independence bill. Though the immigration provisions did not enter into his decision, in his veto message he called for immediate restriction of Philippine immigration.[75] Congress quickly overrode his veto, but the act did not go into operation because the Philippine legislature refused to accept the independence bill. However, the bill, with only minor changes which did not affect the immigration clauses, was passed again by Congress in 1934, approved by President Roosevelt, and accepted by the Philippine legislature on May 1, 1934.[76] On this date the quota of fifty for the Philippine Islands went into effect and the problem of Filipino restriction was settled.

The final disposition of the Filipino immigration question was essentially a compromise. The extreme restrictionists, pressing for the outright exclusion of a colonial people on ethnic grounds, had failed to achieve their immediate goal. They were forced to accept an indirect method of accomplishing their objective, and even then did not gain their complete program. This partial setback indicates that the burning nationalism which was the motivating force of the restriction movement was not without limits. Appeals to nationalism might be successfully employed to justify racial discrimination against foreign immigrants, but chauvinism could not prevail over strong moral considerations of fair play toward a colonial dependency. That is not to say that the granting of Philippine independence was an altruistic act. The spectacle of men advocating independence without regard

73. Ibid. (December 9, 1932), pp. 264–6.
74. "Philippine Independence Bill," *House Report No. 1811*, 72d Congress, 2d Session (Washington, 1932), pp. 7, 9.
75. *Congressional Record* (January 13, 1933), p. 1761.
76. Kirk, pp. 121, 125, 127–8.

to the welfare of the Philippine people in order to achieve immigration restriction is hardly a pleasant one. Yet the whole episode shows that the restrictionist forces were not powerful enough to override the moral conscience of the American people.

Events in succeeding years proved that the restriction of Philippine immigration was a wise decision. As the depression continued, many Filipino laborers in the United States became completely destitute. To remedy this situation, Congress passed a bill in 1934 authorizing the government to pay the passage of indigent Filipinos back to the Philippines.[77] Considering the economic conditions in the 1930's and the violent prejudices of the Americans on the West Coast, the limitation of the Filipino influx was beneficial both for the Filipinos themselves and for American society. It was unfortunate that eventual racial exclusion had been written into the law, since the minute quota had the desired practical effect without injuring Philippine pride. But the principle of complete exclusion of all Asiatics was too firmly entrenched to permit a continued exception in this case.

77. *Congressional Record* (May 20, 1935), p. 7888; (June 25, 1935), p. 10,046.

4. Problems of the 1930's: the Depression

IN MANY WAYS the year 1929 marks a decisive turning point in American immigration policy. Up till that year, immigration restriction was a major issue which commanded a great deal of attention and discussion. The effects of immigration on the ethnic composition of the American people and on the structure of the economy were considered of primary importance, and consequently the question of immigration policy ranked high among the national issues of the 1920's. But with the coming of the depression and the rise of totalitarian governments in Europe, the immigration issue was swiftly displaced from the forefront of public attention by the more fundamental problems of economic and military security. The various aspects of policy were no longer considered as an integral unit but increasingly came to be identified with the more pressing national problems to which they were related.

The major problem of this period was the depression, and it was the economic aspects of immigration which received the greatest attention. Depressions have always resulted in a lessening of immigration, for during such crises the United States loses much of its attraction to the prospective immigrant. Economic dislocations have also been the breeding grounds for restriction, producing demands for the protection of native American labor. In the 1930's both the supporters and opponents of the restriction movement agreed on the need to limit immigration during the depression, but they differed sharply on the method and extent of the necessary restriction. The basic point at issue was whether to limit immigration by administrative or legislative action. The restrictionists urged that Congress reduce the quotas anywhere from 60 per cent to 90 per cent for a period of years, while their opponents favored strict administrative enforcement of existing law to achieve the same ends. The difference in method was important, because there was a strong possibility that further restriction by legislative act might become permanent policy, whereas administrative restriction could be easily terminated when economic conditions improved. This controversy over how to reduce immigration became the basic issue of immigration policy during the depression.

The question of limiting immigration during the depression came under discussion as soon as the seriousness of the economic crisis was evident. In April 1930 Senator Hugo Black of Alabama offered an amendment to the Harris bill to suspend all immigration except for relatives of citizens for five years. Charging that "foreign immigration has been utilized by the big business interests of the country as a direct weapon to break down the price of wages of the people of the land," Black presented a strong case for suspension.[1] Though the Senate finally rejected the amendment, the vote was surprisingly close: 37 to 29.[2] Later in the session President Hoover asked the Congressional immigration committees to formulate legislation to cut the quotas in half during the depression, but the adjournment of Congress in July prevented consideration of this suggestion.[3]

With Congressional action postponed until the next session, Hoover decided to find a way to restrict immigration by administrative enforcement. He presented the problem to the State Department, where a solution was found which grew out of the experience in restricting Mexican immigration. On September 9, 1930, the Department of State announced that effective on that day the consuls would interpret the clause in the 1917 act prohibiting the admission of persons "likely to become a public charge" so as to exclude all but the most prosperous European immigrants.[4] In the words of the press release, "If the consular officer believes that the applicant may probably be a public charge at any time, even during a considerable period subsequent to his arrival, he must refuse the visa."[5] This was a radical change in administrative policy, since previously the public charge clause had not been invoked if the immigrant had the money for passage and expressed the intent of finding employment as soon as he arrived in

1. *Congressional Record* (April 17, 1930), pp. 7211–13.
2. Ibid. (April 20, 1930), p. 7329.
3. *Interpreter Releases*, 7 (September 11, 1930), 217.
4. Department of State, *Press Releases*, 3 (September 13, 1930), 176–7; New York *Times* (September 10, 1930), p. 1. The new policy was announced in the form of a press release and was not an executive order, as was frequently alleged in Congress.
5. Department of State, *Press Releases*, 3, 176–7.

the United States.[6] Immigration statistics soon indicated the effectiveness of the policy. In October only 22 per cent of the available quota numbers were used, in December 13 per cent, and in February less than 10 per cent.[7] Thus within five months the State Department succeeded in cutting European immigration by 90 per cent.

Public reaction to the new policy was generally favorable, with some sharp dissent from liberal quarters. William Green, president of the AFL, wrote a letter to Hoover on September 10 heartily endorsing his action.[8] *Eugenics*, organ of the extreme restrictionists, gave its qualified approval, warning that legislative reduction was a sounder course to follow.[9] According to the *Literary Digest*, the bulk of the nation's press hailed the new measure as "timely common sense." [10] The *Nation*, speaking for the liberals, criticized the policy as an unwarranted extension of executive power and added, "The administration ought to be held to its responsibility concerning unemployment; it is not to be met by excluding a few thousand luckless immigrants." [11] The most outspoken criticism of the new policy came from Representative Dickstein of New York, who labeled it a scheme "contrary to all our tradition; contrary to the Constitution of the United States; and contrary to the spirit of our laws." [12]

President Hoover soon made it clear that he considered the public charge policy a temporary measure to protect the country until Congress enacted legislative reductions in the quotas. In his annual message to Congress in December 1930 Hoover, reviewing the public charge policy, referred to it as a "temporary measure" and stated, "The whole subject requires exhaustive reconsideration." [13] Representative Albert Johnson and Senator David Reed quickly responded by introducing bills to suspend all immigration except that of relatives for two years. Johnson's proposal was the more lenient of the two, allowing the immigration of relatives of both American citizens and resident

6. *Immigration Work of the Department of State* (Washington, 1935), p. 9.
7. *Interpreter Releases*, 8 (March 25, 1931), 96.
8. New York *Times* (September 11, 1930), p. 19.
9. Editorial, "Immigration, Unemployment," *Eugenics*, 3 (October 1930), 395.
10. "Slamming Our Gates," *Literary Digest*, 107 (October 4, 1930), 9.
11. Editorial, *Nation*, 131 (September 24, 1930), 310.
12. *Congressional Record* (January 6, 1931), p. 1501.
13. "Temporary Restriction of Immigration," *House Report No. 2710*, 71st Congress, 3d Session (Washington, 1931), p. 5.

aliens up to 50 per cent of the quota, whereas Reed's measure permitted only relatives of citizens to enter.[14] However, the basic principle behind the two bills was identical—to halt all new stock immigration while unemployment prevailed.

The Senate committee began holding public hearings on the Reed bill in December. Representatives of various organizations sympathetic to immigration appeared to announce their opposition to the proposed measure on the grounds that it worked an injustice on relatives of resident aliens. Spokesmen for religious and charitable societies pointed out that while relatives of citizens were exempt from the quota, wives and children of immigrants who had not yet been naturalized would be excluded by the Reed bill. These witnesses argued that the problem of separated families prevented the assimilation of aliens into American life, and they pleaded for more liberal exemptions in the Reed proposal. Though the majority of these spokesmen opposed the bill in principle, they were willing to accept it if adequate provisions for relatives were added. Few representatives of restrictionist groups sent letters giving their whole-hearted support to the suspension measures.[15] Since both the Senate and House immigration committees had restrictionist majorities, there was little need for witnesses in favor of the bills. Albert Johnson, replying to an offer of support from a local branch of the Junior Order of United American Mechanics, wrote, "About all the various patriotic societies can do now is to urge all the members of the House and Senate, whom they can reach, to use pressure for immediate further restriction." [16]

Just as the prospects for quick action on the suspension bills appeared brightest, Secretary of State Henry Stimson came forward at the Senate hearings with a serious objection to the Reed and Johnson measures. As expected, Stimson approved of legislative action for increased restriction during the depression, stating that his department wished Congress to assume the responsibility for immigration policy. But he surprised the senators by pointing out what he felt was a basic flaw in the Reed and Johnson proposals. These measures, limit-

14. *Interpreter Releases*, 8 (January 3, 1931), 1–2.

15. "Suspension for Two Years of General Immigration into the United States," *Hearings before the Senate Committee on Immigration*, 71st Congress, 3d Session (Washington, 1930), pp. 3, 15–16, 19–26, 28–9, 116–19, 132.

16. Albert Johnson to L. H. Winter (December 23, 1930), House Immigration Committee Papers, File H.R. 71A-F11.

ing immigration solely to relatives, would completely upset the distribution of immigrants established by the national origins provision. Since the great majority of relatives came from the countries of southeastern Europe, the bills "would reverse the percentage which now exists in favor of the northern races to a very large percentage in favor of the southern races." The result, in Stimson's eyes, would be a discrimination against "the Nordic races." In order to restrict immigration further and yet maintain the national origins principle, Stimson suggested a direct 90 per cent reduction of all immigration, including both the quota countries of Europe and the nonquota nations of the Western Hemisphere. He felt that this was the most equitable solution possible, since it would apply equally to all the countries of the world who sent immigrants to the United States.[17]

Reactions to the Stimson proposal varied considerably. Ten organizations sympathetic toward immigrants, headed by the Federal Council of Churches, wrote Stimson a letter of protest. "We believe," they wrote, "that no legislation suspending or limiting immigration should be adopted which raises any additional barrier to the admission and reunion of the families of citizens or aliens already resident in the United States." [18] However, the House Immigration Committee quickly formulated Stimson's suggestions into a bill which they reported on favorably late in January. Representatives Cooke and Dickstein of New York wrote minority reports in which they protested against the separation of families which would result from a 90 per cent reduction in immigration. Praising the public charge policy as a more flexible way of dealing with immigration during the economic emergency, both suggested that the restrictionists had an ulterior motive. Cooke wrote, "I believe that under the claim of duress of economic depression an effort is being made to effect total exclusion of immigration, which may be interpreted to be a definition of the future policy of this Government on that subject." [19]

Though there were many groups which supported the minority position, the great bulk of the letters received by the House and Senate committees were in favor of the 90 per cent reduction bill.

17. "Suspension of Immigration," Senate *Hearings* (1930), pp. 70–8.
18. Senate Immigration Committee Papers, File Sen. 71A-E4.
19. "Restriction of Immigration," *House Report No. 2405*, 71st Congress, 3d Session (Washington, 1931), Pt. I, pp. 1–2; Pt. II, pp. 1–4; Pt. III, pp. 1–2.

The patriotic societies waged an intensive pressure campaign, flooding the committees with telegrams and printed petition forms from the local chapters calling for further restriction.[20] Late in February the Rules Committee issued a rule for immediate consideration of the bill.[21] Now the restrictionists faced one last obstacle—the March 4 adjournment date.

Debate on the 90 per cent reduction bill began in the House on Saturday, February 28, and rapidly degenerated into a name calling contest between southern and western restrictionists and the New York City delegation. Representative La Guardia, irate over slurring remarks about the foreign born, launched into a bitter attack against the restrictionists which became so violent it was omitted from the *Congressional Record.* Representative O'Connor of New York was hardly less temperate in his remarks, calling Albert Johnson a "phlegmatic patriot" and accusing him of anti-Semitism. As for the bill, O'Connor asserted, "It has no merits but must pass to satisfy the howling bigots." These emotional tirades did little credit to the antirestrictionist cause, and Albert Johnson was probably correct when he described the flurry of accusations as delaying tactics designed to obscure the basic issue. Tempers became so heated that the leaders of the House finally decided to postpone further discussion until the following Monday.[22]

When the House took up the reduction bill again on March 2, the restrictionists, feeling confident that an overwhelming majority supported the legislation, moved to suspend the rules, thereby limiting debate to forty minutes. Albert Johnson made a brief statement of the restrictionist case, citing a nationwide demand for the cessation of immigration during the unemployment crisis. Opponents of the bill used up most of the time. Though there was some criticism of the general principle of reduction, the antirestrictionists concentrated their attacks on the relatives issue. Pleading for an amendment to exempt relatives, Representative La Guardia called the bill "the most scientific legislative cruelty ever devised by man." Samuel Dickstein was the principal opposition spokesman, bombarding the representatives with

20. Senate Immigration Committee Papers, Files Sen. 71A-E4, Sen. 71A-S33; House Immigration Committee Papers, Files H.R. 71A-F11, H.R. 71A-H10.

21. *Congressional Record* (February 28, 1931), p. 6574.

22. Ibid. (February 28, 1931), pp. 6576–7; (March 2, 1931), p. 6735; New York *Times* (March 1, 1931), p. 7.

emotional appeals in behalf of relatives. "I am willing to vote to suspend immigration and close our doors," he announced, "but for God's sake let the little babies and the old people whom the Republican platform promised to unite come in." [23] But these pleas were to no avail. Needing a two-thirds vote to pass the bill under the suspension of rules, the restrictionists succeeded by the ample margin of 299 to 82. This was very definitely a sectional alignment, with all but 20 of the negative votes coming from the northeastern representatives. [24] Once again the union of South and West in support of restriction had proved decisive.

The restrictionists acted swiftly to secure Senate approval of their measure. Late on the evening of March 2 Senator David Reed of Pennsylvania presented a motion to place the House bill on the calendar without referring it to the Senate Immigration Committee. After some delay, the Senate approved Reed's motion by a vote of 46 to 13. Then, as the Senate continued to sit in the early morning hours of March 3, Reed asked that the Senate suspend the rules in order to consider the reduction bill. This motion was rejected, 34 to 22, mainly because many senators were more concerned with a copyright bill which was being debated at the time. On the afternoon of March 3 Reed once more tried to get the Senate to consider the immigration bill, but he was blocked by Senator Walsh of Massachusetts. [25] All further attempts to consider the restrictive measure were stymied when Senator Elmer Thomas of Oklahoma began a filibuster on an oil industry investigation bill during the evening of March 3 which lasted until the session ended the following day at noon. [26]

In view of the large majority which supported Reed's original motion there can be little doubt that the Senate would have approved the measure if more time had been available. The series of delays

23. *Congressional Record* (March 2, 1931), pp. 6736–7, 6742.
24. Ibid. (March 2, 1931), p. 6744. The sectional breakdown was as follows:

Section	For	Against
Northeast	52	62
Midwest	115	17
South	104	2
Far West	28	1

25. Ibid. (March 2, 1931), pp. 6712–16, 6720–1; (March 3, 1931), p. 6971.
26. New York *Times* (March 5, 1931), p. 1.

in formulating the final restrictive bill, together with the obstructionist tactics employed in the House on February 28, thwarted what had appeared to be certain triumph for the restrictionists. Never again were they so close to achieving a reduction in the quotas.

The debate over the reduction bill in 1931 marks the high point of the restrictionist tide in the 1930's. Though they pressed vigorously for various bills to suspend or radically limit immigration throughout the decade, they never were able to gain consideration for their measure on the floor of Congress. One reason for this failure was the effective operation of the public charge policy in keeping immigration at a minimum. Even more important was a change in the chairmanship of the House Immigration Committee. In the Congressional elections of 1930 the Democrats won a narrow majority which enabled them to organize the House when Congress convened in December of 1931. As a result Samuel Dickstein, an ardent antirestrictionist, replaced Albert Johnson in the vital role of chairman of the House Immigration Committee. Holding this post throughout the 1930's, Dickstein was able to thwart all efforts of the restrictionists to enact legislative reduction in the quotas. Moreover, after 1933 Dickstein received considerable support for his views from the leaders of the Roosevelt administration, particularly from Secretary of Labor Frances Perkins.

The most serious attempt by the restrictionists to lower the quotas during this period came in 1932. In his annual message to Congress in December 1931 Hoover stated, "I recommend that immigration restriction now in force under administration action be placed upon a more definite basis by law." [27] To achieve this objective, Representative Moore of Kentucky introduced a bill to reduce immigration by 90 per cent permanently.[28] The significant change from temporary to permanent reduction indicated that the restrictionists were confident they could enact their full program in the long session of Congress. At committee hearings the traditional restrictionist groups were present to support the proposed legislation. Representatives of the AFL, the American Legion, and the various patriotic societies, including the American Coalition and the DAR, argued earnestly for restriction.[29]

27. Ibid. (December 9, 1931), p. 21.
28. *Congressional Record* (March 17, 1932), p. 6419.
29. "Suspension and Restriction of General Immigration," *Hearings before the House Committee on Immigration and Naturalization,* 72d Congress, 1st Session (Washington, 1932), pp. 7, 17, 18, 20–33, 41.

The principal argument was the economic one, with constant reference to the ever-increasing number of unemployed. Congressman Thomas Blanton of Texas summarized the restrictionist case when he asserted, "If we permit foreigners to come in here indiscriminately or without any extent of restriction, just to that extent we are going to take that many jobs away from Americans." [30]

Equally vigorous were the opponents of restriction who testified at the hearings. Representatives of social service organizations, mainly Jewish groups, argued that the legislation would bring about a policy of virtual exclusion. They stressed the effectiveness of the public charge policy, an argument on which they received unexpected support when a State Department official asserted that the administrative regulations were working so well that there was "no urgent need for legislation." Rabbi Stephen Wise delivered the most eloquent plea against the Moore bill. "I say to you," he told the committee, "that you will introduce a system of absolute exclusion, and once you get exclusion upon the statute books of America you will set up a new precedent, you will introduce a new method of life into America, and it will be out of keeping with the things that we cherish as American ideals." [31] Further protests were received from a new source, extreme left-wing groups. The Communist party, the Young Communist League, and the National Council for the Protection of the Foreign Born sent strongly worded telegrams to the committee against further restriction. [32]

The House Immigration Committee submitted a favorable report on the Moore bill in April. [33] But Chairman Dickstein opposed the measure, and he succeeded in preventing it from reaching the floor of Congress. The Rules Committee held hearings on the bill, at which Representatives Moore, Johnson, and Dies of Texas urged favorable action. They attacked the public charge policy, Dies asserting that "we ought to put those administrative efforts upon a legal basis so that all foreigners, all aliens seeking admittance, and all nations will understand what the policy of Congress is and will not depend upon various

30. Typescript of an unpublished hearing before the House Immigration and Naturalization Committee (February 23, 1932), House Immigration Committee Papers, File H.R. 72A-D9.

31. Ibid., February 25, 1932; March 8, 1932.

32. House Immigration Committee Papers, File H.R. 72A-H6.

33. "Restriction of Immigration," *House Report No. 1016,* 72d Congress, 1st Session, Washington, 1932.

interpretations of a multitude of consuls scattered throughout the world." Dickstein then rebutted these contentions and claimed that the issue was too controversial for proper debate—"it is going to bring out a lot of dynamite in the House." [34] The Rules Committee bowed to the will of the Immigration Committee chairman and refused to issue a rule for consideration of the bill. Thus the restrictionists were frustrated once more, on this occasion more decisively than the year before.

With the election of Franklin Roosevelt and the beginning of the New Deal, agitation for immigration restriction subsided for a brief interval. In 1934, however, the restrictionists once again began agitating for a legislative reduction of the quotas. Martin Dies of Texas became the spokesman for this resurgence of the restrictionist movement, concentrating on economic arguments. Dies blamed the depression on immigration; at one point he stated, "If we had refused admission to the 16,500,000 foreign born who are living in this country today, we would have no unemployment problem to distress and harass us." [35] He introduced legislation in 1934 and 1935 to reduce the quotas by 60 per cent. "Necessity compels us to adopt and develop a strong nationalistic spirit and policy," he announced. "We must ignore the tears of sobbing sentimentalists and internationalists, and we must permanently close, lock, and bar the gates of our country to new immigration waves and then throw the keys away." [36]

Though many southern and western congressmen applauded the efforts of Dies to tighten up the immigration laws, his proposals met with no practical success. The opposition of the administration, Chairman Dickstein of the Immigration Committee, and the all-powerful Rules Committee prevented any of his bills from reaching the floor of Congress.[37] As Dies became increasingly involved in his Communist investigations, Senator Robert Reynolds of North Carolina took his place as chief agitator on the immigration issue. From 1936 through 1939 Reynolds introduced a series of restrictive bills designed "to preserve American jobs for Americans," but they never progressed

34. "Immigration," *Hearings before the House Committee on Rules,* 72d Congress, 2d Session (Washington, 1932), pp. 4–6, 17–19.

35. *Congressional Record* (June 26, 1935), p. 10,229.

36. Martin Dies, "Nationalism Spells Safety," *National Republic,* 21 (March 1934), 2.

37. *Interpreter Releases, 12* (April 15, 1935), 147.

beyond the committee stage.[38] Thus the decade closed without any legislative changes in the basic character of American immigration policy. The restrictionists, though still a powerful and vocal group, had lost some of the momentum which had brought them victory in the 1920's.

Just as the restrictionists wished to tighten up the immigration laws during the depression, liberal groups endeavored to ease the existing regulations, particularly in regard to relatives. Most of these appeals came from Jewish organizations, which found an able champion in Representative Samuel Dickstein. Though Dickstein praised the public charge policy when arguing against bills to reduce the quotas, at other times he was quite critical of the State Department's administration of this regulation. At a meeting of the American Jewish Congress in 1931 Dickstein claimed that the strict enforcement of the public charge clause in the cases of relatives was responsible for prolonged separation of families.[39] The following year, with immigration reduced to its lowest level since 1831, he warned that the arbitrary use of "Czar-like" powers by American consuls would lead to a policy of permanent exclusion.[40]

In an attempt to liberalize the public charge policy, Dickstein introduced a bill in 1932 to provide a board of review in the United States for cases where relatives were refused visas. At a brief hearing representatives of the YWCA and the Hebrew Sheltering and Immigrant Aid Society supported the bill as a measure "providing for the reunion of families." [41] However, the State Department raised strong objections, and though the bill received a favorable committee report no action was taken by Congress.[42] In order to prevent further criticism the State Department issued special instructions to American consuls later in 1932 ordering them to review all cases in which relatives of citizens and resident aliens had been refused visas on the

38. Ibid., 16 (January 23, 1939), 11; Congressional Record (February 13, 1936), p. 1961.
39. New York Times (October 12, 1931), p. 18.
40. Congressional Record (July 13, 1932), pp. 15,291-2.
41. "Review of the Action of Consular Officers in Refusing Immigration Visas," Hearings before the House Committee on Immigration and Naturalization, 72d Congress, 1st Session (Washington, 1932), pp. 2-7, 9-10.
42. Ibid., pp. 11-14; Congressional Record (June 1, 1932), p. 11,715.

grounds of "likely to become a public charge." [43] These instructions resulted in an immediate liberalization of the immigration of relatives. By 1934 less than 2 per cent of all relatives who applied for admission were being refused visas, and statistics for the years 1932–34 show that relatives made up nearly 60 per cent of the total number of immigrants.[44]

At the same time advocates of a liberal immigration policy pressed for further preferential treatment of relatives. In 1932 and again in 1933 Dickstein introduced bills to exempt elderly parents of American citizens from the quota. These bills were approved by the committee, despite the strong protests of Representative Dies, who contended, "The opponents of restrictive immigration are seeking to do by piecemeal legislation what they dare not seek to accomplish in one general bill." [45] Organized labor and patriotic societies also opposed the parents bill as entering wedges against restriction, while in Congress, Representative Green of Florida claimed that the measure was "the result of years of effort by the alien bloc to break down our immigration laws." Stating that the admission of a few aged parents could hardly be viewed as a reversal of policy, Representative Sabath denounced the opponents of the bill as "professional restrictionists." The House finally passed the bill in drastically amended form, but it died when the Senate failed to act.[46] This marked the end of the relatives issue, for it had become apparent that the liberals would be no more successful in changing the immigration laws than the restrictionists.

The administrative enforcement of the public charge provision remained the basis of American immigration policy throughout the depression. Though Hoover inaugurated this regulation as a temporary expedient, by 1932 he had accepted it as the best means of restricting immigration during the economic crisis. In his campaign for re-election

43. State Department, *Press Releases, 10* (April 14, 1934), 204.

44. State Department, *Immigration Work of the Department of State,* p. 11; *Interpreter Releases, 12* (March 31, 1935), 126.

45. "Exemption from the Quota of Aged Fathers and Mothers of American Citizens," *House Report No. 245,* 72d Congress, 1st Session (Washington, 1932), pp. 1–2; "Exempt from the Quota Parents 60 Years or Over of American Citizens," *House Report No. 52,* 73d Congress, 1st Session (Washington, 1933), Pt. I, p. 1; Pt. II, p. 2.

46. *Congressional Record* (May 31, 1932), pp. 11,691, 11,694; (June 1, 1932), p. 11,756.

in that year he pointed with pride to the public charge regulation, asserting in a speech at Columbus, Ohio, "I propose to continue this policy until the end of the depression." [47] Roosevelt made no public reference to either the public charge policy or immigration during the campaign, but in an interview with a reporter he let it be known that he favored sharp restriction while unemployment prevailed.[48] After taking office, Roosevelt maintained the public charge regulations and assured William Green of the AFL, who feared that Secretary of Labor Perkins might favor a more liberal program, that there would be no change in the policy of strict administrative restriction.[49] In 1937 there was a slight relaxation when the State Department instructed the consuls to be less rigorous in their interpretations of the "likely to become a public charge" clause.[50] This was only a modification of previous policy, however, not a drastic reversal.

The statistics on immigration during the depression decade show the degree of restriction achieved by the public charge policy. As an indication of the significance of the figures given in the accompanying table, the annual number of immigrants had not fallen below 100,000 since the Civil War, or below 30,000 since 1831.[51] In the entire decade, only 528,431 immigrants were admitted, and taking into account the emigration of aliens from the United States, the net increase in the American population through immigration amounted to only 68,693 for the ten-year span.[52] One interesting feature of European immigration during the depression was the national composition of the immi-

47. Myers, The State Papers of Hoover, p. 389; Interpreter Releases, 9 (October 26, 1932), 261.

48. Interpreter Releases, 9 (October 26, 1932), 261; New York Times (October 24, 1932), p. 9.

49. William Green to Roosevelt (September 22, 1933); Roosevelt to Green (December 8, 1933); Franklin D. Roosevelt Papers, File 133, Franklin D. Roosevelt Library.

50. "Deportation of Aliens," Hearings before a Subcommittee of the Senate Committee on Immigration, 76th Congress, 1st Session (Washington, 1939), p. 71; Congressional Record (January 23, 1939), p. 609. The consuls were instructed to refuse visas only when there was a probability that the applicant would become a public charge, not just a possibility.

51. William S. Bernard, ed., American Immigration Policy (New York, 1950), p. 299.

52. Ibid., p. 32; "The Immigration and Naturalization Systems of the United States," Senate Report No. 1515, 81st Congress, 2d Session (Washington, 1950), p. 817.

grant flow. Though the national origins plan established a ratio of five to one in favor of the countries of northwestern Europe, the actual distribution of European immigrants was 57 per cent from the northwestern countries, 43 per cent from the southeastern ones.[53] The much heavier demands against the quota in southern Europe, coupled with the fact that most of the nonquota immigration came from this area, upset the operation of the national origins principle by tending to equalize immigration from the two European regions.[54]

TABLE 2. Immigration into the United States, 1931–40

Year	Quota	Nonquota	Total
1931	54,118	43,021	97,139
1932	12,983	22,593	35,576
1933	8,220	14,848	23,068
1934	12,483	16,987	29,470
1935	17,207	17,749	34,956
1936	18,675	17,654	36,329
1937	27,762	22,482	50,244
1938	42,494	25,401	67,895
1939	62,402	20,596	82,998
1940	51,997	18,759	70,756

Despite the criticisms by extremists, people of moderate views generally hailed the public charge policy as an intelligent solution to the problem of immigration during the economic crisis. The Ellis Island Committee, a group of New York citizens appointed by Secretary of Labor Perkins to study the administration of the immigration laws and to recommend reforms, had nothing but praise for the policy. "Our immigration laws," they reported in 1934, "have met the challenge of the depression. They have permitted the most drastic reduction in immigration and yet have retained a flexibility adapted to changing conditions." [55] In 1936 Senator Marcus Coolidge, Chairman of the Senate Immigration Committee, made a similar appraisal in a radio speech to the nation. Praising the public charge policy, he

53. Calculated from statistics in the *Monthly Review of Immigration and Naturalization Service, 2* (December 1944), 77.

54. For the period 1931–40, 22 per cent of the northwestern European quotas were used, as opposed to 49 per cent of the southeastern ones. *Senate Report No. 1515* (1950), p. 890.

55. *Interpreter Release Clip Sheets, 11* (March 26, 1934), 26.

concluded, "Immigration as such . . . presents no problem to us today." [56] By and large the policy of administrative enforcement was accepted as a sensible compromise of the various viewpoints on immigration control during the depression.

56. *Interpreter Releases, 13* (February 13, 1936), 44–5.

5. Problems of the 1930's: Refugees and Subversives

JUST as the depression raised the issue of limiting immigration during an economic crisis, the rise of totalitarian governments in Europe resulted in two further problems of immigration policy in the 1930's. By far the most important of these problems was the question of refugees fleeing from Hitler's Fascist regime in Germany. The plight of hundreds of thousands of people driven out of Germany by a systematic campaign of political and religious persecution brought about demands for the liberalization of immigration policy on their behalf. A bitter controversy ensued between the liberal and restrictionist viewpoints over the question of granting special consideration to the German refugees. The second problem was the entry of alien subversive elements. The restrictionists, fearing the spread of Fascist and Communist ideologies to the United States, urged the adoption of strict laws to exclude all members of subversive organizations. Near the end of the decade the outbreak of war in Europe and the much-publicized use of fifth-column techniques led to demands for the rigid screening of all immigrants in the interests of national defense, and thus along with the older issue of aiding the distressed of Europe a new concern for the entry of subversive agents was injected into considerations of immigration policy.

"With the growth of democracy in foreign countries political persecution has largely ceased. There is no longer a necessity for the United States to provide an asylum for those persecuted because of conscience." [1] Thus spoke Herbert Hoover in a campaign address in October 1932. A few months later Hitler had come to power in Germany and inaugurated one of the cruelest reigns of persecution the world had yet known. In 1933 approximately 50,000 refugees, mainly Jews but including many Christians hounded for their liberal political views,

1. *Interpreter Releases*, 9 (October 26, 1932), 261.

fled Germany. The mass exodus continued for the rest of the decade, averaging about 25,000 a year down to 1938.[2] This situation raised the question of whether the United States should provide a refuge for these persecuted people. The asylum ideal was an American tradition, yet one which had not been written into the immigration laws. Refugees were not distinguished from other immigrants in existing legislation except in one case—the literacy test could be waived for persons fleeing political or religious oppression. Otherwise, refugees were faced with the same barriers which obstructed the admission of all immigrants—the national origin quotas; the mental, moral, and physical tests; and the public charge clause.[3] For the rest of the decade liberal groups pressed for legislation to implement the asylum ideal by granting special treatment to refugees.

From 1933 through 1938 congressmen friendly to immigration, led by Representative Samuel Dickstein, introduced a series of bills to liberalize the immigration laws in behalf of refugees from Germany. These measures ranged from a bill to exempt refugees from the "likely to become a public charge" clause to a proposal by Congressman Vito Marcantonio to admit refugees outside the quota.[4] Support for these measures came largely from Jewish organizations such as the American Jewish Congress and the Hebrew Sheltering and Immigrant Aid Society,[5] but Protestant and Catholic spokesmen joined in. Harry Emerson Fosdick, a prominent New York clergyman, forwarded a petition to President Roosevelt in 1933 asking him to relax the immigration barriers in behalf of Jewish refugees, and Al Smith wrote in the *New Outlook*, "We must uphold our traditions and vindicate the principles on which this nation was established by making room here for our share of the refugees from Germany."[6] Despite this support

2. Walter Adams, "Extent and Nature of the World Refugee Problem," *Annals of the American Academy of Political and Social Science, 203* (May 1939), 32.

3. Reid Lewis and Marian Schibsby, "Status of the Refugee under American Immigration Laws," *Annals, 203* (May 1939), 74–9; Harold Fields, *The Refugee in the United States* (New York, 1938), pp. 8–9.

4. New York *Times* (March 22, 1933), p. 8; *Interpreter Releases, 12* (July 12, 1935), 288; *14* (April 15, 1937), 97; *Congressional Record*, Appendix (May 18, 1937), pp. 1189–90.

5. New York *Times* (March 20, 1933), p. 5; (March 22, 1933), pp. 8–9.

6. Fosdick to Roosevelt (November 27, 1933), FDR Papers, File 133; Al Smith, "Can We Make Room for the Refugees?" *New Outlook, 162* (November 1933), p. 10.

none of the bills obtained committee approval, and thus the question of relaxing the immigration laws for refugees never received serious consideration in Congress.

The primary reason for the failure of these measures was the opposition of groups traditionally hostile to immigration. When the first refugee measure was introduced, the patriotic societies launched a strong attack upon it. John Trevor, leader of the American Coalition, telegraphed the Senate committee that the proposed legislation would flood the country with Communist agitators and competing workmen.[7] Other patriotic societies took the same stand, and were joined by the powerful AFL. At its annual convention in 1933, the AFL went on record as opposed to any changes in immigration policy in regard to refugees, stating, "There is not a country in the world where there is not religious or political persecutions."[8] In an era of depression and unemployment, the pressures of patriotic societies and organized labor were more than sufficient to prevent any breach in the immigration barrier for refugees.

But while Congress refused to act, President Roosevelt attempted to ease the situation by ordering the American consuls abroad to treat refugees applying for visas with special consideration. The State Department complied with the president's wishes by issuing instructions telling the consuls to give refugees "the most humane and favorable treatment possible under the law."[9] Jewish groups felt that this administrative relaxation was not carried out properly; in 1935, and again in 1936, Governor Herbert Lehman of New York wrote President Roosevelt protesting against unfair treatment by American consuls toward Jewish refugees.[10] In his replies Roosevelt expressed his sympathy for the plight of the persecuted Jews and reiterated the directive to the consuls.[11]

7. Trevor to Senator Marcus Coolidge (March 31, 1933), Senate Immigration Committee Papers, File Sen. 73A-F11.
8. *Proceedings of the 53d Annual Convention of the AFL, 1933* (Washington, 1933), p. 103.
9. State Department, *Press Releases, 10* (April 14, 1934), 204–5.
10. Lehman to Roosevelt (November 1, 1935, and June 15, 1936), FDR Papers, File 133.
11. Roosevelt to Lehman (November 13, 1935, and July 2, 1936), FDR Papers, File 133.

The refugee problem entered a second and more critical stage in 1938. In March Hitler invaded Austria and incorporated that area into the Third Reich. This opened the way to persecution of hundreds of thousands of liberals and Jews in Austria.[12] Meanwhile, attempts to ease the refugee situation by international efforts had proved fruitless. As far back as 1921, the League of Nations had created the autonomous High Commission for Refugees under the leadership of Dr. Fridtjof Nansen to help persecuted Russians and Armenians. When the German refugee problem developed in 1933, the League established a High Commission for Refugees Coming from Germany, headed by an American, James MacDonald. Because of German objections, however, this organization was divorced from the League and continued on private funds. MacDonald resigned in 1935, asserting that no effective work could be accomplished without the authority of the League. In spite of a reorganization in 1938 which established a single High Commission for Refugees, the League continued to be hampered by closely circumscribed powers,[13] and its activities were marked by a singular lack of success.

This was the situation when President Roosevelt made a dramatic move to alleviate the refugee problem. On March 24, 1938, the State Department announced that it had sent notes to twenty-nine European and South American countries asking them to participate in an international conference on German refugees.[14] Since the United States had not taken part in any of the previous international efforts to solve the problem, the new proposal greatly raised the hopes of those sympathetic to the refugees. The State Department made it clear, however, that the contemplated program envisioned no changes in immigration policy. "Furthermore, it should be understood," ran the text of the notes, "that no country would be expected or asked to receive a greater number of immigrants than is permitted by its existing legislation." [15] The next day the president held a press conference

12. Adams, p. 32.
13. Sir John Hope Simpson, *The Refugee Problem* (London, 1939), pp. 191–221; Jacques Vernant, *The Refugee in the Post-War World* (New Haven, 1953), pp. 24–6; Louise Holborn, "The League of Nations and the Refugee Problem," *Annals, 203* (May 1939), pp. 125–35.
14. New York *Times* (March 25, 1938), p. 1.
15. Ibid., p. 1.

at which he spoke of the traditional American ideal of asylum for the politically oppressed of all nations. But he emphasized that this was a statement of principle which in no way foreshadowed any revision of the quota policy.[16]

Reactions to the Roosevelt proposal varied from lukewarm support to outspoken criticism. William Green, speaking for organized labor, praised the suggestion as a humanitarian gesture but stated his opposition to any attempt to increase the quotas.[17] In Congress restrictionists announced their opposition. Representative Jenkins of Ohio warned against becoming embroiled in a European problem, while Rankin of Mississippi asserted, "Almost every disgruntled element that ever got into trouble in its own country has pleaded for admission into the United States on the ground that they were oppressed at home." [18] Spokesmen for patriotic societies and veterans' organizations added their objections, and public opinion appeared to be hostile to any plan for aiding refugees.[19] In a *Fortune* poll in the summer of 1938, 67 per cent of the people interviewed were opposed to the admission of refugees.[20]

Adverse comment did not deter Roosevelt from carrying through with the plan for an international conference. He received many letters from prominent people congratulating him on his action, and in reply to one from Judge Irving Lehman of New York he wrote, "I think that our action in regard to political refugees will have far reaching consequences even though, unfortunately, we cannot take care of more than a small proportion of them." [21] All the nations invited to participate in the plan accepted, and in May, Roosevelt appointed Myron Taylor, former Chairman of the Board of U.S. Steel, as the American representative on the Intergovernmental Committee on Refugees, as the new group was called. Taylor left in June for Evian, France, a small town near the Swiss border, for the first meeting of the new organization.[22]

16. Ibid. (March 26, 1938), p. 1.
17. Ibid.
18. *Congressional Record* (March 28, 1938), p. 4227; (May 20, 1938), p. 7187.
19. New York *Times* (July 3, 1938), p. 8.
20. "The Fortune Quarterly Survey," *Fortune*, 18 (July 1938), 80.
21. Roosevelt to Irving Lehman (March 30, 1938), FDR Papers, File 3186.
22. New York *Times* (May 1, 1938), p. 1; Samuel Rosenman, ed., *The Public Papers and Addresses of Franklin D. Roosevelt* (9 vols. New York, 1938–41), 7, 170.

The Evian conference was marked by many statements of principle but little concrete achievement. Taylor opened the conference with a speech urging international cooperation on the refugee problem, but he reiterated the American view that no changes in the immigration laws of any country should be contemplated.[23] The one solid accomplishment of this conference was the establishment of the Intergovernmental Committee on Refugees as a permanent organization. The committee created a Refugee Aid Bureau in London under the direction of an American, but without a practical plan for the resettlement of the homeless refugees, the work of the Intergovernmental Committee amounted to little more than a pious gesture of sympathy over the plight of these unfortunate people.[24]

A new crisis in the problem came in the fall of 1938. American awareness of the disintegrating European situation was heightened by the events leading to the Munich agreement in September. Two months later, Nazi persecution of Jews broke out in unprecedented fury as a result of the assassination of a German diplomat in Paris by a Polish Jew. President Roosevelt denounced this violent anti-Semitic campaign at a press conference on November 15, 1938, and stated that the American ambassador in Berlin had been recalled.[25] When asked by a reporter if he would recommend that Congress relax the immigration restrictions for Jewish refugees, Roosevelt replied, "That is not in contemplation; we have the quota system." However, three days later he announced that in the case of political refugees temporary visas would be renewed every six months as long as the persecution continued, thereby aiding some 15,000 individuals who had entered the United States as visitors.[26]

Roosevelt still believed that the best solution to the refugee prob-

23. New York *Times* (July 7, 1938), p. 9.

24. In discussing the conference in 1941, Roosevelt placed the blame for essential failure of his plan on the other nations, without mentioning the American refusal to consider any changes in the quotas. "Unfortunately, most of the governments seemed overly cautious in their attitude about receiving these refugees; and while they were generally sympathetic, no constructive plans were submitted." Rosenman, *Public Papers*, 7, 171 (Roosevelt note).

25. Allan Nevins, *The New Deal and World Affairs*, Chronicles of America (New Haven, 1950), pp. 143–65; New York *Times* (November 16, 1938), p. 6; Rosenman, 7, 596–8.

26. Rosenman, 7, 598, 603–4.

lem lay in the Intergovernmental Committee, and he continued to reject the idea of increasing the quotas. In a confidential letter to Myron Taylor, he expressed his hopes for more effective action through the Committee and stated, "I do not believe it either desirable or practicable to recommend any change in the quota provisions of our immigration laws." [27] Taylor announced this policy to the American people in a radio address on November 25. "Our plans do not involve the 'flooding' of this or any other country with aliens of any race or creed," he stated. "On the contrary, our entire program is based on the existing immigration laws of all the countries concerned, and I am confident that within that framework our problem can be solved." [28]

Throughout the winter of 1938–39 and the following spring there was a great deal of public discussion of the refugee issue. Strong pressure developed in liberal circles for a relaxation of the quota laws. Both the *Nation* and the *New Republic* published editorials in favor of admitting refugees into the United States, the latter magazine asserting, "Under the circumstances, common decency requires that the United States should modify its present immigration restrictions." The liberals frequently accused the restrictionists of anti-Semitism in opposing refugee immigration, with one writer stating, "To slam shut the gates of immigration for such a reason is tantamount to admitting that American democracy has failed in the past and no longer exists today." [29] The restrictionists replied forcefully to the liberal arguments. Henry Pratt Fairchild warned that the admission of a large number of Jews would cause latent American anti-Semitism "to burst out into violent eruption." [30] Representative Will Taylor of Tennessee presented the economic argument, claiming that the New Deal showed more concern for the European refugees than for "the 10,-000,000 of American refugees who have been walking the streets of our city in vain." [31] Public opinion appeared to be almost wholly on the restrictionist side. In the *Fortune* survey for April 1939 83 per cent

27. Roosevelt to Myron Taylor (November 23, 1938), FDR Papers, File 3186.
28. *Interpreter Releases, 15* (November 29, 1938), 361.
29. "Refugees and Economics," *Nation, 147* (December 10, 1938), 610; "Let the Jews Come In!" *New Republic, 97* (November 23, 1938), 60; Frank Ritchie, "America Needs Them," *Forum, 101* (June 1939), 320.
30. Henry Pratt Fairchild, "Should the Jews Come In?" *New Republic, 97* (January 25, 1939), 344.
31. *Congressional Record* (November 3, 1939), p. 1376.

of the people polled were opposed to opening the doors to European refugees.[32] The editors interpreted the result as due to fear of economic competition and ruled out anti-Semitism as an important factor. They concluded, "Here is an American tradition put to the popular test, and here it is repudiated by a majority of nearly ten to one." [33]

The debate over refugees reached a climax in the spring of 1939 when the Immigration Committees of both branches of Congress considered legislation dealing with refugee children. The previous year, bills by Representatives Celler and Dickstein proposing to let refugees come in above regular quotas had made no progress.[34] In February, Senator Wagner of New York introduced a new type of refugee measure—a bill that proposed to admit 20,000 German refugee children into the United States over a two-year period as nonquota immigrants.[35] The extensive committee hearings held on this bill afford the clearest picture of the controversy between liberals and restrictionists over the question of refugee immigration.[36]

The people advocating the Wagner bill presented a powerful case which showed that they possessed a realistic understanding of the difficulty in passing a bill liberalizing immigration policy. The most interested supporters formed the Non-Sectarian Committee for German Refugee Children, composed of religious and social leaders of all faiths, which organized and coordinated the liberal efforts. With an eye toward overcoming restrictionist opposition the Non-Sectarian Committee carefully selected and presented the witnesses in favor of the bill. First, they won over organized labor: representatives of both the AFL and CIO testified for the refugee measure. Secondly, they presented as many southern witnesses as possible in order to put

32. "The Fortune Survey," *Fortune*, 19 (April 1939), 102. The exact question was, "If you were a member of Congress would you vote yes or no on a bill to open the doors of the U.S. to a larger number of European refugees than now admitted under our immigration quotas?" Of the people polled, 8.7 per cent answered yes and 8.3 per cent expressed no opinion.

33. Ibid., p. 102.

34. *Interpreter Releases*, 15 (April 18, 1938), 173.

35. Ibid., *16* (February 23, 1939), 56.

36. "Admission of German Refugee Children," *Hearings before the House Committee on Immigration and Naturalization*, 76th Congress, 1st Session, Washington, 1939; "Admission of German Refugee Children," *Hearings before a Subcommittee of the Senate Committee on Immigration and a Subcommittee of the House Committee on Immigration and Naturalization*, 76th Congress, 1st Session, Washington, 1939.

pressure on the southern restrictionists: strong statements in support of the bill by Frank Graham, president of the University of North Carolina, and Homer Rainey, president-elect of the University of Texas, were very effective. Finally, the liberals sought wider popular support by having such celebrities as Helen Hayes and Joe E. Brown appear at the hearings to speak for the bill.[37]

In developing their case, the advocates of the Wagner bill were careful to play down the Jewish question, and Rabbi Stephen Wise was the sole Jewish witness to appear at the hearings. In describing the need for legislation, they continually stressed the fact that the refugees represented every religious creed, asserting that Jews made up only 60 per cent of the total number involved. They revealed their awareness of intolerance as a major obstacle in their path. "I beg of you," a Quaker asked the committee members, "to regard this as being a matter for the relief of children, and children alone, regardless of their parentage, regardless of the question of race or religious affiliations on their part." The plea for tolerance was not wholly successful, for the opponents of the bill on several occasions expressed anti-Semitic viewpoints. Francis Kinnicutt of the Allied Patriotic Societies objected to the Wagner bill because "additional immigration permitted by it would be for the most part of the Jewish race," while another witness declared, "That the Jewish people will profit most by this legislation goes without saying." [38]

The main argument advanced by the liberals was an idealistic one, framed in terms of American history and tradition. They stressed the experience of the United States in succoring the persecuted of Europe. "By long tradition," asserted Senator Wagner, "America has been a haven for the oppressed." "Certainly there isn't any race or any section of this country which is not represented by people who found America a refuge and an escape from European oppression," added another witness. This bill was intended to help refugees, they contended, but even more important as a restatement of fundamental principles it would strengthen America. "The admission of a handful of European children," Wagner stated, "means a great deal, for us and the whole

37. "German Refugee Children," House *Hearings* (1939), pp. 4–15, 27, 31–3, 42–4, 91–7, 109–12; "German Refugee Children," Subcommittee *Hearings* (1939), pp. 70–1.

38. "German Refugee Children," House *Hearings* (1939), pp. 16, 27, 103, 123; "German Refugee Children," Subcommittee *Hearings* (1939), pp. 73, 157, 184.

world, as a symbol of the strength of our democratic convictions and our common faith." The ultimate appeal was not to a national ideal but to a universal aspiration. "After all, we are Americans; but even before we are Americans we are human beings, and we have certain obligations which run with the whole of humanity." [39] This statement by Reid Lewis marked the climax of the liberal argument.

The traditionally restrictionist groups, with the important exception of organized labor, opposed the Wagner bill. Representatives of a great many patriotic societies testified at the hearings, adopting the phrase "charity should begin at home" as their slogan. They frequently cited a phrase from Roosevelt's second inaugural speech—"one third of a nation ill-housed, ill-clad, ill-nourished"—to argue that the United States should take care of its own needy before importing others from Europe. "We have more millions on relief here in the United States," contended a patriot, "than the world has refugees today. These cases of our own should have first consideration." [40] Such arguments reflected, of course, the militant isolationist crusade of the period.[41] A witness for Young Americans bluntly expressed the isolationist viewpoint with the statement, "I say if we are going to keep this country as it is and not lose our liberty in the future, we have got to keep not only these children out of it but the whole damned Europe." The greatest concern of restrictionist witnesses was their fear that the Wagner bill represented an attempt to subvert the basic principles of American immigration policy. They believed that no emergency situation justified temporary exceptions from permanent policy, and they fully agreed with Colonel Taylor, lobbyist for the American Legion, who contended that the Wagner proposal was "nothing more or less than an effort to break down the immigration laws." The complete rigidity of this restrictionist viewpoint was most clearly revealed by a witness who asserted, "We would oppose any increase in any quota to any country." [42]

39. "German Refugee Children," House *Hearings* (1939), pp. 163, 167; "German Refugee Children," Subcommittee *Hearings* (1939), p. 7.
40. "German Refugee Children," House *Hearings* (1939), pp. 67, 124, 186, 227.
41. By 1940 the American Coalition had become more interested in asserting its isolationist views than in defending restrictive immigration policy. *Resolutions Adopted by the American Coalition,* pamphlet, 1940.
42. "German Refugee Children," House *Hearings* (1939), p. 115; "German Refugee Children," Subcommittee *Hearings* (1939), p. 199.

The strong opposition by restrictionist groups evidently impressed the Senate Immigration Committee. After considerable discussion, this group decided to approve the bill with one vital amendment—that the 20,000 children had to enter the United States as quota immigrants. In its report, the Senate committee stated the reason for the drastic change—"The Committee feels that existing quotas should be permitted to stand and would not sanction a breakdown of the existing restrictions." [43] Senator Wagner refused to accept this amendment, stating to the press that "the proposed change would in effect convert the measure from a humane proposal to help children who are in acute distress to a proposal with needlessly cruel consequences for adults in Germany who are in a need of succor and are fortunate enough to obtain visas under the present drastic quota restrictions." [44] Because of Wagner's objections, the amended bill was never officially reported to Congress and so died in committee.

The outbreak of war in Europe in 1939 ushered in the final stage of the refugee problem. In the period before American entry into the war, the administration policy was to help the refugees in every way possible under existing law. In January 1940 Roosevelt asked Commissioner of Immigration James Houghteling to explore the possibilities of Congressional liberalization of the immigration laws on behalf of refugees. Houghteling reported that he had "found a great deal of confusion in the minds of Congressmen on the subject of refugees and of hostility to the admission of any considerable number of aliens to compete for employment with American citizens." [45] Accordingly, Roosevelt did not ask Congress to liberalize the immigration laws. However, in the summer of 1940, after the fall of France, the president moved to help refugees who had fled to Portugal and North Africa. He asked his Advisory Committee on Refugees to prepare a list of eminent refugees in order that the State Department could issue temporary visas to save these individuals.[46] In all, the State Department issued 3268 visitor's visas to "those of superior intellectual attainment,

43. Typescript report, Senate Immigration Committee Papers, File Sen. 76A-E4.
44. New York *Times* (July 3, 1939), p. 4.
45. James Houghteling to Roosevelt (January 5, 1940), FDR Papers, File 133.
46. New York *Times* (July 27, 1940), p. 7; Acting Secretary of State Sumner Welles to Attorney-General Robert Jackson (November 23, 1940), FDR Papers, File 3186.

of indomitable spirit, experienced in vigorous support of the principles of liberal government and who are in danger of persecution or death at the hands of autocracy." [47]

The State Department and the Department of Justice, which had assumed jurisdiction of the Immigration Bureau in 1940, instituted new administrative procedures to aid refugees. In the latter part of 1940 the State Department unblocked the quotas by permitting consuls outside Germany to issue immigration visas to German refugees who were able to procure transportation to the United States. This was a very helpful reform, since previously quota numbers were allocated by priority of application, so that often the recipients of visas were people inside Germany who could not emigrate. Under the new system American consuls in Lisbon, Casablanca, and even Shanghai issued visas to refugees who had fled to those ports.[48] In January 1941 the Justice Department negotiated an agreement with Canada for the benefit of refugees who were in the United States on temporary visas. Under immigration law, an alien could not change his status from that of a visitor to that of an immigrant without leaving the United States. The new regulation, known as Canadian pre-examination, allowed the visitor to be examined in the United States for admission as an immigrant and, if he was approved, to go to Canada, where the American consul issued him a quota visa. Upon re-entry into the United States, the individual became a bona fide immigrant admitted for permanent residence. By this roundabout process many refugees who had sought temporary shelter in the United States were able to stay permanently.[49]

The entry of the United States into the World War in December 1941 marks the end of the prewar refugee problem. The American record in dealing with this human catastrophe is curiously mixed. In

47. State Department press release, quoted in *Interpreter Releases*, 17 (December 20, 1940), 422. Of the 3268 visas, only 1236 had actually been used by January 1941. In many cases, the refugees had not been able to reach a neutral port. Assistant Secretary of State Breckinridge Long to Roosevelt (January 6, 1941), FDR Papers, File 3186.

48. *Interpreter Releases*, 18 (February 5, 1941), 39; "Department of State Appropriation Bill for 1942," *Hearings before the Subcommittee of the House Committee on Appropriations*, 77th Congress, 1st Session (Washington, 1941), pp. 163–4.

49. *Interpreter Releases*, 18 (January 6, 1941), 1–2; (June 1, 1941), 239; New York *Times* (March 28, 1941), p. 21.

Congress, where the restrictionist bloc was powerful, all efforts to liberalize the immigration laws in behalf of refugees failed. But the Roosevelt administration displayed a keen desire to help the refugees in every way possible under law, and as a result administrative policy toward refugees enabled the United States to absorb more refugees than any other nation.[50] Since official statistics do not distinguish refugees from other immigrants, precise figures are unobtainable, but reliable estimates place the number of refugees who entered the United States for permanent residence in this period at about 250,000.[51] In the critical year of 1939, 53 per cent of the total European immigration came from Germany and Austria, while for the period 1934–41, 46 per cent of all quota immigration was German and Austrian.[52] Thus even though Roosevelt's attempts to solve the refugee problem on an international level failed, he was able to thwart the restrictionist majority in Congress and maintain to a very large degree the American ideal of asylum for the oppressed of Europe. Considering that throughout this period the United States was engulfed in the worst depression in its history, the relief given to refugees was a major humanitarian achievement.

On December 1, 1930, 500 Communists and Soviet sympathizers marched on the Capitol in Washington to protest against the restrictive immigration laws. This demonstration, organized by the National Council for the Protection of the Foreign Born, was halted by police using clubs and tear gas.[53] Thus at the very beginning of the decade the problem of the relationship between radical activity and immigration was brought to the attention of congressmen. During the "red scare" in the period immediately following the first World War, Congress had passed legislation excluding all aliens advocating the overthrow of the United States government. But when, with the onset of the depression, Communist activity became more open and militant, a

50. Bernard, *American Immigration Policy*, p. 248.

51. Maurice R. Davie, *Refugees in America* (New York, 1947), pp. 22–7. In addition some 200,000 more refugees entered temporarily. Of these, only 15,000 were still in the United States by 1944.

52. Calculated from statistics given in *Annual Report of the Secretary of Labor, 1940* (Washington, 1940), p. 104, and *Monthly Review of the Immigration and Naturalization Service*, 2 (June 1945), 158.

53. New York *Times* (December 2, 1930), p. 1.

demand arose for a more stringent law which would provide for the automatic exclusion and deportation of any alien who was a member of the Communist party.

The first attempt to exclude Communists specifically was a direct outgrowth of an investigation into Communist activity by a Congressional committee headed by Representative Hamilton Fish during the summer and fall of 1930. In its report the Fish Committee stated, "The fact of a person being a Communist is not a bar to entry into the United States" and consequently recommended that the immigration laws be amended to exclude Communists.[54] In line with this recommendation, Congressman Carl Bachmann of West Virginia introduced a bill in December of 1930 to exclude and deport alien Communists. The House Immigration Committee reported favorably on the measure, but no further action was taken at this session.[55]

The following year Martin Dies introduced a similar bill, which stirred up considerable debate. The House Immigration Committee held a series of public hearings at which Communists and liberal sympathizers violently protested against the Dies bill. The Communists charged that the bill was "a ruling-class" weapon designed to split apart the proletariat by driving wedges between foreign-born and native Americans. They appealed strenuously to the ideal of asylum, claiming that the United States should shelter all radicals expelled from European countries. "We demand the right of asylum," asserted a member of the International Labor Defense, "for all political refugees. We demand the repeal of all laws now on the statute books that restrict immigration or deny the right of asylum." [56]

These militant protests served only to antagonize the committee members, and they quickly reported favorably on the bill. The House of Representatives passed the bill after a brief debate, but it died in the Senate.[57] There was no further effort to legislate on this issue

54. "Investigation of Communist Propaganda," *House Report No. 2290*, 71st Congress, 3d Session (Washington, 1931), pp. 50, 63.

55. "Exclusion of Communists," *House Report No. 7297*, 71st Congress, 3d Session (Washington, 1931), p. 1. Bachmann was a member of the Fish Committee.

56. "Exclusion and Expulsion of Communists," *Hearings before the House Committee on Immigration and Naturalization*, 72d Congress, 1st Session (Washington, 1932), pp. 9–12, 20, 94–5, 127, 134.

57. "Exclusion and Expulsion of Alien Communists," *House Report No. 1353*, 72d Congress, 1st Session (Washington, 1932), pp. 1–4; *Congressional Record* (June 6, 1932), pp. 12,097–108.

until 1935, when Martin Dies introduced a bill to exclude and deport both alien Fascists and Communists. The bill was strongly supported by the AFL and the American Coalition, whose representative told the House Immigration Committee that "we think there is no room in this country for any 'ism' or any word ending in those letters, except Americanism." The committee reported the Dies bill, but once again Congress failed to consider the proposed measure.[58] At the end of the decade, the House passed a bill to exclude all aliens advocating any change in the American form of government, but no action was taken by the Senate.[59] Finally, in 1940 Congress passed the Smith Act, a culmination of a growing anti-Communist feeling throughout the country which had been stimulated by the disclosures of the Dies Un-American Affairs Committee and by the Nazi-Soviet pact. This act made the advocacy of violent overthrow of the government a crime for citizens and aliens alike and required that all aliens register with the government.[60]

Though not directly related to immigration, the Smith Act indicated that in 1940 the fear of subversive elements was spreading through the nation. The fall of France and Norway, and particularly the role of traitors in these German victories, contributed to the general concern over "fifth column" activities. The administration recognized the need for tightening up control over aliens and immigration. On May 22, President Roosevelt submitted to Congress his recommendation that the Immigration Service be shifted from the Department of Labor to the Justice Department. In his message Roosevelt referred to the "startling sequence of international events" and stated, "under existing conditions the immigration and naturalization activities can best contribute to the national well-being only if they are closely integrated with the activities of the Department of Justice." A small minority in the Senate opposed the transfer, claiming that such a move

58. "To Exclude and Expel Alien Fascists and Communists," *Hearings before the House Committee on Immigration and Naturalization*, 74th Congress, 1st Session (Washington, 1935), pp. 2, 9; "Exclude and Deport Aliens Who Are Fascists or Communists," *House Report No. 1023*, 74th Congress, 1st Session (Washington, 1935), p. 1.

59. "Provide for the Exclusion and Deportation of Aliens Who Advocate the Making of Any Changes in the American Form of Government," *House Report No. 259*, 76th Congress, 1st Session (Washington, 1939), p. 1.

60. *Interpreter Releases, 17* (July 8, 1940), 231–2.

would heighten irrational anti-alien prejudices, but a great majority supported the president's recommendation, and on May 31, just nine days after the Presidential message, Congress passed legislation authorizing the transfer.[61]

In a speech of welcome to the Immigration Service on June 14, Attorney-General Jackson explained the significance of the change. He stated that there would be a tightening up of the administration of the immigration laws in the interests of national defense, asserting "that none shall be admitted unless it affirmatively appears to be for the American interest." At the same time Jackson condemned anti-alien prejudice and warned that assaults on the foreign born served only to destroy American unity.[62] This more vigilant attitude toward immigrants was not followed by any basic changes in procedure until the next year. In June 1941 the State and Justice departments worked out a new system to screen all applicants for visas in order to weed out security risks. Under the new regulations all applications for visas were forwarded to a central visa board in Washington composed of representatives of the State Department, Immigration Service, FBI, and Naval and Military Intelligence. The consul abroad was then notified of the board's decision, and if it was favorable, he could proceed to issue the visa.[63] Thus as totalitarian aggression superseded the depression as the primary threat to American well being, the administration established loyalty to the United States as the major determinent in admitting immigrants.

The decade of the 1930's was characterized by startling changes in many spheres of American life. Superficially, it would appear that immigration policy was an exception, since the restrictive program established in the 1920's was maintained throughout this period; yet when one probes deeper, significant transformations in immigration policy become apparent. One of the most important changes was a

61. *Congressional Record* (May 22, 1940), p. 6590; (May 27, 1940), p. 6925; (May 30, 1940), pp. 7198, 7200; (May 31, 1940), p. 7290.

62. New York *Times* (June 15, 1940), p. 9; *Interpreter Releases*, 17 (June 18, 1940), 211–12.

63. "Additional Urgent Deficiency Appropriation Bill, Fiscal Year 1941," *Hearings before the Subcommittee of the House Committee on Appropriations*, 77th Congress, 1st Session (Washington, 1941), p. 138; *Interpreter Releases*, 18 (July 1, 1941), 274–6.

shift in the factors influencing the formulation of policy. The emphasis on ethnic theories, so significant in the development of the quota system, almost wholly disappeared in the 1930's. References to the homogeneity and racial character of the American people were conspicuous by their absence in discussions of immigration matters. Much more stress was laid on the economic aspects of immigration, primarily as a result of the depression. The old cry of "Keep America American" was replaced by the slogan "American jobs for Americans." But the most striking change was the transformation of the nationalistic factor, which remained the dominant consideration. Immigration control came to be thought of not so much as a matter of preserving American culture and the American character from foreign influences as a safeguard for the very existence of the nation. Nationalism in the sense of loyalty and patriotism became the vital consideration in formulating policy. This change was a direct result of the threat to national security posed by the rise of totalitarian governments in Europe and marked a trend which would continue in the postwar period when the question of national survival remained uppermost in American minds.

Important as these changes were, the most significant transformation was the encroachment of the executive branch of the government on Congressional control of immigration policy. Until 1930 Congress had enjoyed a monopoly on the formulation of immigration policy. On several occasions the legislative branch had been able to force through its programs in the face of administration opposition, notably in the case of Japanese exclusion and national origins. But in the 1930's the roles were reversed. The three basic immigration problems of this period were handled by the executive branch. The public charge policy, the help extended to refugees, and the measures taken to prevent the admission of subversives were all administration programs formulated and executed without the consent of Congress. Begun reluctantly by Hoover, this trend toward executive dominance in immigration matters became fully developed under Roosevelt's energetic leadership. By the end of the decade the president, not Congress, controlled the formulation of immigration policy.

This shift in leadership was of great consequence, for it meant a weakening in the power of the restrictionists. Traditionally, the president, acting on the basis of national interests rather than sectional prejudices, had taken a more liberal position on immigration questions than had Congress. The great strength of the restrictionists had always resided in the legislative branch, where provincial dislike of foreigners, particularly on the part of southern and western congressmen, had been an influential factor. Perhaps the most noticeable result of the trend toward executive control over immigration policy was the tendency to view immigration problems as international rather than purely domestic issues. While Congress formulated legislation almost entirely from the standpoint of its effect on the American economy, ethnic character, and social patterns, the administration took into account the possible consequences on relations with foreign countries. Thus the growing dominance of the executive branch in immigration matters resulted in a much greater stress on the foreign relations factor in the determination of policy.

By and large, the decade of the 1930's marks an ebbing of the restrictionist tide. The advocates of restriction had ridden the crest of a nationalistic wave in the previous decade, and it had carried them far along toward their ultimate goal of complete exclusion. Though it had seemed as if the depression might enable them to complete their program, the emergence of executive leadership in immigration policy and the development of the refugee problem prevented this culmination. Whether such a recession was a permanent ebb in the restrictionist surge or merely a brief interval before the final onslaught was a question to be decided in the postwar period.

6. Displaced Persons Legislation: Enactment

THE SECOND WORLD WAR, posing in the most direct form the question of national survival, relegated considerations of American immigration policy to a very secondary place in national affairs. With one important exception there was no governmental action on immigration problems during the war.[1] But with the coming of peace, interest in immigration policy rapidly developed, spurred on by new and pressing problems stemming from the war. Much of this interest centered on a re-evaluation of immigration policy in the postwar world. This trend, which culminated in the passage of the McCarran-Walter Act, will be discussed in later chapters. Of more immediate concern was the question of American policy in regard to displaced persons—the millions of Europeans uprooted by the war and its aftermath. For four years Congress wrestled with this difficult and tragic question until it reached a final decision in the spring of 1950. During that period, the history of American immigration policy is largely the story of the evolution of a displaced persons program.

The displaced persons problem was a direct outgrowth of the war. When the Allies surveyed the population of the liberated enemy territory in the summer of 1945, they found eight million people in Germany, Austria, and Italy who had been displaced from their homes in other parts of Europe.[2] The Nazi policy of importing vast numbers of forced laborers from conquered territory to fill the manpower needs of the German industrial system accounted for the great bulk of these uprooted peoples. The Germans had drawn upon all areas of Europe for involuntary workers, but the majority had come from central Europe, particularly Poland and the Baltic states.[3] A second source of displaced persons was the large number of people who had fled before the Russian advance across Poland and into Germany in 1944 and 1945. Some had retreated into Germany out of fear or hatred

1. The repeal of the Chinese Exclusion Act, discussed in Chapter 8.
2. "Displaced Persons in Europe," *Senate Report No. 950,* 80th Congress, 2d Session (Washington, 1948), p. 8.
3. Eugene Kulischer, *Europe on the Move* (New York, 1948), pp. 261–4. The high point was reached in 1944, when there were eight million foreign workers in Germany.

of Communism, others simply to escape the zone of combat between the opposing armies.[4] The Jewish victims of Nazi persecution who survived the mass exterminations in the concentration camps formed a third and much smaller category of displaced persons. In addition to these people who were in the occupied zones in 1945, there was a continuing stream of refugees which flowed into Germany and Austria from eastern Europe after the war's end. At first largely composed of Jews fleeing from anti-Semitic outbursts in Poland, the movement developed into an exodus by people of all faiths from the Communist nations of eastern and central Europe.[5]

The first attempt to cope with the problem came at the Yalta Conference, where the Allied governments agreed on procedures for the repatriation of displaced persons.[6] In the summer and fall of 1948 seven million people returned to their native countries under this agreement. However, the establishment of Communist regimes in the countries of eastern Europe prevented the easy consummation of the repatriation process. Approximately one million displaced natives of eastern Europe refused to go back to their countries of origin because they feared persecution by the newly instituted Communist governments. The Russians demanded their forcible repatriation, but the American, British, and French governments took a firm stand against involuntary return.[7] This decision in effect committed the three governments to the custodianship of the one million displaced persons in their zones of Germany, Austria, and Italy. Having made the commitment, the democratic nations were faced with the difficult problem of how to dispose of the refugees, and while they groped for a final answer, they supported the homeless in temporary camps, with 600,000 under American care.

The presence of more than four million *Volksdeutsche* or German expellees in Western Germany further complicated the problem.[8]

4. Ibid., pp. 264–73.
5. *Senate Report No. 950* (1948), pp. 11–12.
6. Ibid., p. 8.
7. Ibid., p. 8; "Permitting Admission of 400,000 Displaced Persons into the United States," *Hearings before the Subcommittee on Immigration and Naturalization of the House Committee on the Judiciary*, 80th Congress, 1st Session (Washington, 1947), pp. 335–7, 504.
8. The four million plus figure is for July 1, 1947 (Kulischer, p. 286 n.). By 1950, there were nearly eight million expellees in West Germany, in addition to a million and a half refugees from East Germany. Vernant, *The Refugee*, p. 96.

At the Potsdam conference the democratic nations agreed to a Russian proposal for the transfer of all people of German ethnic origin from Czechoslovakia, Poland, and Hungary to Germany. This entailed not only the movement of Germans living in territory ceded to Poland and Czechoslovakia at the end of the war, but also the transfer of people of German descent who had lived in eastern Europe for centuries. A total of about twelve million people was involved in this gigantic transfer, which resulted in a critical population surplus in Germany.[9] In view of this situation, the American, British, and French governments could not solve the displaced persons problem by disbanding the camps and forcing the displaced persons onto the already overburdened German economy.

By 1947 it had become apparent that the only feasible solution to the problem was to resettle the displaced persons outside of Germany. In order to carry out a resettlement program, the United Nations established the International Refugee Organization (IRO) supported by the United States, Canada, Australia, and the free countries of western Europe.[10] The IRO provided the vehicle for resettlement, but it could be successful only if each of the member nations agreed to accept a portion of the group for permanent residence. In the United States the issue centered on the extent to which this country was to participate in the program. Though the ultimate decision was for a generous allotment, it was reached only after lengthy controversy, which reflected the continuing strength of restrictionist sentiment in Congress.

In the welter of confusion that characterized the months that followed the close of the second World War, the problem of displaced persons went virtually unnoticed in the United States. Not until the end of 1945 did the American government take the first tentative steps toward formulating a policy.[11] On December 22, 1945, President Tru-

9. Vernant, pp. 92–8; Kulischer, pp. 282–6, 301–11.

10. Vernant, pp. 33–4.

11. During the war, there had been one small-scale attempt to aid displaced persons. In June 1944 President Roosevelt authorized the temporary admission of some 1,000 displaced persons liberated in the Italian campaign. This was done as a wartime gesture to hearten those uprooted by the war. Though the admission was designed to be only temporary, in early 1946 President Truman issued orders allowing these displaced persons to become permanent immigrants. New York *Times* (June 10, 1944), p. 1; "Study of Immigration Laws and Problems," *Hearings before the House Committee on Immigration and Naturalization*, 79th Congress, 1st

man opened the issue with a statement announcing a new program to govern the admission of displaced persons. Advising the American people that the United States could not ignore the sufferings of those uprooted by the war, the president outlined a plan to give displaced persons preferential treatment under the existing quotas. By reserving half the quotas of European countries for displaced persons, Truman hoped to admit 40,000 a year.[12] In announcing the new program, Truman carefully attempted to placate restrictionist sentiment in Congress by stressing the limits of his plan. "I wish to emphasize," he wrote, "that any effort to bring relief to these displaced persons and refugees must and will be strictly within the limits of the present quotas as imposed by law."[13] Thus the policy he formulated bore a marked resemblance to Roosevelt's prewar refugee policy—sympathy for the plight of distressed people, but practical help confined within the framework of the quota system.

Truman's cautious plan received a favorable reaction throughout the nation, but its inadequacy soon became apparent. In the first nine months of 1946 only 5,000 displaced persons entered the country under the quota system.[14] Dissatisfied with his first proposal, in October 1946 Truman told reporters he would ask the next Congress to admit displaced persons outside the regular quotas.[15] This disclosure quickly removed the apathy surrounding the displaced persons issue. As long as Truman stayed within the quota system, there was no vital issue at stake, but a proposal to depart from this basic immigration policy made inevitable a showdown battle between the friends and foes of restriction. Both sides began preparing for the struggle in Congress and a controversy was soon under way that would end only after four years of heated debate.

By the end of 1946 the division of opinion over Truman's proposal was evident. Groups favoring the admission of displaced persons organized a Citizens Committee on Displaced Persons composed of many prominent Americans and headed by Earl Harrison, a former

Session (Washington, 1945), p. 64; T. B. Shoemaker, "New Responsibilities of the Service," *Monthly Review of the Immigration and Naturalization Service, 3* (February 1946), 259.

12. *Interpreter Releases, 23* (February 28, 1946), 50.

13. Ibid., 54.

14. Ibid. (November 19, 1946), 285.

15. New York *Times* (October 5, 1946), p. 1.

commissioner of immigration. This specialized lobbying organization was to be the spearhead in the drive for displaced persons legislation, spending over one million dollars in support of its program.[16] In Congress forty-nine senators and representatives issued a statement pledging their support to a measure to open unused wartime quotas to displaced persons.[17] Meanwhile opposition to Truman's proposal quickly developed in restrictionist quarters. National Commander Paul Griffiths of the American Legion issued a statement warning that the entry of displaced persons would deprive veterans of both jobs and houses in the difficult period of postwar adjustment.[18] Strong opposition also developed in Congress. Following the Republican victory in the November elections, Senator Taft asked Senator Chapman Revercomb to submit a report on the displaced persons problem to the Republican steering committee. In his report Revercomb was very skeptical of the Truman plan to admit displaced persons, warning that it "would of course break down the quota system and completely do away with the present plan of allotments by countries and the policy of national origins." [19] While Revercomb did not flatly reject Truman's plan, the tone of the report reflected a hostile attitude toward a liberal displaced persons program.

The formal launching of the campaign to enact emergency displaced persons legislation came with President Truman's state of the union message to Congress in January 1947. After describing the meager results of his attempts to admit displaced persons within the quotas, Truman continued, "I urge the Congress to turn its attention to this world problem, in an effort to find ways whereby we can fulfill our responsibilities to these thousands of homeless and suffering refugees of all faiths." [20] Soon afterward Earl Harrison announced that the Citizens Committee on Displaced Persons would sponsor legislation for the admission of 400,000 refugees over a four-year period.[21] To achieve this goal, the Citizens Committee collected over $200,000,

16. *Interpreter Releases, 24* (January 21, 1947), 25. Among the sponsors were Eleanor Roosevelt, James Farley, William Green, Philip Murray, Herbert Lehman, and Charles Taft.

17. New York *Times* (November 21, 1946), p. 16.

18. Ibid. (November 1, 1946), p. 17.

19. *Congressional Record* (March 25, 1947), p. 2520.

20. Ibid. (January 6, 1947), p. 139.

21. New York *Times* (January 31, 1947), p. 15.

mainly from Jewish contributors, and by June was employing a staff of sixty-five to publicize its program.[22] On April 1, Congressman William Stratton of Illinois introduced the bill sponsored by the Citizens Committee in the House. The Stratton bill proposed the annual admission of 100,000 displaced persons as nonquota immigrants for four years. The bill was very simple in form, requiring only that the displaced persons meet the existing immigration standards and granting preference to close relatives of citizens and war veterans.[23]

The introduction of the Stratton bill placed the issue of displaced persons before Congress for the first time. In the early summer the House Committee on the Judiciary held hearings on the bill which aired the conflicting viewpoints on this controversial question.[24] A great majority of the witnesses—representing the administration, the three major religious groups, and organized labor—urged the enactment of the Stratton bill. The testimony of Secretary of State Marshall, Secretary of War Patterson, and Attorney-General Clark lent great weight to the displaced persons cause. The strong position taken by organized labor was equally significant. William Green, President of the AFL, reversed the traditional restrictionist stand of his organization by a forthright declaration favoring the admission of displaced persons beyond the quota limits. Green apparently believed that the emergency nature of the displaced persons problem justified a temporary departure from his regular quota policy. The defection of the labor unions left only the veterans' organizations and the patriotic societies to uphold the restrictionist viewpoint. Officers of both the American Legion and the American Coalition set forth their vigorous opposition to the displaced persons program, but they were greatly outnumbered by the sponsors of the plan.

The testimony at the hearings revealed that two basic issues were in dispute—the effect of the admission of displaced persons on Amer-

22. *Congressional Record* (October 15, 1949), pp. 14,647–54. This material comes from the lobbying reports of the Citizens Committee submitted to the Clerk of the House of Representatives and made public by Senator Langer of North Dakota during the later stages of the debate.

23. Ibid. (April 1, 1947), p. 2968; New York *Times* (April 2, 1947), p. 11; *Interpreter Releases*, 24 (April 8, 1947), 118.

24. "Permitting Admission of 400,000 Displaced Persons," House *Hearings* (1947). Under the Congressional Reorganization Act of 1946 the House and Senate immigration committees were eliminated and all immigration matters were assigned to the judiciary committees of the two branches.

ican society and the extent to which the United States was obligated
to help these stateless people. On the first point, the proponents of
the Stratton bill argued that the displaced persons were able, freedom-
loving people who would make good citizens. Representative Stratton
presented a strong case for them, asserting, "Most of them represent
a survival of the fittest, having escaped and endured what millions of
their kinsmen could not survive." Both William Green and officials
of the Department of Labor assured the committee that the nation
could easily absorb 400,000 additional immigrants without depriving
American citizens of jobs. The restrictionists, however, sharply dis-
sented from these views. The representative of the American Legion
declared that veterans "should not be forced into competition with
hundreds of thousands of the very people for whose liberation they
made such sacrifice." The opponents of the bill placed the greatest
emphasis on the security argument. Warning that Russia had planted
espionage agents among the displaced persons, one witness asserted
that in addition "there are bound to be numerous and important carriers
of the kind of ideological germs with which it is the aim to infect the
public opinion of the U.S.A." [25] Thus the committee was presented
with two wholly conflicting estimates of the potentialities of displaced
persons as future citizens of the nation.

On the second point, the obligation of the United States to the displaced persons, there was even greater divergence. The advocates of
the Stratton bill argued that the United States had a moral obligation
to accept its "fair share" of displaced persons. This view was based
on both humanitarian and international considerations. Several witnesses invoked the asylum ideal in pleading for humane treatment
of the problem, as Lehman did when he asserted, "The time is long
overdue for us to become mindful with renewed intensity of America's
proud tradition of asylum and hope and opportunity for the oppressed." Secretary of State Marshall put the issue in blunter terms.
"The tasks that are imposed by a declaration of war are not completed when the guns cease fire. This is one of the tasks which we have
not completed." Marshall emphasized the American decision to oppose the forcible repatriation of the displaced persons and warned,
"You cannot assert leadership and then not exercise it." Many other
witnesses took up this theme of the responsibilities of leadership in a

25. Ibid., pp. 2, 164, 167, 322, 383, 445-8, 459.

divided world. Admitting that the United States could not solve the
problem alone, they urged that this country set an example by taking
a generous portion of the displaced persons.[26]

The restrictionist witnesses flatly rejected the concept that the
United States owed any obligation to the displaced persons. Rather,
they argued, the displaced persons should remain in Europe to partake
in the reconstruction of that continent. John Williamson, speaking for
the Veterans of Foreign Wars, asserted that the displaced persons,
"delivered from bondage at the cost of the blood of American youth,
now seek to avoid their share in the responsibility for creating a new
freedom and civilization in Europe." The opponents of the Stratton
bill held that the only obligation was to protect the American people.
"Displaced veterans, displaced Americans have first claim upon America's conscience," declared the American Legion spokesman. John
Trevor, President of the American Coalition, was particularly concerned with the effect of this legislation on the over-all immigration
policy of the United States. Charging that the Stratton bill was "the
spearhead of a drive by the foreign blocs to ultimately abolish the
national-origins quota system," Trevor warned that to upset the
ethnic balance established in 1924 "would accentuate and gravely em-
bitter international racial dissension, and thereby constitute an ever-
growing menace to national unity." [27] Thus the restrictionists replied
to the world leadership argument by asserting that the admission of
displaced persons would weaken the nation internally and thereby
endanger America's leadership of the free world.

The chief result of the hearings was the revelation of the same polar-
ity on the displaced persons question that had characterized previous
immigration debates. The restrictionists viewed the problem from
the domestic standpoint, maintaining that the protection of American
society and the American economy should be the sole determinant of
policy. This was basically an isolationist outlook which ignored the
relationship between displaced persons and American foreign policy.
On the other hand, those advocating the admission of displaced
persons believed that the scope of the issue was fundamentally international. Tending to gloss over the impact on the nation of the admission of displaced persons, they based their argument on the necessity

26. Ibid., pp. 3, 19, 130, 137, 141, 160–1, 175, 190, 282, 384, 497, 504–6.
27. Ibid., pp. 93, 107, 314, 330.

for the United States to take the lead in solving a critical problem which, if left untouched, might destroy American prestige in Europe. These differing viewpoints, clearly defined at the hearings, lay at the heart of the bitter controversy that was to rage in Congress for three years.

Though the hearings had been held promptly and seemed to promise a swift decision, Congressional action was delayed throughout 1947. Despite a special message to Congress by Truman urging haste, the judiciary subcommittee failed to take any action on the Stratton bill. A speech by Representative Ed Gossett of Texas, a restrictionist member of the subcommittee, indicated some of the reasons for the delay. Entitling his remarks "A New Fifth Column or the Refugee Racket," Gossett bitterly denounced both the displaced persons and their sponsors in the United States. "The camps," he charged, "are filled with bums, criminals, black-marketeers, subversives, revolutionaries, and crackpots of all colors and hues." In the Senate the opposition to displaced persons was more subtle but just as real. When a group of eight Democratic and Republican senators introduced a modified version of the Stratton bill, Senator Revercomb countered with a motion to authorize a thorough Senate investigation of all immigration problems, including displaced persons, before discussion of any legislation. Those favoring admission of displaced persons assailed Revercomb's resolution as an inhumane delaying tactic, but after a sharp debate the Senate authorized the investigation and instructed Revercomb to report by January 10, 1948.[28] Thus the restrictionists, fearful of defeat on a showdown vote, succeeded in postponing displaced persons legislation until 1948.

When Congress reconvened in January the outlook for legislation was much brighter, for two events of the fall of 1947 had greatly improved the position of those advocating admission of displaced persons. In late October the American Legion reversed the stand it had taken at the hearings. After a favorable report by National Commander Paul Griffiths, who had toured the camps in Europe during the summer, the National Executive Committee announced that the Legion would support the admission of a limited number of displaced

28. *Congressional Record* (July 2, 1947), pp. 8173–6; (July 7, 1947), pp. 8329–30; (July 23, 1947), p. 9807; (July 26, 1947), pp. 10,350–2.

persons for humane reasons.[29] And the next month a special subcommittee of the House Foreign Affairs Committee which had investigated the problem of displaced persons in Europe for several weeks reported to Congress that after reviewing the whole problem, its conclusion was that resettlement was the only feasible solution, and it accordingly recommended that the United States exert its leadership by calling a conference of the free nations to decide on what share each country should take. Meanwhile, Congress should set the example for other nations by authorizing the admission of displaced persons on an emergency basis.[30]

On January 7 President Truman again urged the adoption of his program, asserting that "the admission of these persons will add to the strength and energy of this nation." [31] The following week the Federal Council of Churches of Christ in America adopted a strong resolution in support of the president. Charging that the delay in the last session of Congress "placed upon the conscience of this nation a great moral burden," the resolution urged Congress "to act favorably and quickly on the Stratton bill." Catholic groups also expressed approval of the administration's program and formed a new organization, the National Catholic Resettlement Council, to coordinate plans for the reception of Catholic displaced persons.[32] Finally, the Citizens Committee continued its activities, both by lobbying in Washington and by stimulating public opinion throughout the country. The Committee's expenditures reached a new high of nearly $300,000 for the first half of 1948.[33]

Faced with this steadily mounting pressure, the Senate Judiciary Committee finally reported out a displaced persons bill on March 2, 1948. The new measure was embodied in the report of the Revercomb subcommittee, which had investigated the displaced persons problem in Europe during the summer and fall of 1947. In the report the sub-

29. New York *Times* (November 1, 1947), p. 5. The Legion recommendation did not state any specific number of displaced persons to be admitted.

30. "Displaced Persons and the International Refugee Organization," *Report of a Special Subcommittee of the House Committee on Foreign Affairs,* 80th Congress, 1st Session (Washington, 1947), pp. 81–4.

31. New York *Times* (January 8, 1948), p. 4.

32. *Interpreter Releases,* 25 (February 9, 1948), 40–1; (January 14, 1948), 16.

33. *Congressional Record* (March 7, 1950), p. 2903. The exact sum was $286,466.

committee came to the conclusion that the displaced persons should be resettled and recommended the admission of a moderate number into the United States under a carefully regulated plan. In the course of this report, the subcommittee revealed considerable skepticism over certain of the claims made on behalf of the displaced persons. The subcommittee regarded the movement of Jews and other refugees from eastern Europe after 1945 as falling outside the scope of the main problem and implied that this exodus was a planned migration organized by Jewish agencies in the United States and in Europe. The report also expressed considerable doubt about the ideology of the displaced persons. Though stating that there were few active Communists in the camps, the subcommittee warned that there might be many "in a dormant state." The subcommittee, furthermore, was skeptical of the assertion that all displaced persons would be persecuted if they returned to their native lands. The report stated that this fear was probably well grounded for the people from the Baltic states and from that part of Poland east of the Curzon line, territory which had been annexed by Russia, but not for those from Poland proper and the Balkan countries.[34]

The bill submitted by the subcommittee reflected the doubts expressed in the report. Adopting the basic principle of admitting displaced persons, the proposed measure contained four restrictive features that were to become the center of controversy in the Senate. First, the bill limited the number to 100,000 over a two-year period, only one-fourth the total in the Stratton bill, on the grounds that a greater number would be harmful to the American economy. In the second place, the subcommittee limited the program to those people who were registered as displaced persons on December 22, 1945, the date of President Truman's directive. This early cut-off date excluded some 100,000 people, mainly Jews, who had entered the camps in 1946 and early 1947. The subcommittee justified this provision on the grounds that help should be extended only to those people who had been directly displaced by the war.[35] Fifty per cent priorities for people from the areas annexed by Russia—the Baltic states and east-

34. *Senate Report No. 950* (1948), pp. 15–16, 20–1, 50–2.

35. Ibid., pp. 54, 56. Under the Truman directive, the cut-off date originally had been December 22, 1945. However, in February 1948 the administration changed the date to April 21, 1947. *Interpreter Releases*, 25 (February 19, 1948), 52.

ern Poland—and for agriculturalists formed a third restrictive feature. The Baltic priority was advocated in the belief that these people would suffer most if repatriated, while the agricultural preference was designed to achieve an even distribution of displaced persons in the United States as well as to meet a shortage of farm labor. Finally, the subcommittee bill required that sponsors of individual displaced persons guarantee both employment and living quarters for the newcomers.[36]

The formulation and approval of a bill by the Senate subcommittee opened a new phase of the displaced persons issue. After nearly two years of delay, Congress now had the opportunity to enact legislation. More important, the new measure indicated a significant shift in the nature of the controversy. The reversal of the American Legion position, the favorable report of the House Foreign Affairs subcommittee, and the heavy pressure from religious and humanitarian organizations convinced the restrictionist groups that the nation favored the admission of displaced persons. As a result, they changed their tactics from outright delay to an attempt to circumscribe the legislation as far as possible. The early cut-off date, the Baltic and agricultural priorities, and the housing and job requirements were all restrictive features designed to limit admissions to a few select groups. With these limitations, the great majority of restrictionists, led by Senator Revercomb, advocated this legislation as the wisest solution to the problem. Caught by the sudden shift of the restrictionists, the original advocates of the displaced persons legislation were put in a difficult position. They were forced to accept the bill in general and concentrate their attack on its restrictive features. Under the leadership of Homer Ferguson of Michigan, a group of eastern and midwestern senators offered a series of amendments designed to liberalize the measure. Though a small group of southern senators objected to the bill in its entirety, the crucial debate concerned the liberal amendments. The question was not whether the Senate would pass a displaced persons bill but whether the bill would be a liberal or a restrictive measure.

In the course of the long and often confusing debate on the Senate floor, the controversy centered about two basic points—the extent of the displaced persons program and the method of selection. On the

36. *Senate Report No. 950* (1948), pp. 52, 55, 57.

first point the restrictionists argued that their bill represented a wise program because it reconciled American obligations to the displaced persons with the best interests of the American people. Senator Revercomb, along with Senator Wiley of Wisconsin, presented the case for .the committee bill. Both men vigorously defended the numerical limit of 100,000 and the restrictions concerning employment and housing. They constantly reminded the Senate that their first obligation was to the American people, warning that a large influx of displaced persons would intensify the housing and employment problems faced by returning servicemen. Senator Wiley summed up the nationalistic viewpoint when he asserted, "We should not, in our zeal to fulfill our humanitarian responsibilities, forget our responsibilities to our own land and to our own people." In sharp contrast, the senators favoring a liberal displaced persons measure stressed the humanitarian and international aspects of the problem. Dismissing the housing and job requirements as the result of "a shallow emotionalism" and an unreasoning dislike of foreigners, Senators McGrath and Ferguson warned that unless several hundred thousand displaced persons were accepted, the future peace of Europe would be endangered. The United States must lead the way, they contended, by taking its fair share of people, which they calculated at a minimum of 200,000. If this were done, "one of the greatest humanitarian efforts in American history [would] be consummated in the spirit of the great American tradition." [37] Nationalism versus internationalism, self-interest versus humanitarianism: this was the crux of the debate.

The disagreement over the method of selection was even greater. The basic points of controversy were the Baltic priority and the cut-off date of December 22, 1945. The advocates of the bill defended these provisions on the grounds that certain displaced persons had suffered much greater hardships than others and therefore were more deserving of American help. Supporting the early terminal date, Senator Revercomb pointed out that the truly displaced people were those whom the Nazis brought into Germany during the war. Minimizing the Polish pogroms in 1946 which caused many Jews to flee to the west, Revercomb contended that a majority of the recent refugees had migrated for economic reasons and not out of a fear of persecution: "the real,

37. *Congressional Record* (May 25, 1948), pp. 6402–4; (May 26, 1948), pp. 6446–7, 6454–5; (May 27, 1948), pp. 6568–9, 6576.

basic reason why we should stick to an earlier date is that we will give the preference to the really displaced persons," he asserted. Revercomb presented much the same argument for the Baltic priority, with strong backing from Senators Taft and Knowland. Stating that many displaced persons could return to the satellite countries without genuine danger of persecution, Revercomb declared that the Baltic people and the eastern Poles faced certain punishment if they went back to their homes in Russian territory. Well aware that these provisions tended to exclude Jewish refugees, Revercomb vehemently denied any intent to slight any racial or religious group: "there is no distinction, certainly no discrimination, intended between any persons because of their religion or their race, but there are differences drawn among those persons who are in fact displaced persons and have been in camp longest and have a preference." [38]

The opposing senators warmly contested the restrictionist contention that there were valid distinctions between different categories of displaced persons. In particular the supporters of a liberal program advocated a later terminal date, April 21, 1947, and a provision to provide for a cross-section method of selection. Senator Smith of New Jersey condemned an early time limit, asserting that the problem "involves those who were displaced because of conditions resulting from the war just as much as those who were displaced forcibly during the conduct of the war." The general argument was that a humanitarian measure of this type should be governed by a spirit of tolerance which avoided any favoritism toward specific groups. The advocates of a liberal bill were particularly concerned over the effect of the restrictive provisions upon Jewish displaced persons, who formed about 20 per cent of the total and yet were largely outside the preferred categories. While refraining from charges of intentional bias, several senators pointed out that the bill would in effect discriminate against Jews, particularly those postwar refugees from eastern Europe who were victims of anti-Semitic campaigns begun by Hitler. Senator Pepper of Florida stated this charge in the bluntest terms when he exclaimed, "Mr. President, I say that if not by design at least by effect the bill discriminates against the Jews." [39]

38. Ibid. (May 26, 1948), p. 6793; (June 1, 1948), pp. 6805–8; (June 2, 1948), pp. 6864, 6866.
39. Ibid. (May 25, 1948), p. 6403; (May 26, 1948), p. 6458; (May 27, 1948), pp. 6579, 6585–6; (June 2, 1948), pp. 6859–63, 6914.

After six days of debate, the restrictionists achieved very nearly a complete triumph. Except on their first amendment, dealing with numerical limits, the senators attempting to liberalize the committee bill met with frustration. On May 27 the Senate voted 40 to 33 to double the number of displaced persons to be admitted, thus authorizing a total of 200,000 for a two-year period. On the next amendment, to eliminate the Baltic priority, twelve Republican senators who had voted for the numerical increase shifted to the restrictionist side. This change, led by Senator Wherry of Nebraska, the majority leader, swung the balance to the supporters of the committee bill, and as a result all the remaining liberalizing amendments were defeated.[40] The Senate did adopt one further amendment, proposed by Senator Langer of North Dakota, which opened 50 per cent of the German and Austrian quotas to the *Volksdeutsche* born in the small-quota countries.[41]

The final vote on the bill came on June 2. The two opposing sides in the debate joined together to pass the measure by a margin of 63 to 13. Twelve of the negative votes were cast by southern senators who, except for Senator Eastland of Mississippi, had kept silent during the debate, evidently hoping that the opposing sides would be unable to reach final agreement on the bill. Before the final tabulation the advocates of a liberal displaced persons program made it clear that they would vote for the committee bill with great reluctance. They expressed hope that the House would pass a more liberal bill which would lead to a modification of the Senate measure in the conference committee.[42] Thus the first debate on displaced persons legislation came to an equivocal ending with the passage of a bill which failed to satisfy those who had first called for action on this issue.

The controversy over displaced persons now shifted to the House. In May the House Judiciary Committee reported out a bill framed by its subcommittee on immigration. The Fellows bill, named for the

40. Ibid. (May 27, 1948), p. 6576; (June 1, 1948), pp. 6810–11. Of these twelve, six were from the Midwest, four from the Far West, and two from the East.

41. Ibid. (June 2, 1948), p. 6894. The committee bill accepted the IRO definition of displaced persons, which specifically excluded persons of German ethnic origin. This amendment, though added to a displaced persons bill, actually dealt with a regular immigration problem under the quota system.

42. Ibid. (June 2, 1948), pp. 6900, 6913, 6916.

chairman of the subcommittee, Representative Frank Fellows of Maine, represented a compromise between the original Stratton bill and the restrictive Senate measure. Setting the number of displaced persons to be admitted at 200,000 the Fellows bill contained no special priorities but instead provided for the selection of displaced persons in proportion to the composition of the total number in Europe. Furthermore, this measure set a terminal date of April 21, 1947. To balance these concessions to the supporters of a liberal displaced persons program, the authors of the bill added one highly significant limitation, the mortgaging of quotas. Rather than permitting the displaced persons to enter as nonquota immigrants, the House measure allowed them to enter immediately but charged them to future quotas of their country of origin, limiting the mortgage to 50 per cent of the quota for any one year.[43] This new feature strongly appealed to the restrictionist members of the House, for it meant that displaced persons could be admitted in reasonable numbers without violating the principle of the quota system.

In contrast to the debate in the Senate, House discussion of the Fellows bill centered on the basic question of admitting displaced persons. A great majority of the representatives rallied around the bill as a reasonable compromise of a controversial issue. The antirestrictionist sponsors of the Stratton bill supported the House measure because they felt it was superior to the Senate version, while many lifelong restrictionists were attracted by the quota-mortgaging feature. Only the most extreme restrictionists, mainly from the South, voiced opposition. Consequently the debate was brief, with the result a foregone conclusion.

The arguments advanced in the discussion of the Fellows bill revealed the compromise nature of the measure. The moderate restrictionists confined their remarks largely to the mortgaging feature. Representative Fellows pointed out that the great merit of the bill was its preservation of the national origins quota system, while several other speakers bluntly stated that they would only support the measure on this basis. On the other hand, the opponents of restriction kept silent on the quota-mortgaging provision and focused their remarks on the

43. "Emergency Displaced Persons Admission Act," *House Report No. 1854*, 80th Congress, 2d Session (Washington, 1948), pp. 2, 20.

liberal features of the legislation. Describing the Senate measure as "a travesty of justice," they advocated passage of the Fellows bill as the best legislation obtainable. The southern spokesmen, however, bereft of support from many of their restrictionist colleagues, resorted to invective in attacking the bill. Representative Gossett of Texas assailed the displaced persons as "human refuse" and warned that their admission would only serve "to inject more poison into the national bloodstream." [44] Other opposing speakers were more temperate in their remarks, but the tenor of their statements indicated that they objected not just to the Fellows bill but to all immigrants and aliens.

The debate ended on June 11 with the passage of the bill by an overwhelming margin. The final tally was 289 to 91, with nearly two-thirds of the negative votes coming from southern representatives.[45] A crippling amendment which would have postponed the operation of the bill until other nations had contracted to accept their share of displaced persons was defeated by a close vote, 88 to 82. The House approved two other amendments. One authorized the entry of 2,000 recent Czech refugees fleeing from Communism, while the second provided for the admission of 3,000 displaced orphans.[46] Thus the Fellows bill, changed only by the inclusion of 5,000 additional people, went to the conference committee for an attempt to frame a measure satisfactory to both houses.

A few days later this committee reported a final bill which represented a complete victory for the restrictionist viewpoint. The measure was essentially the Senate bill, with the only restrictive feature of the House version, the mortgaging of quotas, grafted on. The early cut-off date of December 22, 1945, the housing and employment requirements, and the special priorities were retained, though the Baltic priority was re-

44. *Congressional Record* (June 10, 1948), pp. 7731, 7733, 7737, 7740, 7742–5, 7747, 7759, 7774.

45. Ibid. (June 11, 1948), p. 7887. The sectional breakdown on this vote was as follows:

Section	Yes	No
Northeast	106	4
Midwest	88	28
South	51	57
Far West	44	2

46. Ibid. (June 10, 1948), pp. 7763–5; (June 11, 1948), pp. 7868–9, 7883.

duced to 40 per cent and the agricultural preference to 30 per cent.[47] Four of the twelve conferees, two senators and two representatives, refused to sign the report, while three other representatives signed with great reluctance. Representative Chelf of Kentucky explained to the House the reasons for the surrender to the Senate restrictionists. "However, we had a gun barrel at our heads. That gun barrel was the element of time. . . . I repeat, it was either this compromise or nothing." [48]

The submission of the conference report in the two bodies touched off brief but stormy debates in which the more extreme advocates of a liberal program charged the Senate restrictionists with deliberate intent to discriminate against Jewish displaced persons. In the House, Jewish representatives led the assault, with Emanuel Celler stating that the early cut-off date "would deliberately discriminate against the Jews." Senators Pepper of Florida and McGrath of Rhode Island reiterated these charges in the upper chamber, the latter exclaiming, "Mr. President, the date of December 22, 1945, was deliberately written into this bill because that date prohibited Jews from taking part in this program." Senator Revercomb replied to these charges by stating that there was neither intentional nor accidental discrimination in the bill. Several Republican senators who had supported a liberal displaced persons program defended Revercomb. While deploring the early cut-off date and the Baltic priority as tending to exclude Jews, they vigorously denied that the framers of the bill had deliberately discriminated against any minority groups.[49]

The imminent adjournment of Congress presented the opponents of the bill with a difficult decision. If they succeeded in defeating the conference report, all hopes for displaced persons legislation in 1948 would be lost. The opposing senators finally decided to accept the conference report in order to extend some measure of relief to displaced persons. However, they stated that they would press for amendment of the law in the next session. In the House the extreme anti-restrictionists refused to concede without a struggle. Representative

47. "Authorizing for a Limited Period of Time the Admission into the United States of Certain European Displaced Persons for Permanent Residence," *House Report No. 2410*, 80th Congress, 2d Session (Washington, 1948), pp. 1–6.

48. *Congressional Record* (June 18, 1948), p. 8859.

49. Ibid. (June 18, 1948), p. 8861; (June 19, 1948), pp. 9004–6, 9012–15.

Celler moved to send the bill back to the conference committee. Though the two extremist factions supported this motion, the House voted 266 to 113 to defeat it and then accepted the conference report by a voice vote.[50] The Celler motion marks the only occasion in the history of modern immigration legislation on which representatives from the metropolitan districts of the North voted in harmony with southern restrictionists. This situation indicates that the final bill was a conservative compromise which embodied the views of a moderately restrictionist majority in Congress.

The passage of a displaced persons bill so far removed from his original proposals placed President Truman in a dilemma. On June 25 he signed the bill "with very great reluctance" and at the same time issued a statement condemning the restrictive features of the measure. "In its present form," Truman stated, "this bill is flagrantly discriminatory." Though he criticized all the limiting provisions in the bill, the president concentrated on the early cut-off date as the main source of discrimination. Truman asserted that the 1945 terminal date "discriminates in callous fashion against displaced persons of the Jewish faith," and he also contended that this provision excluded many Catholics. The only reason he could surmise for the choice of this date was "upon the abhorrent ground of intolerance." The president concluded his statement by calling for speedy amendment of the measure. "I have signed this bill, in spite of its many defects, in order not to delay further the beginning of a resettlement program and in the expectation that the necessary remedial action will follow when the Congress reconvenes."[51]

The passage of the displaced persons legislation again revealed the interplay between the four factors influencing immigration policy. Considerations of foreign policy weighed very heavily in the formulation of the program, but foreign policy alone would have called for a much broader and more effective solution to the displaced persons problem. Most congressmen showed a recognition of the need of the United States to carry out its responsibilities toward those uprooted by the war. But this acceptance was tempered by the presence of other

50. Ibid. (June 18, 1948), p. 8863; (June 19, 1948), pp. 9005, 9011, 9014, 9020.

51. *Interpreter Releases,* 25 (July 21, 1948), 252–4.

factors, particularly the strong postwar feeling of nationalism. There was genuine concern over the economic and social effects of the admission of displaced persons, but strongest of all was the fear of contagion from people who had been through the horrors of war. Some feared the displaced persons would be carriers of Communism, while others warned that the shattering experiences of life in forced labor and concentration camps would render these people unfit for a normal life of freedom. This strong concern over the impact of the displaced persons on the nation caused the insertion of limitations in the legislation to protect the American people. By limiting the number and selecting those who could adjust to American patterns most easily, the majority in Congress felt that they could fulfill an international commitment without sacrificing the national interest.

The final law thus represented a compromise between national and international considerations, but a compromise in the direction of a more liberal policy. The law contained serious limitations, and its tendency to exclude Jewish displaced persons, and to a much lesser extent Catholics, left it open to charges of discrimination. As a result, the issue was to remain alive for two more years as the advocates of a generous program strove to remove these restrictions. Yet despite its flaws, the displaced persons legislation was a significant departure from previous immigration policy. For the first time Congress had recognized the plight of distressed people in Europe and had enacted a program designed to extend them special immigration privileges. There would be a continual struggle over the extent and nature of these privileges, but the fundamental principle of admitting displaced persons had been firmly established. A comparison with the Congressional refusal to aid refugees in the late 1930's indicates the degree to which Congress had moved away from absolute restriction. Spurred on by the new position of leadership the United States had assumed in world affairs, Congress had embarked on a cautious policy of aiding the distressed of Europe.

7. Displaced Persons Legislation: Amendment

THE ENACTMENT of the 1948 law marked the halfway point in the controversy over displaced persons. The supporters of a liberal program had gained acceptance of the principle of admitting displaced persons on a special basis, and they now pressed for revision of the law to remove its restrictive features. This movement for liberalization, led by President Truman and the Citizens Committee on Displaced Persons, touched off a renewed controversy as the restrictionists fought bitterly to retain the limited program they had enacted. In the debate that ensued the arguments revolved around the charges of bias and prejudice leveled by the critics of the law. Those favoring amendment claimed that the law discriminated against Jews and Catholics, while the restrictionists maintained that the only bias in the legislation was the exclusion of the *Volksdeutsche* as displaced persons. In developing their charges and countercharges, both sides were guilty of extreme overstatement, and the debate often deteriorated into a morass of name calling. As a result, effective action was continually delayed, and not until 1950 did the supporters of a liberal program finally achieve their objective.

The drive to amend the displaced persons legislation began in June 1948 and immediately became tangled in the political maneuvering leading up to the presidential election. The Republican party defended the law as part of the record of the Eightieth Congress, with the platform adopted at the nominating convention citing "a haven for displaced persons" as an outstanding Republican accomplishment.[1] However, the candidate, Governor Dewey of New York, took a more equivocal position. Though he refrained from charges of discrimination, he announced soon after his nomination that he hoped the displaced persons program could be made "more flexible and less restricted."[2] In contrast, the Democratic platform vigorously denounced the act and pledged the admission of 400,000 displaced persons without discrimination. "We condemn the undemocratic action of the Republican

1. *Interpreter Releases*, 25 (August 18, 1948), 280.
2. New York *Times* (July 14, 1948), p. 1.

Eightieth Congress," asserted the Democrats, "in passing an inadequate and bigoted bill for this purpose, which law imposes un-American restrictions based on race and religion upon such admissions." [3]
Truman supported this stand in his acceptance speech, in which he
referred to the Displaced Persons Act as an "anti-Semitic, anti-Catholic
law." [4]

Meanwhile, the charges of discrimination were being debated outside the political arena. On June 27 the Citizens Committee, speaking
for nearly 200 religious, welfare, and civic organizations, condemned
the displaced persons law, asserting that it smacked of "hate and
racism." [5] Spokesmen for Jewish groups unanimously criticized the
legislation as discriminatory toward people of their faith. Representatives of nine national Jewish organizations sent copies of a joint letter
to President Truman, Governor Dewey, and the chairmen of the
Democratic and Republican national committees in late July, in which
they set forth their objections to the law and suggested eleven basic
amendments.[6] The reaction in Catholic quarters was quite different.
Though Catholic leaders expressed a desire for a more liberal displaced persons program, they denied that the recent law discriminated
against Catholics. Monseigneur Swanson, chairman of the National
Catholic Resettlement Council, issued a public statement on July 14
in which he declared, "No leading Catholic authority or any official
representative of the council ever has spoken of the eightieth Congress
legislation being anti-Catholic." [7] The Catholic magazine *America* reflected the same viewpoint in an editorial calling for liberalization of
the program. "Nevertheless, the existing legislation, though containing
some discriminatory features, is not to be considered basically 'anti-
Catholic,' as some of its critics would have us think. Prominent Catholic leaders have rightly rejected the charges." [8]

Interest in the displaced persons issue began to die down after
the political conventions recessed. During a special summer session
of Congress the president asked for swift revision of the 1948 legisla-

3. *Interpreter Releases*, 25 (August 18, 1948), 280.
4. New York *Times* (July 15, 1948), p. 4.
5. Ibid. (June 28, 1948), p. 5.
6. Ibid. (June 25, 1948), p. 7.
7. Ibid. (July 15, 1948), p. 20.
8. "Congress and the D.P.'s," *America*, 79 (August 14, 1948), 420.

tion, only to meet with complete apathy on the part of Congress.[9] When the presidential campaign began in the fall, the displaced persons question failed to develop as a major issue between the parties. Governor Dewey remained silent on the issue throughout the fall campaign, though he pointedly refused to support Senator Revercomb's bid for re-election in West Virginia, while President Truman referred to the issue only briefly in the course of two minor speeches.[10] The campaign ended on November 2 with Truman's unexpected victory, together with the defeat of Senator Revercomb and a Democratic triumph in Congress. It is very doubtful whether the displaced persons question had any bearing on Truman's re-election, but the New York *Times* attributed Revercomb's defeat to his stand on this issue.[11] In any case, Democratic control of Congress appeared to ensure speedy liberalization of the displaced persons program.

When the new Congress convened in January 1949 the chances for prompt amendment of the Displaced Persons Act seemed very good. Truman emphasized the need for revision in his annual message, and there appeared to be little doubt that the Democrats in control of Congress would carry out their campaign pledge.[12] The first report of the Displaced Persons Commission, submitted to Congress on February 1, further heightened the optimism of those advocating a liberal program. This three-member commission, established to supervise the administration of the act, strongly recommended the removal of the restrictive features from the legislation. Pointing out that the objective of the Displaced Persons Act was to resettle 200,000 people in the United States, the commissioners stated that the restrictive provisions had proved so unworkable from the administrative standpoint that it was very doubtful whether this goal could be achieved.[13] Encouraged by this strong criticism of the existing legislation, Representative Emanuel Celler of New York introduced a bill to admit 400,000 displaced persons virtually without restriction. This new proposal, omit-

9. *Congressional Record* (July 28, 1948), p. 9451; New York *Times* (August 7, 1948), p. 3.

10. New York *Times* (October 26, 1948), pp. 18, 24; (October 27, 1948), p. 20.

11. Ibid. (November 3, 1948), p. 8.

12. *Interpreter Releases, 26* (January 28, 1949), 38.

13. Displaced Persons Commission, *First Semi-Annual Report to the President and to the Congress* (Washington, 1949), pp. 20–1, 55–6.

ting both the Senate limitations and the quota-mortgaging feature, was almost identical with the original Stratton bill.[14]

The administration forces moved quickly in an attempt to pass the Celler bill before the restrictionists could organize opposition. A House Judiciary subcommittee held brief hearings in January at which only congressmen and officials of the Displaced Persons Commission were invited to testify. Representative Celler and Ugo Carusi, chairman of the Commission, were the principal witnesses, and both strongly urged favorable action on the proposed bill. Though no private organizations appeared at the hearings, eighty-two groups submitted written statements containing their views on the Celler measure. With the exception of three statements from patriotic societies, all the groups submitting their views favored liberalization of the act. The most significant written statement came not from an organization but from an individual, Senator Alexander Wiley, former chairman of the Senate Judiciary Committee. Wiley, originally one of the strongest backers of the restrictive Senate bill, now reversed his position. Describing the existing law as "a compromise stop-gap mechanism designed to fill an immediate humanitarian need," Wiley admitted that it had inadvertently caused injustice for some groups, and therefore he urged a liberal revision. "If we revise this law speedily and equitably," he declared, "it will be a real inspiration to all free people. It will be a weapon in our ideological war against the forces of darkness, the forces of Communist tyranny." [15]

Wiley's surprising change in viewpoint, coupled with the overwhelming support from religious and humanitarian groups, ensured a favorable report on the Celler bill. In May the House Judiciary subcommittee approved a modified version of Celler's measure which was very similar to the Fellows bill. The committee compromised on the number, setting a limit of 339,000—300,000 displaced persons plus 39,000 more in special categories. Though the Baltic and agricultural priorities were eliminated, the modified bill retained the quota-mortgaging feature. "The committee," stated the report, "while trying to work out a solution to the displaced-persons problem, was unwilling

14. *Interpreter Releases, 26* (January 28, 1949), 40.

15. "To Amend the Displaced Persons Act of 1948," *Hearings before Subcommittee No. 1 of the House Committee on the Judiciary*, 81st Congress, 1st Session (Washington, 1949), pp. 4–19, 24–5, 30–64, 149–239.

to submit to the House any legislation which would break or circumvent this time-tested basis of our immigration system." To compensate for this restrictive provision, the committee extended the cut-off date to January 1, 1949, to include in the program the ever-increasing stream of refugees behind the Iron Curtain. Three southern members of the committee, headed by Representative Gossett, submitted a minority report in which they condemned the displaced persons. Claiming that the United States had already done more than its fair share to help Europeans, they stated, "To say that we are further bound to open our country to this great additional number of DP's is to insult our patriotism, our intelligence, and our Christianity." [16]

The debate in the House was brief, revealing the same alignment as developed during consideration of the Fellows bill. A coalition of liberals and moderate restrictionists supported the bill, though disagreeing on whether the existing law was discriminatory. Both found common ground on the proposition that the amendment was necessary if the United States was to do its fair share in solving the total problem. Reiterating the "moral obligation" argument, several speakers pointed out that the acceptance of 300,000 displaced persons, coupled with the resettlement activities of other nations, would solve the problem permanently. Representative Celler promised that if the bill were passed, the issue would never again be raised in Congress. The opposition proved to be much weaker than the year before, with only two southerners, Gossett of Texas and Bryson of South Carolina, rising to criticize the bill. Gossett concisely summed up the position of these extreme restrictionists. "That we have a moral responsibility for the DP's is a joke. Our moral responsibility is to retain the strength and security of this country." [17]

The overwhelming support for the Celler bill brought the debate to a swift conclusion. Three hours after the bill was introduced on the floor, the House passed it by a voice vote. Both extremes offered amendments to alter the number of displaced persons, but the moderate restrictionists defeated these proposals.[18] Once again it was this

16. "Amending the Displaced Persons Act of 1948," *House Report No. 581*, 81st Congress, 1st Session (Washington, 1949), pp. 1, 15–18, 20, 49.

17. *Congressional Record* (June 2, 1949), pp. 7169–71, 7173, 7181, 7184, 7186, 7195.

18. Ibid. (June 2, 1949), pp. 7194–9, 7202.

center group which determined the final outcome. The moderate restrictionists acknowledged an American obligation toward displaced persons, but they insisted that the fulfillment of this commitment be harmonized with traditional immigration policy. They approved of an emergency program that operated within the basic framework of the quota system, and it is highly probable that they would have rejected any legislation that failed to include a mortgaging provision. The bill they passed was essentially a liberal compromise.

The prompt action in the House was not to be repeated in the Senate. The primary cause of delay in the upper chamber was the opposition of Senator Pat McCarran, who had replaced Wiley as chairman of the Senate Judiciary Committee. In this influential post McCarran played a dominating role in the determination of immigration policy. Born in Reno, Nevada, in 1876 of Irish parents, McCarran studied at the University of Nevada, and though never attaining a law degree became an eminent jurist. He served on the Supreme Court of Nevada during the first World War, and in 1922 was vice-president of the American Bar Association. Elected to the Senate in 1933, McCarran was primarily interested in aviation legislation until 1943, when he first became chairman of the Judiciary Committee.[19] During the 1948 discussion of displaced persons legislation McCarran had been ill, but he had helped Revercomb frame the Senate bill.[20] An ardent nationalist, McCarran viewed immigrants primarily as a source of danger to American society and believed that immigration policy should be formulated solely in reference to domestic considerations. Impressive in appearance, his head framed by a mane of flowing white hair, McCarran was an experienced and forceful debater who rarely compromised on matters of principle.

Throughout the winter and spring of 1949, McCarran blocked all action on displaced persons legislation in the Senate by holding a series of lengthy hearings on the Celler bill. In contrast to the swift action by the House Committee, the Senate hearings dragged on throughout the summer. The majority of the witnesses, representing

19. *Congressional Directory*, 83d Congress, 2d Session (Washington, 1954), p. 78.
20. *Congressional Record* (June 23, 1949), p. 8186.

patriotic societies and veterans' organizations, opposed any revision of the Displaced Persons Act. The strongest opposition came from the American Legion, whose representative stated that the Celler bill would "totally destroy our immigration laws and immigration policies." [21] As these hearings continued, McCarran found himself under attack on the Senate floor from antirestrictionists who charged him with deliberate procrastination on the displaced persons question. McCarran replied with a blistering assault on the displaced persons and their sponsors which revealed his extreme views on this issue. Warning that a revision of the law would flood the nation with undesirable people, McCarran assailed the Citizens Committee on Displaced Persons. He pointed out that this organization had spent over $800,-000 in lobbying for a liberal DP program and charged that as a result, "there has been disseminated over the length and breadth of this nation a campaign of misrepresentation and falsehood which has misled many public-spirited and well-meaning citizens and organizations." [22]

McCarran's refusal to act thoroughly irritated the supporters of a liberal program in the Senate. After the House passed the Celler bill in June, they tried every possible parliamentary maneuver in an effort to bypass the committee bottleneck, but without success. Then on September 12, Senator McCarran suddenly announced that he was traveling to Europe to conduct a personal investigation of the displaced persons camps.[23] The administration forces, led by Senator Lucas of Illinois, quickly applied pressure to the Judiciary Committee, and on October 12, with McCarran still in Europe, the committee voted 7-3 to report the Celler bill without recommendation.[24] However, the restrictionists, led by Senator Eastland of Mississippi, assailed the Senate leadership for considering displaced persons legislation in McCarran's absence and were able to win the support of many conservative senators. In a showdown ballot on October 15, the Senate

21. "Displaced Persons," *Hearings before the Subcommittee on Amendments to the Displaced Persons Act of the Senate Committee on the Judiciary,* 81st Congress, 1st and 2d Sessions (Washington, 1950), p. 460.

22. *Congressional Record* (April 26, 1949), pp. 5042–3.

23. Ibid. (September 12, 1949), p. 12,769.

24. New York *Times* (October 13, 1949), p. 1; "Amending the Displaced Persons Act of 1948," *Senate Report No. 1163,* 81st Congress, 1st Session (Washington, 1949), p. 1.

voted 36 to 30 to send the Celler bill back to the Judiciary Commit-tee.[25] The recommittal of the measure ended any chance of amending the Displaced Persons Act in 1949. McCarran, by following a policy of delay and evasion, had succeeded in blocking liberalization until the next session of Congress.

The controversy entered its final phase in the winter of 1950. Presi-dent Truman again urged revision of the 1948 legislation in his annual message to Congress, while the Citizens Committee renewed its efforts in favor of a liberal program, running its total expenditures to over one million dollars.[26] When Congress reconvened, the divergence in viewpoint over displaced persons was heightened by the submission of two conflicting reports. On January 20 a special House Judiciary subcommittee issued a favorable report on the effect of displaced per-sons on American society. Reviewing cases of people admitted under the 1948 legislation the subcommittee concluded, "No dangerous or disturbing elements have been injected into our body politic." [27] Meanwhile, Senator McCarran had completed his survey of displaced persons in Europe and gave a totally different description of displaced persons in his oral report to the Senate. This statement, printed up later as a pamphlet entitled *Displaced Persons: Fact versus Fiction,* was in effect a summary of all previous complaints against displaced persons. After listing his objections point by point, McCarran declared, "These facts point to the inescapable conclusion that the floodgates of the nation are being pried open for the entrance of millions of aliens, from the turbulent populations of the entire world, who are seeking admission into the United States under the guise of displaced persons." The result, McCarran concluded, could only be the destruc-

25. *Congressional Record* (October 13, 1949), pp. 14,394–428; (October 14, 1949), pp. 14,490–544; (October 15, 1949), pp. 14,636–75, 14,701. Senators from the Far West cast the decisive votes, supporting the motion by a margin of 11 to 4. In view of their later votes in favor of a liberal program, it is highly probable that the western senators voted for the motion more out of respect for Senator McCar-ran, who was chairman of the Conference of Western Senators, than in opposition to the Celler bill.

26. *Interpreter Releases,* 27 (January 10, 1950), 25; *Congressional Record* (June 7, 1950), p. 8213.

27. "Displaced Persons in Europe and Their Resettlement in the United States," *House Report No. 1507,* 81st Congress, 2d Session (Washington, 1950), pp. 128–9.

tion of all immigration barriers and the inundation of the country by a flood of aliens.[28]

Though McCarran's views had only been strengthened by his European trip, the senator decided that he could no longer continue postponing action on the Celler bill. Instead he altered his policy in an attempt to emasculate the House measure. With McCarran's approval, the Senate Judiciary Committee approved a heavily amended version of the Celler bill which retained many of the restrictive features of the existing act. Though the late cut-off date of January 1, 1949, was retained, the committee amendments re-established the Baltic and agricultural priorities. The most controversial amendment was a new provision which redefined displaced persons to include the *Volksdeutsche*. Previously, Congress had accepted the IRO definition, which specifically excluded all persons of German ethnic origin, and had dealt with the *Volksdeutsche* separately by giving them a preference under the German and Austrian quotas. The committee justified its amendment on the ground that the exclusion of a large number of uprooted people because of their ethnic origin was discriminatory.[29] Thus the restrictionists, who had repeatedly attacked their opponents for attempting to flood the nation with aliens, now expanded the category of displaced persons to embrace several million more people.

Three members of the committee filed a minority report in which they advocated the passage of the Celler bill in its original form. The minority objected to the retention of the priorities, which they criticized as both unworkable and unfair, but their principal complaint dealt with the inclusion of the *Volksdeutsche*. They pointed out that the new definition would be disadvantageous to the displaced persons in the IRO camps, since they would have to compete with millions of German expellees for the additional 100,000 visas authorized in the bill. The report expressed sympathy for the *Volksdeutsche* but urged that they be treated as a separate problem. In addition to this minority report, four other members of the committee who had voted to report out the bill expressed their dissatisfaction with the final version and stated their intention of supporting a movement to liberalize the measure on the Senate floor.[30] It was clear that a majority of the

28. *Congressional Record* (January 6, 1950), pp. 113–14.

29. "Amending the Displaced Persons Act of 1948," *Senate Report No. 1237*, 81st Congress, 2d Session (Washington, 1950), Pt. I, pp. 1–3, 6.

30. Ibid., Pt. II, pp. 1–2, 8, 12–13.

committee favored a liberal displaced persons program and had assented to the restrictive amendments only to avoid further delay by Senator McCarran.

The final debate on the displaced persons issue began on the last day of February and after a long postponement finally came to a conclusion in early April. The discussion revolved around the committee amendments to the Celler bill, particularly the one regarding the *Volksdeutsche*, but the basic issue at stake was whether or not Congress would adopt a liberal displaced persons program. Thus in essence this debate was a recapitulation of the entire displaced persons controversy, with the lines tightly drawn between the opposing sides. Senator McCarran was the chief spokesman for the restrictionist group, while Senator Kilgore of West Virginia, together with Herbert Lehman, who had recently been elected to the Senate from New York, led the advocates of the Celler bill.

A central point of conflict between the two groups was the question of whether the United States had done its "fair share" in resettling displaced persons. The supporters of a liberal program claimed that the United States had failed to accept a number consistent with the wealth and stature of the nation. They asserted that this country had "a solemn obligation" to clear up the entire problem by taking a generous number. One senator warned that "the avoidance of such a solemn obligation with the United Nations and the world at large could bring only dishonor upon our way of life and our integrity as a nation." In response to this argument, the restrictionists contended that the United States had already done its fair share toward solving the displaced persons problem. Limiting displaced persons to those actually uprooted prior to the war's end, Senator McCarran claimed that there were only 11,000 war-displaced persons left unsettled in Europe. All others, he maintained, were refugees who had fled westward after the close of hostilities. Other senators, notably Jenner of Indiana and Cain of Washington, echoed McCarran's views. They attacked the 1949 cut-off date as a "gigantic fraud" designed to break down the protective quota system by labeling all European immigrants "displaced persons." [31] The restrictionists thereby replied to the arguments

31. *Congressional Record* (February 28, 1950), p. 2478; (March 1, 1950), p. 2548; (March 6, 1950), pp. 2843, 2847; (April 3, 1950), pp. 4581, 4597; (April 4, 1950), p. 4659; (April 5, 1950), pp. 4725, 4736–41.

of moral commitment and world leadership by raising the specter of a host of aliens flooding the nation.

The question of discrimination, which had bulked so large in the 1948 presidential campaign, also received attention during the debate. The advocates of a liberal program stressed the importance of a late cut-off date and the elimination of the Baltic priority in order to remove any possible bias from the program, though they admitted that there were so few Jewish displaced persons still unsettled that these provisions were no longer discriminatory in effect.[32] Senator Kilgore brought up the discrimination charges but carefully stated that the bias in the 1948 law was accidental and not intentional. It was the restrictionists who now made the strongest assertions about discrimination. "There has been much talk of religious and racial discrimination in the present displaced persons law," Senator McCarran declared. "There is no question that the law was discriminatory with respect to the German expellees. . . . To oppose the committee in this regard is to advocate racial discrimination." Senator Eastland made the same charge, asserting that the exclusion of the Volksdeutsche from the displaced persons program was "a slander against every individual through whose veins flows Germanic blood."[33] It became apparent as the debate progressed that the restrictionists advocated the inclusion of the Volksdeutsche primarily in order to embarrass the proponents of a liberal program. By injecting this new issue into the debate, they tried to turn the question of discrimination to their favor.

The debate reached a climax on April 5 when the Senate began voting on the committee amendments. A bipartisan coalition of senators from the Northeast, Midwest, and Far West defeated all the amendments supported by Senator McCarran, including the key one relating to the inclusion of the Volksdeutsche in the definition of eligible displaced persons. The Senate then approved by a vote of 49 to 25 a group of substitute amendments put forward by Senator Kilgore in opposition to the committee amendments. The Kilgore amendments, opposed mainly by southern senators, made some slight changes in

32. Ibid. (March 6, 1950), pp. 2844–5; (April 3, 1950), pp. 4588–9; (April 5, 1950), p. 4734. The creation of the new state of Israel in 1948 had provided an outlet for a large portion of the Jewish displaced persons.

33. Ibid. (February 28, 1950), p. 2479; (March 3, 1950), p. 2736; (April 5, 1950), p. 4743.

the Celler bill, the most important being a provision to admit 10,000 refugees from Greece. Then the Senate finally passed the amended Celler bill by a vote of 58 to 15, with only the staunchest restrictionists refusing to concur.[34]

For nearly two months a conference committee worked on the problem of harmonizing the measures that had been approved by the two branches of Congress. On June 2, 1950, this committee reported a final bill which embodied the liberal program President Truman and the Citizens Committee had called for. The conference measure

TABLE 3. Comparison of the Numbers Authorized under the Displaced Persons Acts of 1948 and 1950 *

Categories	Act of 1948	Act of 1950
IRO displaced persons	200,000	301,500
Volksdeutsche	27,377	54,744
Polish veterans in exile	——	18,000
Greek displaced persons	——	10,000
European refugees from China	——	4,000
Venezia-Giulia refugees (Italian)	——	2,000
Displaced orphans	3,000	5,000
Other European orphans	——	5,000
Recent refugees	2,000	500
Adjustment of status (displaced persons in the United States temporarily)	15,000	15,000
Total	247,377	415,744

* Slightly modified from a table in the Congressional Record (June 6, 1950), p. 8198.

established January 1, 1949, as the cut-off date, eliminated the Baltic and agricultural priorities, and provided for the selection of displaced persons without regard to their race, religion, or national origin. The most complicated section of the bill dealt with the various categories of people to be admitted. In addition to slightly over 300,000 regular displaced persons, the program was expanded to include special groups of Greek, Polish, and Italian refugees, as well as orphans and European refugees stranded in Asia. The committee compromised on the question of accepting recent refugees from behind the Iron Curtain, setting a limit of 500 in order to provide relief for special

34. Ibid. (April 5, 1950), pp. 4749, 4753, 4760, 4761, 4798–9. The vote on the Volksdeutsche amendment was 48 to 37.

cases. Finally, the conference bill doubled the number of *Volks-deutsche* who were given special preference under the German and Austrian quotas and authorized American participation in an international conference to study possible solutions to this grave problem.[35]

In submitting their report to Congress, the members of the conference committee stated, "It is the considered opinion of the conferees that the enactment of this legislation constitutes the final contribution of the United States toward a satisfactory solution of the displaced persons problem. . . ."[36] Both the House and the Senate accepted this view and the conference report was approved without further debate.[37] On June 16 President Truman signed the bill in the presence of the Congressional leaders, with Senator McCarran conspicuously absent. At the conclusion of the ceremonies, the president distributed the twelve pens he had used in signing the measure as souvenirs and then praised the bipartisan movement which had brought about the liberalization of the previous law.[38] On this harmonious note, in marked contrast to the discord which surrounded the signing of the act of 1948, the long controversy over the extent of American participation in the resettlement of displaced persons came to a close.

The struggle to liberalize the displaced persons program revealed the same basic core of disagreement that had been present in the debate over the passage of the original act. The advocates of a liberal program stressed the international aspects of the problem and America's role of leadership in the postwar world, while their opponents viewed the question almost exclusively from the standpoint of the internal structure of the nation. Insofar as the extreme restrictionists did admit the necessity for the United States to help displaced persons, they wished to limit this assistance to those people who had been uprooted as a direct consequence of the war. Their opponents, on the other hand, believed that the presence of a large number of stateless people in western Europe, regardless of whether displaced by the war or its aftermath, endangered the economic stability of nations which

35. "Amending the Displaced Persons Act of 1948," *House Report No. 2187*, 81st Congress, 2d Session (Washington, 1950), pp. 1–12.
36. Ibid., p. 12.
37. *Congressional Record* (June 6, 1950), p. 8197; (June 7, 1950), p. 8222.
38. New York *Times* (June 17, 1950), p. 1.

they viewed as vital bulwarks against the expansion of Soviet power. The decision in favor of a broader program signified that a majority of congressmen, many of whom were restrictionists at heart, believed that the resettlement of all displaced persons was essential for the proper conduct of American foreign policy in western Europe.

However, it would be a mistake to assume that the enactment of a generous displaced persons program marked a retreat from the restrictive immigration policy established in the 1920's. The majority in Congress made clear their belief in the need for restriction by refusing to admit displaced persons outside the quota limits. Acknowledging an emergency situation, they were willing to suspend temporarily the restrictive quotas in order to solve the immediate problem, but they invoked the mortgaging provision to maintain the fundamental principle of the quota system. The advocates of a liberal program, who originally had proposed the admission of displaced persons outside the quota limits, were able to enact their major objectives only by jettisoning the nonquota proposal. The displaced persons dispute revealed very clearly that Congress considered the quota system the indispensable core of American immigration policy.

The final liberalization of the act of 1948 removed all traces of discrimination from the displaced persons program. Though it is quite obvious that the cut-off date, and to a lesser extent the Baltic priority, tended to exclude Jewish displaced persons, there seems to be little basis for concluding that the framers of the bill drew up these provisions to discriminate against people of the Jewish faith: the expressed motive of the restrictionists, to limit the program to those people displaced during the course of the war, appears to be a valid explanation for these provisions. The tendency of Jewish groups to attribute the exclusion of many of their coreligionists to anti-Semitic bias is understandable; however, the extreme charges of discrimination made during the 1948 presidential campaign lead one to suspect that the northern wing of the Democratic party was using this issue to attract votes from members of minority groups. Certainly Truman's assertion that the 1948 law was anti-Catholic, made in the face of Catholic denials, indicates that political expediency had a great deal to do with the emphasis on the discrimination issue. The restrictionists used a similar tactic in asserting that the liberal proposals were discriminatory because they failed to include the *Volksdeutsche* as eligible displaced persons. It seems fair to conclude that in the heat of debate both sides resorted to the discrimination issue as an appeal to the emotions in order to win popular support for their position.

The displaced persons program enacted by Congress terminated on June 30, 1952. Though originally scheduled to conclude a year earlier, Congress extended the time limit of the program in June 1951 in order to ensure the utilization of all visas authorized by law.[39] In the four years the program was in effect the United States accepted 337,244 displaced persons as permanent residents, in addition to some 50,000 more German expellees.[40] There can be little doubt that the generous American participation in the resettlement of displaced persons was the major factor in the final solution of the problem. From 1947 until its demise at the end of 1951, the International Refugee Organization resettled slightly more than one million displaced persons. The American share in this gigantic population transfer was approximately one-third, equaling the portion taken by the next two largest receiving countries, Australia and Israel, combined. Though by the end of 1951 there were still some 400,000 people under the care of IRO who had not been resettled, the great majority were recent refugees from eastern Europe.[41] Thus the United States displaced persons program achieved its major goal—the complete resettlement, through the stimulus of American participation, of the million-odd people left stateless by the war.

The resettlement of displaced persons solved the most critical problem of postwar Europe. There were two persisting problems, however, that continued to hamper the recovery of the western European countries, namely the stream of refugees that flowed westward from the Communist nations and the critical overpopulation of West Germany and of Italy. On March 24, 1952, President Truman asked Congress to admit 300,000 people from western Europe as nonquota immigrants in order to ease the refugee and overpopulation problems.[42] No action resulted then from this proposal, but President Eisenhower sponsored

39. *Congressional Record* (May 9, 1951), p. 5114; (June 21, 1951), p. 6857.
40. Displaced Persons Commission, *Memo to America: the DP Story* (Washington, 1952), p. 366. Including the 41,379 admitted under the Truman directive, the grand total of displaced persons admitted from December 1945 until June 1952 was 378,623.
41. Vernant, pp. 37–8.
42. New York *Times* (March 25, 1952), p. 1.

a similar program which was enacted in the summer of 1953. Though the evolution of this legislation is beyond the scope of the present study, it is significant to note that the displaced persons program served as a model for later policy. The use of immigration legislation to strengthen the countries of western Europe, pioneered in the displaced persons program, became an established part of American foreign policy in the continuing power struggle with Soviet Russia.

8. *The Postwar Debate over Immigration Policy*

WHILE the displaced persons issue was the most important immigration problem in the immediate postwar period, several other aspects of immigration policy received Congressional attention in the 1940's. The spirit of international cooperation which pervaded the country during the war and immediately afterward led many people to believe that the time had arrived for a liberalization of the immigration laws. American participation in the United Nations, and later the development of a foreign policy which placed the first line of defense in western Europe, encouraged those who felt that international considerations should dominate in the formulation of immigration policy. On the other hand, the growing severity of the cold war with Russia stimulated a concern for national security among many Americans. The restrictionists resisted all efforts to liberalize the immigration laws, in the belief that such action would only weaken the nation during a critical period in its history. The final clash between these conflicting viewpoints occurred in the debate over the McCarran omnibus immigration bill in 1952. Before examining this debate, however, it is necessary to survey the developments in the 1940's which led up to the final climax in the next decade.

Three major problems of immigration policy confronted Congress in this period. First, there was the question of oriental exclusion. The wartime alliance with China and the postwar concern for the spread of communism in Asia caused a fundamental re-evaluation of previous policy toward oriental immigrants. In the second place, the never-ending controversy over the limits and nature of the quota system continued throughout the postwar years. Once more the restrictionists attempted to reduce the quotas, while the liberals countered by attacking the basic premise of restriction by means of national quotas. Finally, the climate of crisis engendered by the threat of Russian aggression stimulated concern for the entry of subversive immigrants. The restrictionists renewed their efforts to amend the existing law to provide for the specific exclusion of Communist and Fascist applicants for admission.

146

The passage of the Immigration Act of 1924 with its provisions for the exclusion of all persons ineligible for citizenship had closed the issue of oriental immigration for nearly twenty years. Nevertheless, two groups, religious leaders concerned with missionary work in Asia and businessmen engaged in Far Eastern trade, had felt the repercussions of the exclusion policy and had repeatedly expressed a desire for a change in the Asiatic immigration laws.[1] After Pearl Harbor the alliance between the United States and China introduced a new factor into the situation which enabled the interested parties to develop a campaign for the repeal of the Chinese exclusion laws and the extension of a minimum quota of 105 to China. With the United States and China fighting Japan, those favoring Chinese immigration had a powerful argument for the reversal of traditional policy.

The movement for repeal began in 1942 among a group of people in New York interested in promoting American good will in China. The most active participant was Richard Walsh, editor of the magazine *Asia and the Americas*.[2] In February 1942 Walsh published an article by Charles Nelson Spinks which called for immediate repeal of the Chinese exclusion laws. The article produced a favorable reaction in many quarters and brought forth offers for active help in achieving this goal.[3] Soon similar appeals appeared in Walsh's magazine, in the *Christian Century*, and in the *New Republic*.[4] A visit by Madame Chiang Kai-shek to the United States in the winter of 1942–43 generated an atmosphere of enthusiasm for the Chinese which led

1. In 1930 business interests and religious groups began agitating for a repeal of the oriental exclusion laws. This campaign proved abortive. In 1934 Representative Kramer of California introduced a bill to extend quotas to the Asian countries, but no action was taken on this measure. New York *Times* (May 24, 1930), p. 6; "Rectifying the Japanese Immigration Mistake," *Christian Century*, 47 (September 10, 1930), 1076; Griswold, p. 378; *Interpreter Releases*, 11 (March 6, 1934), 68.

2. Fred W. Riggs, *Pressures on Congress* (New York, 1950), pp. 47–64. This book is a detailed study of the repeal of the Chinese exclusion laws written as a case study in pressure group techniques.

3. Charles Nelson Spinks, "Repeal Chinese Exclusion," *Asia and the Americas*, 42 (February 1942), pp. 92–4; Riggs, p. 48.

4. The more significant articles include Richard Walsh, "Our Great Wall against the Chinese," *New Republic*, 107 (November 23, 1942), and "Repeal Exclusion Laws Now," *Asia and the Americas*, 43 (June 1943); editorial, "Are We Afraid to Do Justice?" *Christian Century*, 60 (June 9, 1943); and Oswald Garrison Villard, "Justice for the Chinese," *Christian Century*, 60 (May 26, 1943).

Representative Kennedy of New York to introduce a bill in Congress
providing for the repeal of the Chinese exclusion laws. The group led
by Walsh, composed mainly of social workers and publicists, intensified its efforts to win support for the repeal proposal, hiring a professional lobbyist in Washington and finally forming a Citizens Committee to Repeal Chinese Exclusion in late May 1943.[5] The Citizens
Committee established contact with people of similar views in California and worked diligently to stimulate support for repeal on the West
Coast. Throughout the summer and fall this catalytic pressure group
publicized repeal as a vital war measure by means of a press and radio
campaign, while behind the scenes its members exerted influence on
key figures in the House and Senate.[6]

Meanwhile, several more bills proposing repeal of the exclusion
laws and the granting of a quota to China were introduced in Congress. In May the House Immigration Committee decided to hold
hearings on the proposed legislation.[7] The usual alignment between
restrictionist and antirestrictionist groups developed, with the latter
predominating. Representatives of religious organizations, businessmen interested in postwar foreign trade, and members of the Citizens
Committee supported the bills. Labor was split on this issue, with
the more liberal CIO backing repeal and the traditionally restrictionist
AFL opposing it. The patriotic societies and the veterans' groups objected strongly to any change in policy, but the Citizens Committee
succeeded in neutralizing West Coast opposition. No hostile witnesses
appeared from this region, while a California congressman, Will
Rogers, Jr., and several Pacific Coast business groups even testified
for repeal.

The advocates of repeal presented their case on two levels—the
moral and the practical. The religious leaders stressed the moral considerations, stating that repeal would end the unjust racial discrimination against the Chinese. Several witnesses spoke of the inconsistency of
waging war on behalf of the four freedoms of the Atlantic Charter and
at the same time denying equality of treatment to an Asian ally. "If

5. Riggs, pp. 52–7.
6. Ibid., pp. 58–64, 82–8, 140–4.
7. "Repeal of the Chinese Exclusion Acts," *Hearings before the House Committee on Immigration and Naturalization,* 78th Congress, 1st Session, Washington,
1943.

this is a war for world unity and world freedom," asserted a Hindu witness, "then the United States cannot practice double standards of international morality—one for the whites and the other for the Asiatics." The dominant argument, however, was that repeal would help the war effort by strengthening Chinese morale. Citing Japanese propaganda broadcasts to China based on the theme that Asians should unite against the Western countries which considered them inferior, several witnesses stated that repeal was of crucial importance. They warned that China might give up the long struggle against Japan unless heartened by equal treatment from its allies. One of the most vigorous advocates of these bills, Congressman Walter Judd of Minnesota, claimed that repeal "would invigorate and galvanize them into more active effort and resistance, as no amount of pronouncements or Atlantic Charters or even of planes and guns can do." [8]

The restrictionists replied by asserting that immigration policy was purely a domestic concern unrelated to the war effort. Representatives of patriotic societies and veterans' groups argued that the only effective way to help China was to send her planes, guns, and tanks. Instead of reversing a traditional policy while under the influence of "war hysteria," Congress should wait until the postwar period, they contended. Several witnesses warned that opening the gates to the "Chinese hordes" would gravely endanger the nation's economy, claiming that repeal was only the first step in a campaign to break down all existing immigration barriers. Though all the opposing witnesses carefully stated that they were not motivated by racial considerations, hints of prejudice crept into their statements. James Wilmeth of the Junior Order of United American Mechanics stated that he feared repeal "would renew a stream of yellow people, unfitted and unsuited for American citizenship." Bias was most evident among the southern members of the committee, who bristled whenever the words "racial equality" were used. At one point Representative Gossett of Texas asserted that he "and the rest of the boys down below the Mason-Dixon line do not like the idea of trying to tie this thing up with social equality and racial equality." [9]

At the conclusion of the hearings in June, the House Immigration

8. Ibid., pp. 31, 37, 56, 68–70, 78–80, 92–3, 119–23, 133–4, 145, 153, 197.
9. Ibid., pp. 48–9, 65, 107–8, 168–76, 178–80, 217–19.

Committee decided to postpone making a decision on reporting out legislation until after the summer recess. Nevertheless, the publicity efforts of the Citizens Committee succeeded in creating a growing popular demand for repeal of the Chinese Exclusion Act, and in the fall the House Immigration Committee favorably reported the repeal bill. This measure provided a quota of 105 annually for the Chinese race, including Chinese born in all parts of the world as well as those native to China. This significant departure from the standard country-of-birth formula used for European quotas was designed to prevent an influx of Chinese born in Hong Kong or the countries of the Western Hemisphere. The racial quota for China meant that the repeal legislation, while eliminating race as a bar to the entry of Chinese, did not provide completely equal treatment for China. In reporting the bill, the majority of the committee expressed regret over past misunderstandings caused by the exclusion laws and concluded, "It is fitting that the incongruity of discriminatory legislation, inconsistent with the dignity of both our peoples, should be eliminated." [10]

With the repeal bill now beyond the committee bottleneck, the administration leaders moved quickly to secure passage of the measure. On October 11 the Rules Committee issued a rule for the immediate consideration of the bill in the House. On the same day President Roosevelt sent a message to Congress endorsing repeal. "I regard this legislation," the president declared, "as important in the cause of winning the war and of establishing a secure peace. By the repeal of the Chinese exclusion laws we can correct a historic mistake and silence the distorted Japanese propaganda." [11] With this strong endorsement, the House took up the repeal issue in late October, and the Senate debated the question the following month. The more heated debate occurred in the lower branch, but the basic issues were the same in both houses and the two debates can be analyzed together.

A prominent issue was the question of discrimination. The advocates of repeal concentrated their remarks on the need to remove discriminatory legislation from the statute books, but there was a significant divergence in their ranks. The more liberal spokesmen attacked the existing policy as embodying racist concepts contrary to American

10. "Repealing the Chinese Exclusion Laws," *House Report No. 732*, 78th Congress, 1st Session (Washington, 1943), Pt. I, pp. 1–4.
11. *Congressional Record* (October 11, 1943), pp. 8176, 8193.

ideals. Representative McCormack of Massachusetts made such a charge, and then described the repeal bill as "a denial of the false doctrine of racism and a reiteration of the American principles of equality of opportunity for life, liberty, and happiness for mankind." Many moderate supporters of repeal, particularly southerners, played down the racial issue. They acknowledged the fact that the exclusion policy slighted the Chinese, but they attributed the origin of the policy to economic, not racial factors. Pointing out that the small quota would achieve the needed economic restriction, the moderates backed repeal in order to remove the unintentional racial stigma against the Chinese. Finally, the opponents of repeal tried to hedge on the racial issue by asserting that the basic issue was one of assimilation, not discrimination. They contended that the Chinese, because of a widely divergent cultural background, could not be easily absorbed into American society. Thus Senator Holman of Oregon declared, "I base my thoughts on the subject not on the ground of inferiority of any race or group but on the ground of incompatibility when in large unassimilable groups they settle permanently among us." [12]

The other major issue in the debate was the propriety of repealing the Chinese exclusion laws during the war. Those favoring repeal flatly declared that the bill was a vital part of the war effort. Representative Gossett of Texas reversed his usual restrictionist stand to lead in the fight for repeal. "The bill under consideration," Gossett exclaimed, "is not an immigration bill. This bill is a war measure and a peace measure." Several speakers supported this position, stating that repeal would counter the Japanese "Asia for the Asiatics" propaganda and ensure continued Chinese participation in the war. The restrictionists answered by charging that liberal groups were using the war situation to breach the immigration barriers. "It is one of a succession of attempts to punch the first hole in the immigration dike," asserted one speaker. Representative Elmer of Missouri was more caustic. "The copious tears shed for the Chinese are only a few drops compared to the dramatic climax of The Rains Came that is to follow," he exclaimed. Behind this assertion lay the restrictionist belief that the existing immigration policy was sound and any change might be harmful. This belief was best expressed by Representative Bennett

12. Ibid. (October 20, 1943), pp. 8575, 8579, 8585, 8593, 8599; (November 26, 1943), p. 9989.

of Michigan, who declared, "I am opposed to the pending bill because it nullifies a basic, thoroughly sound, and long-established rule of immigration in the midst of a world war." [13]

The attempts of the restrictionists to postpone consideration of repeal until the postwar period failed. On October 21, 1943, the House passed the repeal measure by voice vote, and the Senate acted favorably the following month.[14] Less than two months after his message to Congress, President Roosevelt signed the bill he had endorsed. "It is with particular pride and pleasure," the president stated, "that I have today signed the bill repealing the Chinese exclusion laws. The Chinese people, I am sure, will take pleasure in knowing that this represents a manifestation on the part of the American people of their affection and regard." [15]

It is highly debatable whether or not the repeal of the Chinese exclusion laws was really a free expression of American good will toward China. The exclusion laws had been in existence for decades with only a few missionaries and businessmen favoring their repeal. Suddenly, after the onset of a war in which the United States faced a common foe with China, a movement for repeal developed which quickly culminated in complete success. The debates in Congress revealed that the supporters of repeal were primarily concerned with the effect of this action in furthering the defeat of the common enemy. The few who saw repeal as a renunciation of racist concepts and an effort to realize American ideals were very definitely in a minority, and it is most improbable that the liberals could have secured their objective on these moral and idealistic grounds. Representative Gossett was correct when he stated that the bill was a war, not an immigration, measure. Yet its passage stands as one of the turning points in American immigration policy. For the first time Congress liberalized its rigid policy of exclusion toward an Asiatic people, giving hope to those who favored placing all Orientals upon a quota basis.

The repeal of the Chinese exclusion laws stimulated sentiment for the extension of quotas to other Asian countries. Though no congressman proposed a complete reversal of the oriental exclusion policy,

13. Ibid. (October 20, 1943), pp. 8581–2, 8584, 8588, 8591–2, 8594, 8603; (November 26, 1943), p. 9995.

14. Ibid. (October 21, 1943), p. 8635; (November 26, 1943), p. 10,019.

15. "An Act of Good Will toward China," *Monthly Review of the Immigration and Naturalization Service, 1* (January 1944), 4.

several bills were introduced in 1944 to place India, Korea, and Siam on a quota basis. The measure to repeal exclusion of the people of India, introduced by Representative Emanuel Celler of New York in 1944 and again in 1945, met with the strongest support.[16] The House Immigration Committee held hearings on the Celler bill in March 1945, with all the witnesses except an AFL representative supporting the legislation.[17] Despite this favorable testimony, the committee at first voted to table the bill. However, the administration applied pressure on the committee, and after a special session at which William Phillips, the president's personal representative to India, testified in secrecy, the members reversed their stand. On July 3, 1945, the committee reported the Celler bill, which provided the same racial quota for India that had been granted to China.[18]

Congress began consideration of the Celler bill in 1945, and after brief debates which recapitulated the arguments expressed during the discussion of a quota for China, finally acted favorably in 1946. The debates revealed that the major reason for passage was the feeling that the bill would aid American foreign policy in Asia. The advocates of a quota for India stressed the need to counter Communist propaganda in Asia by removing discrimination from our immigration policy. The restrictionists replied with their usual contention that immigration is solely a domestic concern. They warned that the Celler bill represented another wedge directed at the total breakdown of the protective immigration system, but the numbers involved were so slight that their argument made little impression. The easy passage of the bill by voice votes in both houses indicated that Congress was willing to ease immigration barriers to help foreign policy as long as no great change in the number of immigrants resulted.[19] And though the law meant another step toward eliminating race as a barrier to the admission of immigrants, it was passed not for moral reasons but out of regard for national interests abroad.

16. *Interpreter Releases, 21* (May 16, 1944), 176; 22 (March 31, 1945), 75.

17. "To Grant a Quota to Eastern Hemisphere Indians," *Hearings before the House Committee on Immigration and Naturalization,* 79th Congress, 1st Session, Washington, 1945.

18. *Interpreter Releases,* 22 (March 31, 1945), 75; "Authorizing the Admission into the United States of Persons of Races Indigenous to India," *House Report No. 854,* 79th Congress, 1st Session (Washington, 1945), pp. 1–2.

19. *Congressional Record* (October 10, 1945), pp. 9521–32; (June 14, 1946), p. 6918.

In passing the India quota bill, the Senate added a provision granting Filipino immigrants the right to become naturalized citizens, passed by the House as a separate bill the year before.[20] The effect of this measure was to prevent the exclusion of Filipinos upon the completion of Philippine independence, which was scheduled for July 4, 1946. Four days after the proclamation of independence, President Truman established a quota of one hundred for the new nation.[21] Since the Philippine quota was based on the country-of-birth formula rather than on race, this action gave the Philippine Islands a privileged position in comparison to India and China.

The quotas granted to China, India, and the Philippines inevitably led to demands for the renunciation of the entire policy of oriental exclusion. In 1947 Representative Walter Judd of Minnesota introduced a bill to repeal the Asiatic exclusion laws and extend the quota system to Asia. The Justice Department endorsed Judd's approach in 1948 when it objected to a bill providing a quota for Siam on the grounds that a complete re-evaluation of policy, not another special exception, was required.[22] Judd proposed to solve the problem by setting up an Asia-Pacific triangle which would encompass all the countries inhabited by oriental peoples. His bill provided a racial quota of one hundred for each country within the triangle, based on the formula used for China and India, and in addition established a quota of one hundred for the entire region to take care of people of mixed oriental ancestry and inhabitants of colonial dependencies.[23] This ingenious scheme achieved the major goal of eliminating outright racial exclusion of Asians and yet at the same time severely restricted oriental immigration. By employing quotas based on race rather than on country of birth, however, Judd's measure did not provide for complete equality of treatment between European and Asian immigrants.

20. Ibid. (June 14, 1946), p. 6933; (April 17, 1945), p. 3454. There was no debate in either house on this measure.

21. *Interpreter Releases*, 23 (August 15, 1946), 198.

22. "Authorizing the Admission into the United States of Persons Indigenous to Siam," *House Report No. 1432*, 80th Congress, 2d Session (Washington, 1948), p. 2.

23. "Providing for Equality under Naturalization and Immigration Laws," *Hearings before the Subcommittee on Immigration and Naturalization of the House Committee on the Judiciary*, 80th Congress, 2d Session (Washington, 1948), pp. 18–19.

Congressional consideration of the Judd bill began in 1948 when the House Judiciary Committee conducted hearings on the measure. Representative Judd explained the purpose of the bill, stating that it "will work to remove the stigma that at present attaches to complete prohibition of immigration of certain races, and yet will make sure that there will not be any flooding of America with people of lower economic standards or other cultural patterns." Representatives of the State Department strongly endorsed the bill. They pointed to the damage which the exclusion policy had caused in the past and stressed the need to win Asian friendship in the struggle to contain Communist expansion. Joseph Grew, former ambassador to Japan, claimed that the small size of the quota was unimportant in winning good will, asserting, "The question is one of principle, of recognition of the innate equality of peoples, of giving force to our own democratic beliefs." Both the American Legion and the American Coalition registered their opposition to the Judd bill, but a more significant criticism came from another quarter. A representative of the American Jewish Congress condemned the racial quotas as inconsistent with the basic objective of removing racial discrimination from the immigration laws. "The obvious purpose and effect of this inconsistency is to discriminate against Asiatics," he maintained.[24]

The Judiciary Committee issued a favorable report on the Judd bill at the close of the hearings, and in March 1949 the House began discussion of the measure.[25] The ensuing debate was one of the most harmonious ever held on an immigration bill. Not one speaker opposed the granting of quotas to all Asian nations, and even the California delegation expressed its complete approval of the reversal in policy. Judd voiced the basic reason for this wholehearted agreement when he stated that the bill would "influence greatly the battle for men's minds and hearts that is going on between the two philosophies of life and government that are locked in mortal struggle in our world." There were no objections from liberal quarters to the use of racial quotas for Asia, and indeed one champion of minority rights exclaimed, "I have never seen such a fine atmosphere of good will and brotherhood in terms of race relations since I have been in Congress."

24. Ibid., pp. 8, 20, 36–7, 43, 151.
25. "To Make Immigration Quotas Available to Asian and Pacific Peoples," *House Report No. 65*, 81st Congress, 1st Session, Washington, 1949.

Though there was some heated debate over a minor provision of the bill, harmony prevailed and the House passed the bill by voice vote on March 1, 1949.[26]

The advocates of the Judd bill hoped for prompt consideration of their measure in the Senate, but other factors prevented the consummation of the movement to end oriental exclusion at this time. In 1947 the Senate had authorized a subcommittee headed by Pat McCarran to conduct a complete investigation of the immigration laws. This investigation was still in progress when the Judd bill reached the Senate in 1949 and the Judiciary Committee decided to table all immigration measures until the subcommittee reported its findings.[27] The final report, delivered in 1950, accepted the basic principles of the Judd bill and incorporated this measure into an omnibus immigration bill that was the forerunner of the McCarran Act.[28] Thus the question of terminating oriental exclusion became involved in the larger problem of re-evaluating the over-all immigration policy of the United States.

While the final step in the reversal of American policy toward Asian immigrants was postponed until the next decade, the 1940's did witness a remarkable change in Congressional sentiment on this issue. The overwhelming approval of the Judd bill in the House indicated that the great majority of congressmen had accepted the principle of extending the quota system to Asia. The debate on the measure revealed once again that the primary motivation was a desire to implement American foreign policy in Asia by removing a source of friction. To quiet the fears of the restrictionists over a large-scale influx of oriental immigrants, the sponsors of the legislation compromised by providing small racial quotas for the Asian countries. The compromise formula removed the basic source of discrimination yet at the same time did not accord the Asians equality of treatment with European immigrants. This inconsistency went unchallenged during the debates

26. *Congressional Record* (March 1, 1949), pp. 1680, 1688, 1691–2. The only controversy was over a provision to limit all immigration from colonies to 100 of the mother country's quota. Representatives from Negro districts of the Northeast objected on the grounds that this provision discriminated against Negro immigrants from the West Indies.

27. *Interpreter Releases, 26* (April 18, 1949), 137.

28. *Senate Report No. 1515* (1950), pp. 457–8.

in the 1940's, but it was to become the center of controversy in future discussions of immigration policy.

Discussion of the oriental exclusion issue represented only one aspect of the postwar reassessment of American immigration policy. The war had cut short the controversy over the nature of the quota system, but the advent of peace was accompanied by a renewed interest in this problem. As early as 1944 the restrictionists had put forth proposals for the reduction and even the suspension of immigration. In the following year five restrictive bills were introduced in Congress, two calling for reductions in the quotas and three providing for the complete suspension of immigration for five years. Both the American Legion and the Daughters of the American Revolution advocated a policy of suspension until unemployment dropped below the million mark and all veterans had found peacetime jobs.[29] The restrictionists justified this program by asserting that the postwar years would constitute a difficult period of economic readjustment during which immigration could only complicate domestic problems.[30]

At the same time, proponents of a more liberal immigration policy spoke of the need for sweeping revision of the quota system. In 1944 Commissioner of Immigration Earl Harrison advocated a consideration of "the international implications" of immigration policy in an address to a conference of social workers. "It might be well to consider the possibility of adopting a more flexible type of quota regulations which would enable us to meet situations of an urgent nature," Harrison declared. This concern for an international approach to immigration policy was echoed by Harrison's successor, Commissioner Ugo Carusi, in an address in May 1945. Speaking at the time when the United Nations Organization was being founded at San Francisco, Carusi exclaimed, "There is no reason why the new concept of international cooperation should not extend to our policy with respect to immigration." [31] While neither spokesman outlined specific recom-

29. *Interpreter Releases, 21* (April 17, 1944), 151; (May 8, 1944), 169; (May 16, 1944), 176; *22* (January 25, 1945), 12; *Summary of Proceedings of the Twenty-Sixth Annual Convention of the American Legion* (Chicago, 1944), p. 65.

30. *Congressional Record*, Appendix (January 26, 1944), p. A405; (August 11, 1944), p. 6906.

31. *Interpreter Releases, 21* (June 5, 1944), 191–3; *22* (August 27, 1945), 233.

mendations, both urged the formulation of a new policy based on conditions outside the United States.

Congress took the first concrete step toward reassessing immigration policy in 1945 when the House authorized the Immigration Committee to conduct a study of the immigration laws. Representative Dickstein of New York headed a special subcommittee which held hearings in various cities during the summer of 1945. In each city, groups for and against immigration testified, airing their widely divergent views. Local representatives of veterans' organizations and patriotic societies stated their opposition to any liberalization of the quota system and reiterated the proposals to suspend immigration during the postwar period of economic readjustment. Spokesmen for local civic groups and immigrant-aid societies presented a totally different line of argument. Beginning with the premise that immigration was the foundation of American greatness, they attacked the quota system as discriminatory toward southeastern Europeans and urged the adoption of a more flexible method of selection based on the individual merit of the immigrants. Several witnesses spelled out a plan of pooling quotas by which quota numbers unused by countries with large allotments would be distributed among the small-quota nations of southeastern Europe.[32]

In the fall the subcommittee submitted a report on its investigations of immigration problems. The members of the subcommittee, stating that the hearings revealed a broad cross-section of conflicting opinion on the quota system, concluded "that no widespread popular demand exists for immediate, drastic changes in the existing law, and that, in fact, no such changes are now required." The report recommended a full-scale study of existing immigration laws and practices by "experts qualified to undertake impartial and complete research and analysis into all phases of the problems presented." Until such a study was conducted, the subcommittee felt it would be unwise to embark on any major changes in the immigration system.[33] Thus the

32. "Study of Problems Relating to Immigration and Deportation and Other Problems," *Hearings before Subcommittee I of the House Committee on Immigration and Naturalization*, 79th Congress, 1st Session (Washington, 1945), pp. 178–9, 253–4, 263–4, 274, 277–9, 283, 294, 449, 454–7. Hearings were held in New York, Cleveland, Chicago, San Francisco, Los Angeles, and Miami.

33. "Immigration and Naturalization Laws and Problems," *House Report No. 1312*, 79th Congress, 1st Session (Washington, 1945), pp. 4–7, 14–15.

first postwar survey of immigration policy resulted in no positive proposals aside from a plea for further investigation. The neutral tone of the report suggests that the sterility of the subcommittee's findings was due largely to an impasse between its restrictionist and liberal members.

Dissatisfied with this report, the restrictionists tried once more to secure a reduction of quota immigration. In 1946 Representative Gossett added a clause reducing quotas by 50 per cent for five years to a bill dealing with another aspect of immigration. Hearings on this measure produced the usual conflict in viewpoint between restrictionists and people favoring increased immigration. However, one surprising reversal of position occurred that was of major significance. Organized labor came out strongly in opposition to the reduction proposal, with representatives of both the CIO and the AFL stressing the need for continued immigration to avoid "national isolationism." The strong stand against the quota-cutting bill taken by the AFL was of special importance. Since its inception in 1885, this organization had been the single most influential member of the restrictionist coalition. Yet at the hearings, the AFL representative declared: "We need people. We cannot get enough of them." This witness emphasized his belief that immigration was a vital part of American foreign policy in a period of crisis, and it seems clear that the cause of this sudden change in labor's views was primarily a new international outlook on the immigration issue.[34]

This dramatic shift in organized labor's viewpoint proved a deathblow to Gossett's proposal: at the conclusion of the hearings the House Immigration Committee voted 10 to 7 against the quota-reduction scheme.[35] Never again did any of the restrictionist proposals for reducing or suspending immigration receive serious consideration.

In 1947 the issue of displaced persons crowded out all discussion of general quota policy. Meanwhile, in the Senate the McCarran subcommittee proceeded with its investigation of the over-all problem of immigration policy. Though the House considered some minor

34. "Denying Admission to the United States of Certain Aliens and to Reduce Immigration Quotas," *Hearings before the House Committee on Immigration and Naturalization*, 79th Congress, 2d Session (Washington, 1946), pp. 1–2, 79–84, 87–96. The bill in question, discussed below, concerned the exclusion of Nazi party members and German soldiers.

35. *Interpreter Releases*, 23 (May 8, 1944), 89a.

phases of immigration policy in this period, no final decisions on major issues could be reached while the Senate awaited the subcommittee report, finally released in the spring of 1950. Thus, as was the case with Asiatic exclusion, the culmination of the postwar debate on the quota system was postponed until the next decade.

The significance of the controversy over quota policy in the 1940's lies in its clear delineation of conflicting viewpoints. The restrictionists, starting from the premise that immigration weakened rather than strengthened the nation, concentrated their arguments on the impact of immigrants upon the internal problems of the United States. Their opponents, accepting the proposition that immigration had been and continued to be a source of national vigor, contended that immigration policy should be viewed in the larger context of a world situation in which the United States had assumed responsibilities of leadership. The advocates of a liberal policy had successfully blocked the postwar restrictionist drive for the lowering of quotas. The unresolved issue was whether this group could achieve its further goal of liberalizing a quota system which the restrictionists considered the *sine qua non* of immigration policy.

The third aspect of postwar discussion of immigration problems involved the denying of alien Fascists and Communists admission into the United States. At the war's end the restrictionists revived their earlier campaign for the specific exclusion of all members of totalitarian parties. A heightened public concern for the infiltration of subversive elements into American society and government, stemming from a general fear of Communism, greatly aided this campaign. In the early postwar years the major issue was the exclusion of former Nazis, with both liberals and restrictionists in agreement on the need for a strict policy. As the Russian menace grew in intensity, attention shifted to a concern for the entrance of Communist agents in the guise of immigrants; in the controversy that developed, the restrictionists favored much severer limitations than their liberal opponents. The climax came in 1950 with the passage of the Internal Security Act, which encompassed Communist infiltration from both within and without the nation.

The House investigating subcommittee established in 1945 included the problem of former Nazis in its survey of the immigration laws. At the hearings Chairman Dickstein proposed that the German quota be abolished for a number of years so as to guarantee the exclusion of all Fascists. The majority of witnesses felt that this was too drastic a remedy and instead urged a rigid screening of all German immigrants to keep out confirmed Nazis.[36] The investigating committee finally rejected Dickstein's proposal, but in 1946 Representative Gossett reopened the issue by introducing a bill to exclude all Nazis and all Germans who had voluntarily borne arms during the war. Congress held hearings on this measure, and the witnesses, led by the American Legion, voiced their approval.[37] The House passed Gossett's bill without discussion, but the Senate failed to act on it.[38] Though Gossett introduced the measure again during the next session, no further action was forthcoming in Congress, and the immediate postwar drive to exclude Nazis subsided without achieving concrete results.

For the next two years the displaced persons problem absorbed the attention of Congress. But in 1949 Senator McCarran reopened the issue of subversive immigrants by introducing legislation to make membership in the Communist party or any of its subsidiaries a specific ground for exclusion. Stating that the existing laws, which excluded anyone advocating the violent overthrow of government, were inadequate, McCarran asserted, "We must bring our immigration system into line with the realities of Communist tactics." [39] At hearings on this bill in the summer of 1949, ex-Communist witnesses such as Elizabeth Bentley and Louis Budenz testified that the real control of the party in the United States was in the hands of foreign agents who entered and left the country at will. Maurice Malkin, another former Communist, declared, "The Communist Party of the United States was organized and has been led by aliens since its inception in 1919." These witnesses recommended much more stringent immigration laws in regard to subversives in order "to cut the lifeline of the party." [40]

36. "Study of Immigration Problems," House *Hearings* (1945), pp. 1, 12–13, 20–2, 31–3, 105.

37. "Denying Admission," House *Hearings* (1946), pp. 2, 9–10, 68–9, 108.

38. *Congressional Record* (July 2, 1946), p. 8163.

39. Ibid. (April 25, 1949), p. 4993.

40. "Communist Activities among Aliens and National Groups," *Hearings before the Subcommittee on Immigration and Naturalization of the Senate Judiciary Committee*, 81st Congress, 1st Session (Washington, 1949), pp. 116, 123, 472, 783.

As a result of these hearings, the Senate subcommittee investigating the immigration system devoted a special section of its report to the problem of subversives. The basic premise of this report was that "the Communist movement in the United States is an alien movement, sustained, augmented, and controlled by European Communists and the Soviet Union." To remedy this situation, the subcommittee adopted the recommendations of the witnesses at the hearings and advocated new legislation to exclude specifically any member of a Communist or totalitarian organization. This prohibition applied to both past and present membership in Communist and Fascist parties and any of their affiliates.[41]

During the summer of 1950 the Senate Judiciary Committee decided that the exclusion of subversive immigrants was an urgent matter which should be acted upon immediately. Instead of postponing action by including the proposals for tightening the exclusion laws in the omnibus immigration bill, the Committee reported out a separate bill on this subject.[42] In early August the Senate, without any debate or discussion, passed this bill, making membership in either Communist or Fascist organizations a bar to admission to the United States.[43] Then the Judiciary Committee adopted a further change in procedure by combining the exclusion measure with bills dealing with subversive activity by native Americans in order to encompass the entire problem of internal security in one comprehensive piece of legislation.[44]

For several weeks Congress debated the internal security bill, but there was virtually no discussion of the immigration features of the measure. The opponents of the bill concentrated their criticisms on other sections, while the restrictionists, approving the exclusion provisions, remained silent. Finally both chambers passed the bill and on September 20 sent it on to President Truman. Two days later the president vetoed the bill. The veto message dealt in part with the immigration sections, the president objecting to the exclusion of past members of totalitarian organizations who had renounced their former

41. *Senate Report No. 1515* (1950), pp. 787, 797–9.

42. "Exclusion and Expulsion of Subversive Aliens from the United States," *Senate Report No. 2230*, 81st Congress, 2d Session (Washington, 1950), p. 1.

43. *Congressional Record* (August 9, 1950), p. 12,060.

44. "Protecting the Internal Security of the United States," *Senate Report No. 2369*, 81st Congress, 2d Session (Washington, 1950), pp. 1, 10–11.

ideology. "Instead of trying to encourage the free movement of people, subject only to the real requirements of national security," the president declared, "these provisions attempt to bar movement to anyone who is, or once was, associated with ideas we dislike, and in the process, they would succeed in barring many people whom it would be to our advantage to admit." In the debate over the veto, several speakers referred to the need for greater flexibility in the exclusion provisions, but again the discussion centered on other features of the bill. The proponents of the bill succeeded in mustering the necessary two-thirds majority in both houses and on September 23 overrode Truman's veto.[45]

In the passage of the Internal Security Act of 1950 the restrictionists finally achieved one of their oldest objectives, the specific exclusion of Communists and Fascists from admission into the United States. While this action embodied only a slight change in existing legislation, it marked a highly significant shift in the formulation of immigration policy. Previously the primary motivation of the restrictionists had been racial and cultural nationalism—the desire to preserve the predominant cultural patterns and ethnic composition of the United States by limiting immigration. With the rise of totalitarian governments and the crisis of the second World War, a new stress on nationalism in its most fundamental meaning, the security of the nation, became evident. Beginning in 1940, when the jurisdiction over immigration affairs was transferred from the Department of Labor to the Department of Justice, the intense concern for the loyalty of immigrants developed and grew, reaching a peak with the coming of the cold war with Russia. The fear of Communistic infiltration, which played such a large role in mid 20th-century American life, permeated discussions of immigration legislation and tended to replace the old fear of ethnic invasion as the dominating concern in immigration policy. Thus the Internal Security Act, with its nearly obscured immigration provisions, symbolized a vital change in attitude toward immigration that would become even more evident in the passage of the McCarran-Walter Act.

45. *Congressional Record* (September 12, 1950), p. 14,628; (September 20, 1950), pp. 15,260, 15,297; (September 22, 1950), pp. 15,631–2; (September 23, 1950), p. 15,726.

9. The McCarran Act

THE DECISIVE TURNING POINT in the postwar debate on American immigration policy came in 1950. In the first five years after the war discussion of many of the basic issues had revealed a fundamental conflict between the restrictionists and those favoring a liberalization of the immigration system. However, except on the issue of subversive immigrants, this controversy had not led to any legislative results and had served only to widen the gulf between the two traditional approaches to immigration policy. This period of preliminary sparring ended in 1950 when the McCarran subcommittee concluded its investigation of the immigration laws and submitted a comprehensive bill covering all aspects of immigration policy. Embodying almost completely the restrictionist views on the basic points in dispute, the McCarran bill engendered a lengthy and vigorous debate which proceeded with increasing heat until the final enactment of the measure in the spring of 1952. The long controversy over the re-evaluation of American immigration policy, sterile and unfruitful during the 1940's, swiftly reached a climax in the first two years of the next decade.

The McCarran bill was a complex and highly technical measure which codified the entire system of immigration laws, which had developed in a haphazard fashion since the late 19th century. For this reason, the debate over the bill covered a wide range of immigration problems, some of primary significance, others of much more limited importance. Yet out of the welter of details and technicalities which encumbered the discussion, certain basic issues emerged as primary points of dispute. The principal issue was the retention of the national origins quota system. The antirestrictionists, hoping for a modernization of immigration policy, bitterly protested the continuation of a method of choosing immigrants which they believed was basically discriminatory and therefore inconsistent with the nation's new role as leader of the free world. On the other hand, the sponsors of the bill equated the quota system with the principle of numerical restriction and refused to consider any modification of a system which they felt had become a vital national institution. A second important issue was the question of limiting Asiatic immigration by means of racial quotas. The restrictionists defended this formula on the basis of protection against an inundation by oriental peoples, while their opponents advocated a policy of complete equality of treatment between Asian and European immigrants. Other controversial issues of lesser significance included the broadening of exclusion provisions in regard to subversives and the extent of power wielded by administrative officials.

Behind all these specific issues lay the fundamental divergence in viewpoint between the two opposing groups. The restrictionists, believing that immigration was a source of potential danger to the nation, argued that the basic aim of immigration policy should be to protect the institutions and traditions of the United States. Their opponents denied the premise that immigration might weaken the country and contended that immigration policy should express a spirit of friendliness and generosity to the less fortunate people of the world. The conflict between such diametrically opposed conceptions of immigration policy formed the core of the debate over the McCarran bill.

The origins of the omnibus immigration bill date back to the summer of 1947 when Senator Chapman Revercomb introduced a resolution authorizing a subcommittee of the Senate Judiciary Committee to investigate the immigration laws. The Senate approved the resolution with little discussion, thereby establishing the first thorough Congressional study of immigration problems since the investigation by the Dillingham Commission near the beginning of the century.[1] During the first year of its existence the subcommittee concentrated its attention on the displaced persons issue, but after the election in 1948, when Senator McCarran replaced Revercomb as chairman of the body, the investigation of general immigration problems got under way. For nearly two years the committee staff gathered testimony from members of the Immigration Service, the Foreign Service, and interested private organizations. Staff members traveled to all parts of the United States and to the principal emigration centers in Europe, transcribing testimony for the use of the subcommittee. After

1. *Congressional Record* (July 26, 1947), p. 10,352.

a thorough study of this evidence, the subcommittee compiled a 900-page report which surveyed the basic problems of immigration policy and included recommendations which were embodied in an accompanying omnibus bill.[2]

The subcommittee report contained both a sociological survey of the effect of immigration on American society and a detailed discussion of the various features of existing immigration policy. The survey of the foreign born in the United States represented a fairly straightforward and objective analysis, yet evidence of bias on the part of the subcommittee members did creep in. The stereotypes of "old" and "new" immigrants were used to differentiate between people from northwestern and southeastern Europe, with an invidious distinction in favor of the "old" immigrants. The members of the subcommittee emphasized the large number of Jewish people among the new immigrants. "The population of the United States has increased three-fold since 1877," the report stated, "while the Jewish population has increased twenty-one-fold during the same period." The report discussed the question of population growth at considerable length, warning that many experts placed the optimum population of the United States at less than the existing number. Though the subcommittee did not formulate any final conclusions on the relationship between immigration and population growth, there was a clear implication that an increase in population due to heavy immigration would run counter to the national interests.[3]

The most significant section of the subcommittee report dealt with an evaluation of the national origins quota system. Reviewing the statistics of immigration, the subcommittee concluded that insofar as the quota system was designed to restrict the number of immigrants, it had proved successful. However, the members of the subcommittee felt that there was a second and more fundamental objective, the preservation of the ethnic composition of the nation, which had not been fully achieved. Their report stated that a study of the passage of the 1924 law showed that "one of the motivating reasons behind the enactment of the law was the restriction of immigration from southern and eastern Europe in order to preserve a predominance of persons of northwestern European origin in the composition

2. *Senate Report No. 1515* (1950), pp. 2–4.
3. Ibid., pp. 231–5, 241, 284–5.

of our total population." An examination of the statistics revealed that the tendency of the people from southwestern Europe to utilize their quotas to a much greater degree than those from the northwestern section had upset "the contemplated pattern for immigration from Europe." [4] In this analysis the members of the subcommittee indicated a basic sympathy for the goal of preserving the existing ethnic balance in the United States, though they did not express their approval of this concept explicitly.

In their final recommendations, the members of the subcommittee advocated the retention of the national origins system "without giving credence to any theory of Nordic supremacy." The principal justification was that the quota system provided a selective formula "automatically resistant to pressures for special treatment." Observing that each minority group sought advantages for its own members, the subcommittee concluded that the national origins scheme provided the only practical way of avoiding continuous agitation by these groups. However, in rejecting a suggestion for the pooling of unused quotas, the members of the subcommittee revealed their true beliefs on this issue. "To distribute the unused quotas on the basis of registered demand would shift more quota numbers to the countries of southern and eastern Europe," the report stated. Just as in the 1920's, the basic motivation of the advocates of the national origins system was a desire to limit the immigration of people from southeastern Europe. But in the 1950's theories of racial superiority were no longer in fashion and the restrictionists attempted to hedge on the philosophy behind the quota system. At several points in the report there were references to "the similarity of cultural background" as a reason for favoring immigrants from northwestern Europe, but the subcommittee carefully avoided any statement concerning the racial qualities of the different categories of immigrants.[5] This refusal by the restrictionists to discuss one of their basic reasons for supporting national origins became one of the characteristic features of the debate over the Mc-Carran bill.

The subcommittee rejected the alternative plan advanced by liberal groups to choose immigrants solely on the basis of their individual merits, without reference to national origin. However, the members

4. Ibid., pp. 442, 445–6.
5. Ibid., pp. 65, 441, 448–9, 455.

agreed on the need for a greater degree of positive selection of immigrants, and they recommended a system of economic selection within the quotas. Instead of granting priority to relatives of citizens and resident aliens, the report suggested that the first 30 per cent of the quota be reserved for immigrants whose services were needed by industries, universities, or governmental agencies in the United States. The rest of the quota would be allotted to relatives of citizens and resident aliens, with only 10 per cent open to nonpreference applicants. This plan, which Secretary of Labor James Davis had suggested back in the 1920's, represented a practical approach to the problem of selecting immigrants in line with the restrictionist belief that immigration should be regulated so as to further the economic well being of the country. In the words of the subcommittee report, "more emphasis should be placed upon the interests and needs of the United States in determining who among the applicants for admission should be admitted." [6]

The report dealt more briefly with other aspects of immigration policy. The subcommittee accepted the reversal of policy toward oriental immigrants embodied in the Judd bill, including the racial quotas, with the statement that "exclusion on the basis of race is no longer necessary." The members of the subcommittee also advised the continuation of Western Hemisphere immigration on a nonquota basis. Though expressing some doubts as to the wisdom of this policy, the report stated, "Quota restrictions are not compatible with our good neighbor policy." A minor recommendation, yet one which the antirestrictionists had long advocated, was the decision to end discrimination between the sexes by granting nonquota status to the alien husbands of American women. Finally, the subcommittee urged the broadening of the grounds for excluding undesirable aliens. The section of the report dealing with subversives has been discussed earlier, but in addition to this category, the subcommittee suggested a strengthening of the provisions barring criminals and the diseased.[7]

To carry out the recommendations made in the report, the subcommittee prepared an omnibus bill which codified all existing laws into one measure. Named for the subcommittee chairman, the McCarran

6. Ibid., pp. 449, 456–7; James J. Davis, *Selective Immigration* (St. Paul, 1925), pp. 209–12.

7. *Senate Report No. 1515* (1950), pp. 373, 412–17, 457–8, 473.

bill was essentially a restrictionist measure recapitulating the protective policy which had evolved in the course of the century. The most significant feature was the retention of the national origins quota system as the basic method of limiting immigration. Though the bill did introduce several major changes, the new features did not represent a liberalization of policy but instead harmonized with the restrictionist conception of immigration control. The system of economic selection within the quotas, together with the tightening of the exclusion provisions, furthered the goal of protecting the economy and the social structure of the nation. Even in the case of granting quotas to Asian countries, basically a liberal proposal, the fact that these quotas were based on race rather than nationality reflected a desire to keep oriental immigration at a minimum. The most liberal change was the granting of nonquota status to alien husbands of American citizens, but this new provision affected only a few hundred immigrants a year.

While the Senate subcommittee was formulating the McCarran bill, antirestrictionist groups were putting forth their own programs for the modification of the immigration laws. The most significant of these originated with the National Committee on Immigration Policy, an organization formed by a group of citizens in 1945 to study immigration problems. Early in 1950 William Bernard reported the findings of this group in a book entitled *American Immigration Policy—a Reappraisal*. The major portion of the book was devoted to a survey of the influence of immigration on economic, social, and population trends in the United States. In contrast to the Senate subcommittee report, this study denied the existence of differences between "old" and "new" immigrants and strongly suggested the need for increased immigration to prevent a future decline in population growth. From the standpoint of the internal factors stressed by the restrictionists, Bernard concluded that a more liberal immigration policy would be beneficial to the nation.[8]

The major point brought out in Bernard's study was the liberal be-

8. Bernard, pp. 107–8, 176–98. This book was a collaborative work with Bernard, who was the executive director of the Committee, acting as editor. There were evidently close links between this group and the Citizens Committee on Displaced Persons, since Earl Harrison was chairman of both organizations and Bernard served on the staffs of the two committees.

lief that existing immigration policy was anachronistic. Charging that the national origins quota system "implies the doctrine of racialism," Bernard called for the modernization of this method of choosing immigrants by bringing immigration policy into line with the democratic ideals and concepts which the United States advocated for the world. The specific recommendations advanced by the National Committee on Immigration Policy consisted of proposals to increase the number of quota immigrants—possibly doubling the existing limit of 154,000 annually—and to make the national origins system more flexible by pooling unused quotas. Under the latter suggestion, the unused numbers would be distributed among the small-quota countries and to refugees fleeing persecution. It is interesting to note that these recommendations did not include a complete elimination of the national origins scheme. Though at one point Bernard stated, "Some more equitable method can surely be devised," neither he nor the National Committee offered an alternative plan. The best they could do was to suggest the establishment of a joint Congressional immigration committee to work out an acceptable substitute for the national origins quota system.[9]

The contrast between this liberal program and the omnibus bill explains the bitterness of the dispute which ensued in Congress. The McCarran bill dashed the hopes of the antirestrictionists for a postwar modification of immigration policy. The decision to maintain the basic features of existing legislation denied the premise that the nation's new international responsibilities demanded a recasting of the immigration laws. In particular, the retention of the national origins quota system conflicted with the plan to alleviate discrimination against southeastern Europeans by pooling the unused quotas. For the next two years the groups favoring a liberalization of policy fought against the adoption of the McCarran bill and attempted to replace it with measures embodying their own program. Realizing that the enactment of the omnibus bill would sound the death knell on the postwar movement to liberalize the immigration laws, the opponents of restriction made a supreme effort to prevent its passage.

The McCarran omnibus bill did not reach the floor of the Senate in 1950. Instead the Senate Judiciary Committee continued working

9. Ibid., pp. 259–60, 272–3, 275–8.

on the bill to perfect the many technical details involved in the codifi-
cation of all existing immigration statutes. At the opening of the next
session of Congress in January 1951 Senator McCarran introduced a
refined version of the bill. In spite of many minor changes suggested
by administrative officials, the revised measure closely resembled the
original bill.[10] The only significant change relaxed the rigid provisions
excluding members of subversive organizations. In the case of past
members of Communist or Fascist parties, the bill allowed the
Attorney-General to admit immigrants who had renounced their former allegiance and had actively opposed this ideology for the last
two years. Further, the bill recognized that many inhabitants of
countries with Fascist or Communist regimes were forced to hold
nominal membership in the ruling party in order to secure jobs or ra-
tion cards. A special provision exempted such persons from the ban
on members of totalitarian parties.[11] All other major provisions of the
McCarran bill remained unaltered.

In addition to the McCarran bill, two other omnibus immigration
measures were presented to Congress. Representative Walter of Pennsylvania, a member of the House Judiciary Committee, introduced a
bill which was designed as a House version of McCarran's legislation.
Though the Walter measure differed in some minor details, it followed
the Senate bill on all major points. To counterbalance these restrictionist measures, Representative Celler, Chairman of the House Judiciary Committee, submitted a liberal omnibus bill in February
1951. Celler accepted many features of the McCarran and Walter
measures, but on the key issue of national origins quotas he proposed
the adoption of a pooling system whereby unused quotas would be
allotted to the small countries of southeastern Europe at the end of
each year.[12] This was quite obviously a compromise proposal, with
Celler giving in on many points in order to achieve the basic objective
of antirestrictionists—the modification of the national origins quota
system.

In order to avoid duplication, the Senate and House Judiciary Committees decided to hold joint hearings on the three omnibus bills in

10. "Revision of Immigration, Naturalization, and Nationality Laws," *Joint
Hearings before the Subcommittees of the Committees on the Judiciary*, 82d Congress, 1st Session (Washington, 1951), p. 3; *Interpreter Releases*, 28 (February 1,
1951), 47.

11. *Interpreter Releases*, 28 (February 21, 1951), 67.

12. Ibid., 28 (February 21, 1951), 64–7; (March 3, 1951), 76–7.

the spring of 1951.[13] The great bulk of the testimony at these hearings consisted of criticisms of the McCarran and Walter bills. Representatives of patriotic societies, veterans' organizations, and the American Federation of Labor endorsed the omnibus legislation, but they confined their remarks to general statements of approval. In contrast, spokesmen for a wide variety of groups sympathetic to immigration undertook extensive and detailed criticism of every aspect of the McCarran and Walter bills. Minority groups spearheaded the attack on the omnibus measures, with Jewish and Italian organizations predominating. In addition a host of other organizations, ranging from the National Catholic Rural Life Conference and the American Friends Service Committee to the Americans for Democratic Action and the American Committee for the Protection of the Foreign Born sent representatives to oppose the McCarran and Walter bills. Most of these groups expressed their approval of the Celler bill, though many witnesses had further liberalizing amendments they wished to see included in it.

The critics of the McCarran bill focused their objections on the retention of the national origins quota system. Witnesses representing Italian and Jewish organizations charged again and again that the national origins scheme represented a racist concept out of harmony with the democratic ideal that men should be judged solely on the basis of their individual merit. "Under the cloak of governmental policy," asserted an Italian leader, "we have permitted 'nativist' enemies in our Nation to enunciate and promulgate an unscientific and dangerous racialist doctrine that is at its roots subversive and undemocratic." One witness pointed out that recent scientific study had proved the falsity of the racial theories which were so widely accepted in the 1920's. "Mental or moral characteristics cannot be associated with race," he continued, "however broadly or narrowly that dubious concept is interpreted, or with national origin." These minority spokesmen further charged that the favoritism toward northwestern European immigrants completely ignored the realities of the European population problem. Because of the national origins system, the countries where the pressure for emigration was heaviest received the smallest quotas, and thereby were deprived of a needed outlet for their surplus population.[14]

13. "Revision of Immigration Laws," Joint *Hearings*, 1950.
14. Ibid., pp. 233, 333–4, 379–83, 390–5, 743, 779–82.

While all the witnesses opposing the McCarran bill agreed on the evils of the national origins system, they advanced two different remedies to the problem. The more militant wing favored the complete eradication of the quota system. The representative of the American Jewish Congress declared that the retention of national origins in any form would be "a political and moral catastrophe" and recommended a policy of individual selection without quotas. Carol King, speaking for the American Committee for the Protection of the Foreign Born, endorsed this suggestion, exclaiming, "A quota based on national origins is and can be based only on racial discrimination." However, the majority of the witnesses proposed only that the national origins system be modified by distributing the unused quotas among immigrants from southeastern Europe. This plan would retain the maximum limit of 154,000 a year, yet it would allow all nationalities to "share more equitably in immigration to the United States." Reid Lewis, director of the Common Council for American Unity, asserted that "this matter of utilizing unused quotas it seems to me is a way of making our whole quota system more flexible, more responsive both to national needs and humanitarian needs." In addition, the representative of the Americans for Democratic Action proposed that the national origin quotas be calculated on the basis of the 1950 census. The advocates of these changes admitted that their plans would not remove discrimination from the immigration laws.[15] Realizing that national origins was too deeply entrenched for a successful assault, they compromised with an oblique attack aimed at lessening the discriminatory effects of the quota system.

The section of the McCarran bill dealing with Asian immigration also received a good deal of attention during the hearings. All the witnesses, including representatives of patriotic societies, expressed approval of the decision to end the policy of oriental exclusion. Representative Judd testified in support of this long-sought goal, stressing the need to win the friendship of Asian peoples in the struggle against Communism, which by this time had broken out into open warfare in Korea. "In the fierce contest for people's loyalties," he declared, "this is a step of the utmost importance." However, most witnesses felt that the McCarran bill did not go far enough toward granting equality of treatment between European and Asian immigrants. They contended that the use of racial quotas continued a policy of discrimina-

15. Ibid., pp. 336–7, 351–2, 394–5, 423, 538, 639, 755.

tion toward the Asian peoples which would prevent any rise in American prestige in the Orient. Even the AFL representative, who approved the retention of national origins, expressed dissatisfaction with the quota formula for Asia. "This form of discrimination may still be a serious impediment to good diplomatic relations with Asian countries and could be used by the Communists to great advantage to hurt our position in Asia," he asserted. Rejecting the notion that the country might be flooded with oriental peoples born in the Western Hemisphere, the critics of the bill urged the extension of the country-of-birth formula to Asia.[16]

Finally, there was considerable discussion of the sections of the omnibus bills dealing with the exclusion of subversives, particularly the new provisions which permitted the entry of nominal and past members of subversive parties. The witnesses who criticized other portions of the McCarran bill praised these new features which liberalized the existing Internal Security Act. Representatives of the Immigration Service and the Justice Department objected to these changes, however, claiming that it was impossible to ascertain the true status of people who came from countries behind the iron curtain. These administrative officials admitted that the present regulations tended to exclude many nonsubversive aliens, but they contended that it was better to err in favor of American security. On other points concerning the exclusion of subversives, the liberal witnesses were extremely critical of the bill. In particular they objected to a provision which enabled the Attorney General to exclude aliens suspected of subversive affiliations without an airing of the charges made against them. The few restrictionist witnesses who testified at the hearings expressed their belief that strict exclusion provisions formed the most vital part of the bill. Mrs. C. D. Wright, representing the General Federation of Women's Clubs, summed up the restrictionist viewpoint when she stated, "This is a fine bill, and we certainly hope that in helping the people of Europe you will put the security of the United States first." [17]

A long period of delay followed the conclusion of the hearings while the two Congressional committees and the authors of the bills

16. Ibid., pp. 32–5, 231–2, 381, 587–8, 618, 630–3, 664.

17. Ibid., pp. 12–15, 27, 127–8, 145, 196, 280–1, 419–20, 427, 597, 662, 683, 713.

worked out further revisions of the omnibus legislation. Finally, in January 1952 at the beginning of the second session of the Eighty-Second Congress, the two committees reported favorably on the Mc-Carran and Walter bills. A statement in the opening paragraph of the Senate report indicated the acceptance of the restrictionist viewpoint by the judiciary committees. "Today, as never before, a sound immigration and naturalization policy is essential to the preservation of our way of life because that system is the conduit through which a stream of humanity flows into the fabric of our society." Liberal members of the committees rejected this conception of immigration regulation in their minority reports. Asserting that the proposed legislation "fails to modernize our anachronistic quota system," they called for modification of the bills to provide an immigration policy consistent with the strength and traditions of the nation.[18] Meanwhile, Senators Herbert Lehman of New York and Hubert Humphrey of Minnesota introduced a liberal omnibus bill as a substitute for the McCarran-Walter measure.[19] A comparison of these two bills reveals the extent of the disagreement between the opposing sides on the fundamentals of immigration policy.

The final version of the McCarran-Walter bill contained three major sections dealing with immigration.[20] The first pertained to European immigrants, providing for the retention of the national origins plan and introducing a new method of allotting numbers within each country's quota. The preferential treatment of immigrants from northwestern Europe continued, with approximately 85 per cent of the total European quota assigned to this region. Under the plan for economic selection, half of each quota was reserved for applicants possessing special skills in demand in the United States, while relatives of citizens and resident aliens had a priority on the remaining places. Nonpreference applicants received consideration only when the priorities were unfilled. Secondly, the bill extended quotas of one hundred to the countries of Asia, stipulating that these quotas include both people born in the Asian countries and those born elsewhere of oriental

18. "Revising the Laws Relating to Immigration, Naturalization, and Nationality," *House Report No. 1365*, 82d Congress, 2d Session (Washington, 1952), pp. 326–8; "Revision of Immigration and Nationality Laws," *Senate Report No. 1137*, 82d Congress, 2d Session (Washington, 1952), Pt. I, p. 1, Pt. II, pp. 1–11.

19. *Interpreter Releases*, 29 (April 21, 1952), 104.

20. This bill also dealt with deportation and naturalization.

ancestry. To provide for people of mixed oriental ancestry and for Asian immigrants from European colonies such as Hong Kong, a special Asia-Pacific triangle quota of one hundred was established. Finally, the McCarran-Walter measure broadened the grounds for exclusion of applicants with criminal records and chronic diseases. The bill continued the prohibition on the entry of subversive aliens contained in the Internal Security Act, making a special exception for nominal members of totalitarian parties and those who for the last five years had actively opposed their former party.[21]

The Humphrey-Lehman bill differed radically from the McCarran-Walter measure. Though retaining the basic principle of national origins, the liberal bill provided for the pooling of unused quotas, which consisted chiefly of numbers assigned to Great Britain and Ireland. At the end of the year, these quota numbers were to be distributed equally among four classes of immigrants—refugees, relatives, skilled laborers, and special hardship cases—without regard to national origin. Furthermore, the bill provided for redetermining the quotas on the basis of the 1950 census, which would increase the total quota limit of 154,000 by approximately 60,000 because of the growth of the American population since 1920. In regard to oriental immigrants, the Humphrey-Lehman measure eliminated the Asia-Pacific triangle and established regular country-of-birth quotas of one hundred for the Asian countries. Finally, this bill modified the exclusion provisions by stipulating that an alien could be excluded only on the basis of factual evidence, not merely on the opinion of administrative officials. To prevent the arbitrary exclusion of immigrants, the bill established a central board to review the decision of consular officers in denying visas to applicants for admission.[22]

The differences between these two measures indicate the gulf that separated the restrictionists from the advocates of a liberal immigration policy. The basic points of divergence were the national origins quota system, the racial quotas for Asia, and the power of administrative officials to exclude undesirable aliens. Behind these specific issues lay totally different conceptions of the fundamental objectives of immigration policy. The final showdown between the opposing groups, brewing since the end of the war, arrived with the emergence of omnibus legislation on the floor of Congress.

21. *House Report No. 1365* (1952), pp. 37, 39, 45, 49–50.
22. *Interpreter Releases,* 29 (April 21, 1952), 104–5.

Congressional discussion of the McCarran and Walter bills began in April and continued through the spring until a decision was reached in late June. Though the House acted first, the key debate took place in the Senate, where the absence of limits on discussion enabled the opponents of the legislation to air their criticisms at great length. In the upper chamber a group of liberal senators led by Lehman and Humphrey attempted to win over a majority to their viewpoint by delivering a detailed critique of every aspect of the McCarran bill. The restrictionists countered this move by deliberately ignoring the liberal criticisms. At many points in the debate only a handful of sympathetic senators remained in the chamber. Throughout the discussion Senator McCarran presented the restrictionist case single-handedly, and only at the very end was he joined by other senators who supported the bill. In the House, brevity and frequent exchanges of opinion between a broad range of speakers characterized the debate. The antirestrictionist minority was much weaker in the lower chamber, and the inevitability of the final outcome somewhat dampened the enthusiasm of the discussion. Despite these differences in externals, the two debates dealt with identical issues and can be analyzed together.

Though the debate over the McCarran bill dealt with many specific immigration problems, the fundamental controversy stemmed from two conflicting conceptions of immigration policy. The restrictionists began with the premise that immigration was a potentially dangerous process which demanded careful regulation. Describing immigrants as "a stream of humanity [which] flows into the fabric of our society," Senator McCarran asserted, "If that stream is healthy, the impact on our society is salutary; but if that stream is polluted, our institutions and our way of life become infected." With millions of aliens seeking admittance to the United States, the nation had to maintain an attitude of "everlasting vigilance" in order to preserve its basic character. The McCarran bill, contended its supporters, was framed with the security of the country uppermost in mind, and they denied that it was motivated by any prejudice or hostility toward immigrants. Instead, they asserted that only by preserving its internal strength could the nation exert a positive force for good in the world. Senator McCarran declared, "The cold, hard fact is . . . that this Nation is the last hope of Western civilization; and if this oasis of the world shall be overrun, perverted, contaminated, or destroyed, then the last flickering light of humanity will be extinguished." [23] Extremely conscious of a crisis in world affairs, the restrictionists viewed the McCarran bill as a vital measure designed to protect the integrity of the nation.

The advocates of liberal legislation rejected the restrictionist conception of immigration policy and in its place advanced their own beliefs. Denying the proposition that immigration was potentially dangerous, the antirestrictionists asserted that immigration was a source of strength. "I believe," declared Representative Addonizio of New Jersey, "that our immigration legislation should be based on the assumption that the infusion of fresh new blood, of a selected stream of immigration, is good for the economic, spiritual, and cultural growth of our country." Seeing no danger to the nation through immigration, the opponents of restriction asserted that the policy adopted by Congress should express the fundamental principles of the American way of life to the people of the world. "In short," exclaimed Senator Lehman, "we cannot pass an omnibus immigration bill without taking an irrevocable stand, not only on immigration, but also on the whole complex of beliefs and practices which we call our basic institutions and traditions." The McCarran bill, described as a "restrictive, exclusionist, and oppressive" measure founded on xenophobia, would deny rather than reaffirm American ideals, contended the antirestrictionists. The result would be "the blackening of the name of America all over the world" and a loss in prestige abroad that would have a disastrous effect on the conduct of American foreign policy.[24] Viewing the struggle with Soviet Russia as primarily an ideological conflict, the antirestrictionists called for a generous immigration policy which would extend the principles of democracy beyond the narrow confines of the United States.

Here, then, was the nub of the controversy. The restrictionists advocated a stringent immigration policy designed to protect the basic institutions of the country, while their opponents charged that such a program represented a denial of the ideals and principles upon which these institutions rested. Throughout the debate the antirestrictionists concentrated their criticism on what they felt were repudiations of basic

23. *Congressional Record* (May 13, 1952), pp. 5089–90; (May 16, 1952), pp. 5330–1; (June 11, 1952), p. 7017; (June 26, 1952), p. 8215; (June 27, 1952), p. 8263.

24. Ibid. (April 23, 1952), pp. 4308, 4311; (May 13, 1952), pp. 5100, 5110; (May 15, 1952), pp. 5217, 5230.

American ideals in the McCarran bill. In their view, the greatest fault was the continuation of racial discrimination against the people of Asia and southeastern Europe. Seizing the initiative in the debate, they pressed their charges of discrimination in the face of a consistent refusal on the part of the restrictionists to discuss this question.

The opponents of the bill dealt at greatest length with the inequities of the national origins quota system. Claiming that racial equality was "an essential element of our democratic faith," the advocates of a liberal policy condemned the preferential treatment of northwestern European immigrants as undemocratic. They asserted that the national origins plan embodied a theory of Nordic supremacy which had been an integral part of German Fascism. Democracy in the United States, with a population drawn from all quarters of the globe, rested upon a belief in the innate equality of all men regardless of race, religion, or national origin, the antirestrictionists contended. By drawing a distinction between various European nationalities, the national origins plan represented "a slur and an insult" to many of the minority groups in the population and therefore tended to weaken the unity of the American people. Representative Yates of Illinois stated the ideal which the critics of national origins felt should be expressed in immigration legislation:

> Mr. Speaker, the district which I have the honor to represent draws its population from many parts of Europe and the Orient. We are cosmopolitan and proud of that fact, because we believe that we embody the essence of America—peoples of every ethnic and economic group, of all races and creeds and religions, fused in freedom and working to achieve the great American ideal of equal justice under the law.[25]

While advancing idealistic arguments which indicated their desire to repeal the national origins system entirely, the opponents of the bill limited their practical proposals to the plans for the pooling of unused quotas and the use of the 1950 census as the basis for determining the allotments. These amendments to the existing system would correct the outstanding evils by removing some of the inequal-

25. Ibid. (April 23, 1952), p. 4305; (May 13, 1952), pp. 5102, 5111; (May 14, 1952), p. 5159; (May 16, 1952), p. 5334; (May 22, 1952), p. 5774; (June 10, 1952), p. 6989; (June 27, 1952), pp. 8256, 8261.

ities in distribution among the European countries and by permitting quota immigration to reach the legal maximum, the antirestrictionists asserted. Pointing out that "almost 50 per cent of the quotas go to waste each year while human beings live in alternate currents of hope and despair," one speaker urged adoption of the liberalizing amendments in order to help the refugees from behind the iron curtain and the overcrowded populations of such strategic anti-Communist countries as Greece and Italy. While admitting that the use of the 1950 census would increase the quota limit to about 230,000 annually, Senators Lehman and Benton denied that they favored unrestricted immigration into the country. However, at one point Senator Benton declared, "Frankly, I wish that the limitation of 230,000 in our bill were a great deal higher." [26] It is evident that the antirestrictionists would willingly have followed the logic of their basic argument to the point of advocating a policy of complete individual selection with much higher numerical limits if there had been any chance for its adoption. But faced with strong restrictionist sentiment in both chambers, they compromised with plans to modify, but not radically change, existing policy.

Senator McCarran replied to the liberal criticisms by equating national origins with the principle of restriction. Refusing to discuss the equity of the national origins plan, Senator McCarran flatly asserted that any departure from the traditional quota formula "would tear down the protective immigration system." The adoption of the quota system in the 1920's had saved the nation from the disaster of continued unregulated immigration, McCarran claimed, and with some 18 or 19 million people seeking admission to the United States, any attempt to alter the system by a pooling arrangement would be inviting tragedy. "The times, Mr. President, are too perilous for us to tinker blindly with our basic institutions." McCarran carefully avoided the question of discrimination raised by the critics of national origins, but at one point he indicated his fundamental beliefs on this issue: "if we scrap the national origins formula," he asserted, "we will, in the course of a generation or so, change the ethnic and cultural composition of this Nation." [27]

26. Ibid. (April 23, 1952), pp. 4305, 4310; (May 14, 1952), pp. 5157–8; (May 19, 1952), pp. 5415–17; (May 21, 1952), pp. 5604–5.
27. Ibid. (May 16, 1952), p. 5330; (May 21, 1952), p. 5624; (May 22, 1952), pp. 5772–3.

Other supporters of the bill were less cautious than McCarran in stating the ethnic considerations which underlay the restrictionist position. Representative Wood of Idaho answered the antirestrictionist argument with a revealing statement. "It seems to me," he exclaimed, "that the question of racial origins—though I am not a follower of Hitler—there is something to it. We cannot tie a stone around its neck and drop it into the middle of the Atlantic just because it worked to the contrary in Germany." Wood and several other speakers justified the national origins system on the ground that the people of northwestern Europe shared a common cultural background with Americans and therefore provided better material for citizenship than southeastern European immigrants. The latter, according to Representative Jenkins of Ohio, "were less sympathetic to the ideals of the United States and a very large portion of them were non-Christians who had no intention whatever of accepting the ideals of western Christian civilization." The racial bias evident in this assertion was brought out even more clearly by Senator George of Georgia who declared, "Mr. President, I hope the time has not come when one must apologize for being a hateful Anglo-Saxon." A veteran of the original debate on the adoption of the quota system, George continued, "The basic purpose back of the immigration act which we finally enacted in 1924 was to preserve something of the homogeneity of the American people." [28] Though most congressmen refused to disclose their views on this point, there can be little doubt that their support of the national origins plan rested on a continuing belief in the ethnic theory so popular in the 1920's.

In regard to the provisions of the McCarran bill dealing with Asiatic immigration, the antirestrictionists advanced the same argument they had employed in criticizing the retention of the national origins plan. By establishing an arbitrary quota formula for Asian peoples based on race, the restrictionists were violating a basic democratic ideal, the critics of the bill contended. "The key and heart of the democratic philosophy is recognition of the dignity of the human kind, and of the brotherhood and fraternity of mankind," declared Senator Humphrey in pleading for equal treatment of all immigrants. Denying the danger of any inundation of the country by oriental immigrants, the opponents of restriction claimed that the continued discrimination

28. Ibid. (April 23, 1952), p. 4314; (April 25, 1952), p. 4442; (May 22, 1952), pp. 5768, 5773–4.

against Asians would give the Communists a valuable propaganda weapon in their attempt to win all Asia. The restrictionists answered this criticism by charging that their opponents were arguing on idealistic grounds completely divorced from the realities of the situation. Senator McCarran read a telegram from the major oriental organizations in the United States endorsing the principle of racial quotas and rejecting the proposals for complete equality of treatment as "ill-advised, impractical, and not in the best interests [of] persons of Asian ancestry." [29] McCarran also pointed out that the State Department had approved the bill without registering any objection to the racial quotas. Warning that some 600,000 inhabitants of the Western Hemisphere of Asian descent would be eligible for nonquota admission under a country-of-birth formula, he described this proposal as "fantastic" and concluded that his measure provided "the only fair and reasonable solution to this problem." [30]

The final point of dispute in the debate concerned the strict provisions of the McCarran bill in excluding subversive and other undesirable aliens. The critics, while agreeing on the necessity of keeping out elements harmful to American society, contended that the McCarran bill was too stringent, barring the innocent as well as the guilty. In particular they objected to the arbitrary power of the consuls and the Attorney General to deny visas and exclude aliens. Senator Moody of Michigan declared, "One man should not have the power of life and death over human beings in this way." To remedy what they termed "administrative absolutism," the antirestrictionists urged the establishment of a visa review board and a statutory board of immigration appeals.[31] These proposals shocked the restrictionists, who considered the strengthening of the exclusion provisions as the most vital part of the McCarran bill. "Our present laws are shot through with weaknesses and loopholes," asserted Senator McCarran; ". . . criminals, Communists, and subversives of all descriptions are even now gaining admission into this country like water through a

29. Ibid. (April 23, 1952), p. 4316; (May 15, 1952), pp. 5234–5; (May 21, 1952), p. 5624; (May 22, 1952), pp. 5760–2. The four organizations were the Japanese-American Citizens League, the Chinese-American Citizens League, the Filipino Federation of America, and the Korean National Association.

30. Ibid. (May 21, 1952), pp. 5623–4; (June 27, 1952), p. 8254.

31. Ibid. (April 24, 1952), p. 4400; (April 25, 1952), p. 4431; (May 22, 1952), pp. 5778–80. A Board of Immigration Appeals existed within the Justice Department, but this body possessed only advisory powers and could be overruled by the Attorney General.

sieve." Pointing out that the administrative officials who knew the situation best had recommended the provisions of his bill dealing with exclusion, McCarran rejected the liberal proposals as dangerous to national security.[32]

Despite the vigorous opposition of the antirestrictionists, Congress passed the McCarran-Walter bill by overwhelming majorities. The House acted first, approving the Walter bill on April 25 by a margin of 206 to 68. Prior to the vote, numerous liberalizing amendments were offered and rejected, in each case the House following the lead of Representative Walter. The Senate began consideration of the McCarran bill in the middle of May. At first the antirestrictionist minority tried to recommit the bill, claiming it had not received adequate consideration by the Judiciary Committee, but the restrictionists defeated this motion, 44 nays to 28 yeas. Then the advocates of a liberal policy attempted to substitute the Humphrey-Lehman measure for the McCarran bill, only to meet with defeat again by a vote of 51 to 27. As the debate entered its second week, the antirestrictionists offered their proposals as separate amendments, but when the restrictionist lines held firm, they changed their tactics and conceded passage of the bill. Realizing that at best they could only muster votes of one-third of the Senate for their position, Senators Humphrey and Lehman announced that they would conserve their strength for a final showdown after the expected presidential veto. Thus on May 22, with only a dozen senators present, the upper chamber passed the McCarran bill by a voice vote.[33] Two weeks later both houses approved a conference report ironing out minor differences between the two omnibus bills and sent the measure on to President Truman.[34]

Intense pressures were applied to the president as he debated what course to follow in regard to the McCarran-Walter bill. Organizations

32. Ibid. (May 22, 1952), p. 5778; (June 27, 1952), p. 8254.
33. Ibid. (April 24, 1952), pp. 4409, 4414, 4416; (April 25, 1952), p. 4444; (May 19, 1952), p. 5427; (May 21, 1952), p. 5630; (May 22, 1952), pp. 5803–4; New York *Times* (May 23, 1952), p. 1.
34. *Congressional Record* (June 10, 1952), p. 6991; (June 11, 1953), p. 7019. The final bill differed from the original McCarran measure only in one important particular. The conference committee added a clause from the Walter bill establishing a Joint Committee on Immigration and Nationality Policy to supervise the administration of the immigration laws and study all matters bearing on immigration policy.

representing minority groups, particularly Jewish societies, sent a continuous stream of telegrams and resolutions to the White House urging a veto, while government agencies concerned with immigration, including the State Department, advised the president to approve the bill.[35] Finally, on June 25, President Truman returned the bill to Congress accompanied by a strong veto message. Stating that the legislation failed to achieve the necessary modernization of immigration policy, the president focused his criticism on the retention of the national origins quota system. This scheme of restriction kept immigration at an extremely low level, the president asserted. "The greatest vice of the present quota system, however, is that it discriminates, deliberately and intentionally, against many of the peoples of the world," he continued. "It is incredible to me that, in the year 1952, we should again be enacting into law such a slur on the patriotism, the capacity, and the decency of a large part of our citizenry." Truman concluded by calling for the adoption of legislation creating an immigration system that would be "a fitting instrument for our foreign policy and a true reflection of the ideals we stand for, at home and abroad." [36]

The veto message touched off the final debate in Congress. In a statement to the press, Senator McCarran asserted that the message conformed to the Communist party line and he termed the veto "one of the most un-American acts I have ever witnessed in my public career." [37] On the floor of Congress the restrictionists stressed the fact that the government agencies in direct contact with immigration problems had approved the bill and implied that political expediency was the sole reason for the veto. Representative Walter, unwilling to attack the leader of his party directly, charged that the veto message was written "by the President's ghost writers who have neglected to do one thing—read the bill." The antirestrictionists responded by praising the veto message as a brilliant recapitulation of their criti-

35. New York *Times* (May 24, 1952), p. 12; (June 12, 1952), p. 18; (June 16, 1952), p. 5. The State Department recommendation was disclosed on the floor of Congress when Senator Benton stated that he had telephoned Secretary of State Acheson, who told him that he had reluctantly agreed with the decision of the experts in the department approving the bill. *Congressional Record* (June 27, 1952), p. 8258.

36. *Congressional Record* (June 25, 1952), pp. 8082–3.

37. New York *Times* (June 26, 1952), p. 1.

cisms of the legislation. Realizing that their only chance to sustain
the veto lay in the Senate, the advocates of a liberal policy engaged
in an all-out assault on the McCarran bill in the upper chamber. They
used every tactic at their command, including threats of reprisal by
minority groups at the polls. Senator Benton, warning that the foreign born were enraged over the retention of national origins, declared, "If the Presidential veto, by some misadventure, is not sustained today . . . I predict that more than one seat in this chamber
is going to change hands, based on this vote alone." [38]

The final protests by the antirestrictionists were of no avail. On
June 26 the House, as expected, overrode the president's veto by the
decisive margin of 278 to 113. The next day, in a tense roll-call vote,
the Senate passed the McCarran-Walter bill, 57 yeas to 26 nays.[39]
The shift of two affirmative votes would have sustained the veto, but
the restrictionist lines held firm in the final test. Characteristically, an
analysis of the vote reveals a sectional rather than a party alignment
in both houses. A majority of congressmen from the Northeast supported the veto, but legislators from the other three sections of the
country, led by the southern representatives, voted overwhelmingly
in favor of the McCarran-Walter measure.[40] The continuing alliance
between the southern and western restrictionists in Congress dashed
the hopes of the antirestrictionists for a modernization of the immigration system. Though the opponents of the bill persisted in their agitation for a liberal policy, the passage of the McCarran-Walter bill by
decisive majorities made any major revisions extremely unlikely in
the near future.[41] Thus the long postwar debate over the nature of

38. *Congressional Record* (June 26, 1952), pp. 8214–18; (June 27, 1952), pp.
8254–8.

39. Ibid. (June 26, 1952), p. 8225; (June 27, 1952), p. 8267.

40. The sectional breakdown was as follows:

Section	Senate		House	
	YES	NO	YES	NO
Northeast	8	10	56	66
Midwest	15	8	96	32
South	19	3	91	3
Far West	15	5	35	12

41. On September 4, 1952, President Truman issued an executive order establishing a special Commission on Immigration and Naturalization. Composed of
seven men, the presidential commission held hearings in the major cities of the

American immigration policy terminated in a complete triumph of the restrictionist viewpoint.

The controversial nature of the McCarran-Walter Immigration Act makes' it difficult to assess the significance of the legislation. The critics of the law interpreted it as a denial of democratic beliefs and an expression of a racist philosophy alien to American ideals. The restrictionists viewed it as a beneficial measure which dealt realistically with the dangers inherent in immigration. Both these interpretations represented extreme viewpoints highly colored by the partisan emotions engendered in the heat of controversy. To gain an objective understanding of the true import of the measure, we must discard both versions and examine the problem from a different angle. Perhaps the most instructive approach would be to compare the McCarran Act with previous immigration legislation, particularly with the original quota law of 1924, from the standpoint of the four factors involved in the formulation of immigration policy.

The economic factor received the least emphasis in the passage of the McCarran bill. Considerations of the impact of immigrants on the wage scale and employment conditions, as well as the broader question of the relationship between immigration and population trends, had been uppermost in the minds of restrictionists in the late 19th and early 20th centuries. During the debate over the quota system in the 1920's, the economic aspect of immigration received less attention than previously, but the onset of the depression in the next decade elevated this factor to a position of primary importance again with demands for "American jobs for Americans." Yet in the postwar period the restrictionists, perhaps because of the continuation of war-induced prosperity, did not emphasize this factor. To be sure, a plan of economic selection was incorporated into the McCarran bill, but neither the supporters nor the opponents of the bill appeared to con-

United States during the fall of 1952 at which the overwhelming burden of the testimony was in favor of the liberalization of immigration policy. The commission recommended sweeping revision of the immigration laws, including the elimination of the national origins system, in its report submitted in January 1953. Despite President Eisenhower's concurrence with these views, no legislative action has yet resulted. *Hearings before the President's Commission on Immigration and Naturalization,* Washington, 1952; President's Commission on Immigration and Naturalization, *Whom We Shall Welcome,* Washington, 1953.

sider this new concept as a matter of vital importance. Demands for the protection of the native American worker and references to competition from cheap foreign labor were conspicuous by their absence during the debate over the McCarran Act. A split in the ranks of organized labor, with the AFL supporting restriction, though much less strenuously than before, and the CIO opposing it, helps explain this situation. However, the basic reason for the lack of interest in the economic aspect of immigration was an engrossing concern on the part of both restrictionists and their opponents with other considerations. Thus it seems safe to assert that the primary motivation of the McCarran Act was not a desire to protect the American wage earner and his high standard of living.

A second factor in the formulation of immigration policy is the social and ethnic one, comprehending the problem of the assimilation of immigrants. The role of this factor in the passage of the McCarran Act is extremely difficult to assess because of the reticence of the restrictionists to disclose their views. In the debates over the quota system and the national origins plan in the 1920's and in the discussions of the Mexican and Filipino immigration problems of the early 1930's, the restrictionists had openly avowed their belief in a theory of racial differences. Stating that the people of northwestern Europe were endowed with qualities better suited to the American way of life, and implying, though rarely openly proclaiming, the innate superiority of the "Nordics," the restrictionists had urged severe limitation on the influx of southeastern Europeans and Mexicans and outright exclusion of all oriental races. In the postwar period only the most extreme restrictionists voiced these beliefs, and many moderate supporters of restriction indicated a willingness to end the Asiatic exclusion policy. Yet even the moderates insisted upon the retention of a quota system based on the racial theories they no longer expressed openly. Referring guardedly to the need for the preservation of the ethnic and cultural composition of the American population, the restrictionists favored continuing the preferential treatment of immigrants from northwestern Europe. The conclusion appears inescapable that ethnic considerations played an important role in the passage of the McCarran Act.

At this point it might be useful to inquire into the part played by such considerations among the opponents of restriction. Proclaiming a belief in complete racial equality, the antirestrictionists urged the elimination of all discriminatory features from the immigration laws. The question arises whether this position stemmed from a genuine belief in the ideal or resulted from the fact that these men were members of minority groups or represented districts composed of minority groups which felt they had been slighted by the national origins system. During the debate over the national origins plan in the 1920's, the spokesmen for minority groups had revealed less interest in ideals than in the practical effect of the quota system on the nationalities they represented. The strong objections of Jewish and Italian organizations to the McCarran bill, as well as the geographical pattern of the final vote, indicates that much of the opposition to the bill stemmed from special group interests of ethnic blocs in the Northeast. This is not to deny that many antirestrictionists held a genuine belief in the ideal of ethnic equality, but it does seem clear that the principles espoused by the opponents of the bill rested upon the same pragmatic and emotional foundations which underlay the restrictionist viewpoint.

In connection with the social and ethnic factor, there arises the question of the role of religious prejudice in the formulation of immigration policy. The national origins system tended to favor immigration from predominantly Protestant countries and to limit the influx from areas with large Jewish and Catholic populations. Reluctance of congressmen to manifest religious bias in public makes it difficult to generalize on this question. Anti-Semitism may be guessed but cannot be proved as a factor furthering the national origins system. It may be that the outspoken Jewish criticism of the McCarran bill reinforced this bias. Anti-Catholic feeling is much less evident, though probably the southern congressmen considered Protestantism as one of the important aspects of the cultural complex which they wished to preserve. However, McCarran himself was a devout Catholic, two of his daughters having become nuns, and the National Catholic Welfare Conference endorsed his bill.[42] Other Catholic spokesmen opposed the measure, but there is no evidence to show that the Church considered the McCarran bill a manifestation of anti-Catholicism. It would appear that if religious considerations had a bearing on the formulation of

42. *Congressional Directory* (1954), p. 78; *Congressional Record* (May 19, 1952), p. 5408.

the restrictionist policy, they were subsidiary to the ethnic aspect.

Consideration of the influence of immigration policy on foreign relations forms a third factor, one which received a great deal of emphasis
during the debate over the McCarran bill. Traditionally, the restrictionists have tended to minimize the relationship between foreign policy and immigration legislation, arguing that immigration is solely
a matter of domestic concern. The adoption of Japanese exclusion in
1924 over the protests of the State Department and the Japanese ambassador marks the most notable example of this trend. However, in
the postwar period, the restrictionists retreated somewhat from this
extreme viewpoint by grudgingly approving the admission of displaced persons and agreeing to the termination of the oriental exclusion policy. Nevertheless, they still maintained that domestic considerations were of paramount importance. It was their opponents who
placed the primary stress on the foreign policy factor by asserting
that immigration legislation was an expression of American ideals to
the world. Protesting that the McCarran bill expressed a spirit of hostility toward foreigners, the antirestrictionists warned that the passage
of the bill would lower American prestige abroad. Though the State
Department approved the measure, probably because it repealed
Asiatic exclusion, the McCarran Act was essentially a denial of the
liberal premise that international considerations should play a dominating role in the determination of immigration policy.

Nationalism is the fourth factor, and there can be little doubt that
this aspect was the decisive consideration in the passage of the Mc-
Carran bill. Concern for the integrity of the nation has always been
the driving force behind the restriction of immigration. In the 1920's
the advocates of restriction linked nationalism with ethnic theory in
arguing for a quota system which would preserve the racial homogeneity, and thereby the fundamental unity, of the American people.
A basic change occurred in the late 1930's, which developed more
fully in the postwar period. Instead of viewing nationalism solely from
the standpoint of the ethnic composition of the population, the restrictionists, fearing the spread of Communism and Fascism to the
United States, came to emphasize nationalism in the sense of loyalty
to the nation. After the war, the basic concern of the restrictionists
was with the internal security of the United States, which they believed
was menaced by Communist infiltration into American society. The

most direct expression of this concern was the passage of the Internal Security Act of 1950 with its stringent provisions barring the entry of subversive aliens. In the debate over the McCarran bill, the nationalistic emphasis on security received a broader application. The suspicion with which the restrictionists regarded all immigrants implied a belief that loyalty to the nation stemmed from birth in the United States and could not be easily instilled in the foreign born. Alarmed by the continuing intensity of the cold war with Soviet Russia, the supporters of the McCarran bill believed that strict control of immigration was essential for the preservation of national security.

This survey of the four factors bearing on the formulation of immigration policy indicates that the motivating force behind the McCarran Act was a concern for the integrity of the nation during a critical period in its history. The legislation did continue an immigration system which in effect discriminated against people of Asia and southeastern Europe, but there is little evidence to show that racial prejudice was the primary reason for the passage of the act. Undoubtedly the more extreme restrictionists, especially the southerners, actively approved of this aspect of the McCarran bill. But the moderate supporters of restriction appear to have been motivated more by a reluctance to alter a time-tested method of limiting immigration than by racial prejudices. The national origins quota system had been in existence for nearly thirty years, and in the course of that time had reduced immigration very effectively. Fearful that changes in the national origins plan might endanger the nation by increasing the flow of immigrants, the majority of congressmen registered a decision in favor of preserving the status quo in immigration policy. Thus the passage of the McCarran bill was in essence an act of conservatism rather than of intolerance.

In the last analysis, the McCarran Act represented the triumph of nationalism over international considerations in the determination of American immigration policy. Both restrictionists and antirestrictionists agreed that immigration legislation should be framed in reference to the ideological and power conflict with Soviet Russia which dominated the minds of all Americans in the middle of the 20th century. The opponents of restriction believed that the expansion of Russia could be halted only by combating the doctrines of Communism throughout the world, and therefore they advocated an immigration policy designed to foster good will in foreign countries. Thus in his final plea in the debate, Senator Humphrey declared, "The issue is whether we shall have the respect of people all around the world." On the other hand, in his concluding speech Senator McCarran exclaimed, "If we destroy the internal security of this country by opening the floodgates of unlimited immigration, without screening and without curtailment, we will have destroyed the national security of the United States." [43] Convinced that the maintenance of the United States as a bastion against Communism was of paramount importance in the cold war, the restrictionists insisted upon an immigration policy which sought to protect the internal strength of the nation. By casting their votes for the McCarran bill, a majority of congressmen recorded their conviction that the primary objective of immigration policy was to preserve the national integrity of the United States.

43. *Congressional Record* (June 27, 1952), p. 8267.

APPENDIX A: *Sources of Immigration, 1820-1950*

THE TABLE BELOW lists the ratio of immigrants from northwestern Europe to those from southeastern Europe by decades. The third column lists the percentage from other areas of the world, including the Western Hemisphere, Asia, Africa, and Australia–New Zealand. Note particularly the reversal of the ratio in the 1890's, when the new immigration first assumed heavy proportions. The advent of restriction again altered the pattern in the 1920's, with the non-European areas becoming important contributors to the immigrant flow. It should be borne in mind that the higher percentages for non-European areas after 1920 reflect a relative increase in proportion to European immigration, not an absolute rise in numbers.

Decade	Percentage from Northwestern Europe	Percentage from Southeastern Europe	Percentage from Non-European Areas
1820–30	68.0	2.2	29.8
1831–40	81.7	1.0	17.3
1841–50	93.0	0.3	6.7
1851–60	93.6	0.8	5.6
1861–70	87.8	1.5	10.7
1871–80	73.6	7.2	19.2
1881–90	72.0	18.3	9.7
1891–1900	44.6	51.9	3.5
1901–10	21.7	70.8	7.5
1911–20	17.4	59.0	23.6
1921–30	31.2	29.1	39.7
1931–40	37.4	28.6	34.0
1941–50	47.3	12.7	40.0
1820–1950	48.4	36.2	15.4

Sources: U.S. Immigration and Naturalization Service, *Monthly Review, 2* (December 1944), 77; *Annual Report* (1950), table 4.

APPENDIX B: *Quota and Nonquota Immigration, 1925-52*

THE TABLE BELOW shows the proportion of quota to nonquota immigrants in the annual immigration to the United States. The nonquota figures include both Western Hemisphere immigrants and relatives of American citizens from European areas. The heavy influx of war brides accounts for the rapid rise in nonquota immigration in the late 1940's. It should be noted that from 1950 until 1952 quota immigration exceeded the annual limit of 154,000 because of the admission of displaced persons mortgaged against future quotas.

Year	Quota Immigrants	Nonquota Immigrants	Total Immigrants
1925	145,971	148,343	294,314
1926	157,432	147,056	304,488
1927	158,090	177,105	335,175
1928	153,231	154,024	307,255
1929	146,918	132,760	279,678
1930	141,497	100,203	241,700
1931	54,118	43,021	97,139
1932	12,983	22,593	35,576
1933	8,220	14,848	23,068
1934	12,483	16,987	29,470
1935	17,207	17,749	34,956
1936	18,675	17,654	36,329
1937	27,762	22,482	50,244
1938	42,494	25,401	67,985
1939	62,402	20,596	82,998
1940	51,997	18,759	70,756
1941	36,220	15,556	51,776
1942	14,597	14,184	28,781
1943	9,045	14,680	23,725
1944	9,394	19,157	28,551
1945	11,623	26,496	38,119
1946	29,095	79,626	108,721
1947	70,701	76,591	147,292
1948	92,526	78,044	170,570
1949	113,046	75,271	188,317

Year	Quota Immigrants	Nonquota Immigrants	Total Immigrants
1950	197,460	51,727	249,187
1951	156,547	49,170	205,717
1952	194,247	71,273	265,520
Total*	2,145,961	1,678,356	3,824,317

Sources: U.S. Immigration and Naturalization Service, *Monthly Review, 3* (August 1945), 189; *4* (January 1947), 85; *Annual Report* (1950), table 7; (1952), tables 1, 3.

Bibliographical Essay

RECENT YEARS have witnessed a considerable growth of interest in the history of immigration in the United States. Both historians and sociologists have contributed to an expanding body of literature, though these scholars have tended to neglect the question of governmental policy toward immigrants. Despite the lack of secondary treatments of immigration policy, there is a wealth of source material which has formed the basis of the present study. Because of the varied character of the immigration problems covered in this study, it has been thought best to analyze briefly the nature of the source material and then proceed with a more detailed description under several major subject headings.

I. Nature of the Source Material

MANUSCRIPT SOURCES

Three manuscript collections have been consulted, primarily for material in the period prior to the second World War. The Papers of the House and Senate Immigration Committees in the National Archives constitute the most extensive and useful collection. Petitions from individuals and organizations, letters from the committee chairmen to constituents, memoranda from various members of the committees, and unpublished hearings and reports comprise the bulk of the material. All help to provide a clearer understanding of the pressures on the committees and the views of individual members. The Roosevelt Papers in the Franklin D. Roosevelt Library, Hyde Park, New York, form a second important source of material. The White House files for the 1930's shed considerable light on Roosevelt's views on immigration problems. The Coolidge Papers in the Library of Congress proved much less helpful; this small collection contains only a few items bearing on immigration.

GOVERNMENTAL SOURCES

Government documents, particularly the record of Congressional transactions, comprise the most important sources for a study of immigration policy. The *Congressional Record,* with its complete reporting of all speeches and votes in Congress, is of fundamental importance. Though the debates are often dull and repetitious, they provide the best means of determining the views of congressmen on legislation. The *Hearings* of Congressional committees are an equally significant source, indicating what interests support and oppose individual measures. The frequent cross-examination of witnesses at the hearings often reveals the underlying motives behind legislation. Somewhat less valuable are the committee *Reports,* which explain the nature and objectives of proposed bills. The *Reports* tend to justify measures rather than state openly the reasons for the committee's action.

Though mainly concerned with the administration of the laws, the Immigration and Naturalization Service has played some part in the formulation of policy. The *Annual Reports of the Commissioner-General of Immigration* (Washington, 1925–32), first published separately, then summarized in the *Annual Reports of the Secretary of Labor* (Washington, 1933–40), and finally printed as *Annual Reports,* U.S. Immigration and Naturalization Service (Washington, 1941–52), contain considerable material on immigration policy as well as a wealth of statistics. The *Monthly Review* of the Immigration and Naturalization Service, published from 1943 until 1952, is a valuable supplement to the official reports.

PERIODICALS

Interpreter Releases (Foreign Language Information Service, 1924–40; Common Council for American Unity, 1941–52) is an indispensable guide to developments in the field of immigration legislation. Published by a New York organization interested in furthering the assimilation of aliens, this information bulletin chronicles from time to time the legislative proceedings on all measures relating to immigrants. In addition, the files of the New York *Times* were examined from 1924 to 1952 for supplementary material on legislative and executive action.

II. The Development of Restriction

GOVERNMENTAL SOURCES

There is a considerable body of material on the enactment of the quota system. For the 1921 law, "Percentage Plans for Restriction of Immigration," *Hearings before the House Committee on Immigration and Naturalization,* 66th Congress, 1st Session (Washington, 1919) and "Restriction of Immigration," *House Report No. 4,* 67th Congress, 1st Session (Washington, 1921) are valuable. "Immigration and Labor," *Hearings before the House Committee on Immigration and Naturalization,* 67th Congress, 3d Session (Washington, 1923) contains the views of business interests and organized labor. The most important hearings in this period are "Restriction of Immigration," ibid., 68th Congress,

1st Session (Washington, 1924) and "Selective Immigration Legislation," *Hearings before the Senate Committee on Immigration,* 68th Congress, 1st Session (Washington, 1924), which contain voluminous testimony on the quota system. "Japanese Immigration Legislation," ibid., 68th Congress, 1st Session (Washington, 1924) deals with the problem of oriental exclusion. The best statement of the philosophy behind the quota system is given in "Restriction of Immigration," *House Report No. 350,* 68th Congress, 1st Session (Washington, 1921).

For the earlier period, the 42 volumes of the Dillingham Report represent a landmark in the development of the restrictionist movement. *Abstracts of the Reports of the Immigration Commission* (2 vols. Washington, 1911) is a useful summary which contains the recommendations and conclusions of this investigating committee.

CONTEMPORARY ARTICLES AND BOOKS

Two series of popular magazine articles played an important role in influencing attitudes toward immigration in the 1920's. Kenneth Roberts stressed the dangers of a postwar flood of immigrants in the *Saturday Evening Post* in 1920–21, the most significant articles being "Plain Remarks on Immigration for Plain Americans," *203* (February 12, 1921) and "The Existence of an Emergency," *203* (April 30, 1921). Equally influential was the series written by Gino Speranza in the *World's Work, 47* (November 1923–February 1924). Entitled "The Immigration Peril," these articles applied the theory of racial homogeneity to immigration problems.

The key book in the transit of European ethnic theories to the United States is Madison Grant, *The Passing of the Great Race* (New York, 1916). Other elaborations of this theme include Lothrop Stoddard, *The Revolt Against Civilization* (New York, 1922) and Charles Gould, *America, a Family Matter* (New York, 1922). Two books by psychologists which fostered the growth of racist theory are Carl Brigham, *A Study of American Intelligence* (Princeton, 1923) and William MacDougall, *Is America Safe for Democracy?* (New York, 1921).

GENERAL WORKS

A satisfactory general history of American immigration has yet to be written. George Stephenson, *A History of American Immigration* (New York, 1926) is sketchy but does contain the best over-all summary of the development of restriction down to 1924. Carl Wittke, *We Who Built America* (New York, 1939) concentrates on immigrant contributions to American life. The best comprehensive account of immigration as an international phenomenon is Maurice Davie, *World Immigration*

(New York, 1936). Henry Pratt Fairchild, *Immigration* (New York, 1925) deals at length with immigration policy, but this book is marred by a strong restrictionist bias, while Jeremiah Jenks and W. Jett Lauck, *The Immigration Problem* (New York, 1917) stresses the economic aspects of immigration.

The only book dealing solely with the general history of immigration policy is Roy L. Garis, *Immigration Restriction* (New York, 1927). Written by an avowed restrictionist, this work is of value mainly for its full description of the various laws regulating immigration. A recent book by John Higham, *Strangers in the Land: Patterns of American Nativism, 1860–1925* (New Brunswick, 1955), is a highly perceptive study of the evolution of the restrictionist philosophy. A doctoral dissertation, Joseph Taylor, "The Restriction of European Immigration, 1890–1924" (University of California, 1936) treats of the legislative development of the quota system.

Of the numerous books on racial theory, the most useful are Louis Snyder, *Race, a History of Modern Ethnic Theories* (New York, 1939) and M. F. Ashley Montague, *Man's Most Dangerous Myth: the Fallacy of Race* (New York, 1948). David Bowers, ed., *Foreign Influences in American Life* (Princeton, 1944) contains a series of essays and critical bibliographies on the impact of immigrants on American society. The essay by Stow Persons, "The Americanization of the Immigrant," a penetrating analysis of popular attitudes toward immigrants, is the most valuable item in this collection. T. J. Woofter, *Races and Ethnic Groups in American Life* (New York, 1933) is another useful treatment of this subject.

The standard work on the problem of Chinese immigrants is Mary Coolidge, *Chinese Immigration* (New York, 1909), while Yamoto Ichihashi, *Japanese in the United States* (Stanford University, 1932) deals fully with immigration from Japan. Thomas Bailey, *Theodore Roosevelt and the Japanese-American Crises* (Stanford University, 1934) and A. Whitney Griswold, *The Far Eastern Policy of the United States* (New York, 1938) cover the diplomatic aspect of American policy toward Japanese immigrants. Also useful on the question of Japanese immigration are Raymond Buell, "The Development of Anti-Japanese Agitation in the United States," *Political Science Quarterly*, 37 (1922), 605–38, and 38 (1923), 57–81, and "Japanese Immigration," *World Peace Foundation Pamphlets*, 8 (Boston, 1925), 281–380. On the enactment of Japanese exclusion, Rodman Paul, *The Abrogation of the Gentlemen's Agreement* (Cambridge, Mass., 1936) is an excellent concise study.

III. National Origins

MANUSCRIPT SOURCES

The files of the House and Senate Immigration Committees for the years 1927–29 in the National Archives are very helpful in tracing the pressure applied for and against the national origins plan. A series of letters from Albert Johnson to persons interested in this issue provide an insight into the views of this key figure.

GOVERNMENT SOURCES

The calculations used in determining the national origins quotas are given in the reports of the Quota Board, "National Origin Provision of the Immigration Act of 1924," *Senate Document No. 190,* 69th Congress, 2d Session (Washington, 1927); "Immigration Quotas on the Basis of National Origin," ibid., *No. 65,* 70th Congress, 1st Session (Washington, 1928); and ibid., *No. 259,* 70th Congress, 2d Session (Washington, 1929). Of these, the report for 1928 gives the fullest explanation of the methods employed.

The views of groups and organizations were revealed at three hearings held on this question, "National Origins Provision, Immigration Act of 1924," *Hearings before the House Committee on Immigration and Naturalization,* 69th Congress, 2d Session (Washington, 1927); "National Origins Provision of Immigration Law," *Hearings before the Senate Committee on Immigration,* 70th Congress, 1st Session (Washington, 1928); and "National Origins Provision of Immigration Law," ibid., 70th Congress, 2d Session (Washington, 1929). "Repeal of 'National Origins' Provision of Immigration Act of 1924," *House Report No. 2029,* 69th Congress, 2d Session (Washington, 1927) and "Postponement of 'National Origins' Provision of the Immigration Act of 1924," *Senate Report No. 2260,* 69th Congress, 2d Session (Washington, 1927) give the opinions of committee members on the national origins question.

CONTEMPORARY ARTICLES AND BOOKS

The files of *Eugenics* and the *Minute Man,* official bulletin of the Sons of the American Revolution, for this period reveal the viewpoint of the eugenicists and the patriots on the national origins question. The positions of the veterans and organized labor are made clear in the *Summary of the Proceedings of the National Conventions of the American Legion, 1925–1930* and the *Reports of the Proceedings of the Annual Conventions of the American Federation of Labor, 1925–1930.*

Albert B. Hart gave a moderate statement of the restrictionist position in "The National Origins Plan for Restricting Immigration,"

Current History, 30 (1929), 480–2, while Madison Grant asserted the extreme racist argument in "America for Americans," *Forum, 74* (1925), 346–55; Albert Hopkins, "Which Races are Best?" *Scientific American, 132* (1925), 77–9; and Ales Hrdlicka, "The Choice of Future Americans," *Outlook, 154* (1930), 99. Jerome Dowd, "The Protection of National Culture as the Proper Basis of Immigration Restriction," *Scientific Monthly, 23* (1926), 206–9, represents an attempt to justify restriction on cultural rather than racial grounds.

Henry Pratt Fairchild, *The Melting Pot Mistake* (Boston, 1926) is a reasoned statement of the theory of racial homogeneity. Less temperate is Lothrop Stoddard, *Reforging America* (New York, 1927). Edward Lewis' *America, Nation or Confusion* (New York, 1928) was written as a defense of the national origins plan and is the most persuasive assertion of the restrictionist case. A less able defense is Martha Ragsdale, *The National Origins Plan* (1928), with a foreword by Roy Garis. The most significant critique of the Nordic theory written in this period is Frank Hankins, *The Racial Basis of Civilization* (New York, 1926).

GENERAL WORKS

There is no scholarly analysis of the national origins controversy in print. The American Council of Learned Societies published the "Report of the Committee on Linguistic and National Stocks in the Population of the United States" in the American Historical Association, *Annual Report, 1931, 1* (Washington, 1932), 103–441. This report describes the role of the Council in assisting the Quota Board to determine national origins, and defends the methods employed. William Myers and Walter Newton, *The Hoover Administration, a Documented Narrative* (New York, 1936) contains information on Hoover's role in the national origins controversy.

IV. Mexican and Philippine Immigration

MANUSCRIPT SOURCES

The Coolidge Papers in the Library of Congress contain letters from Secretary of State Kellogg to President Coolidge on thè issue of Mexican immigration which help clarify the position of the State Department on this issue.

GOVERNMENT SOURCES

Very extensive hearings were held on the general subject of Western Hemisphere immigration from 1925 to 1930 at which the major concern was the influx of Mexicans. The most important of these hearings are "Seasonal Agricultural Laborers from Mexico," *Hearings before the House Committee on Immigration and Naturalization*, 69th Congress, 1st Session (Washington, 1926); "Immigration for Countries of the Western Hemisphere," ibid., 70th Congress, 1st Session (Washington, 1928); "Western Hemisphere Immigration," ibid., 71st Congress, 2d Session (Washington, 1930); and "Restriction of Western Hemisphere Immigration," *Hearings before the Senate Committee on Immigration*, 70th Congress, 1st Session (Washington, 1928). Briefer and of less significance are "Immigration from Latin America, the West Indies, and Canada," *Hearings before the House Committee on Immigration and Naturalization*, 68th Congress, 2d Session (Washington, 1925) and "Immigration from Mexico," ibid., 71st Congress, 2d Session (Washington, 1930). The three committee reports dealing with legislation in this field are "Subject Certain Immigrants, Born in Countries of the Western Hemisphere, to the Quota under the Immigration Law," *Senate Report No. 1343*, 70th Congress, 2d Session (Washington, 1928); "Immigration from Countries of the Western Hemisphere," *House Report No. 896*, 71st Congress, 2d Session (Washington, 1930); and "Restriction of Immigration from the Republic of Mexico," ibid., *No. 1594*, 71st Congress, 2d Session (Washington, 1930).

There was only one hearing on the question of direct exclusion of Filipinos, "Exclusion of Immigration from the Philippine Islands," *Hearings before the House Committee on Immigration and Naturalization*, 71st Congress, 1st Session (Washington, 1930). However, the immigration issue received considerable attention at two hearings on Philippine independence bills, "Independence for the Philippine Islands," *Hearings before the House Committee on Insular Affairs*, 72d Congress, 1st Session (Washington, 1932) and "Independence for the Philippine Islands," *Hearings before the Senate Committee on Territorial and Insular Affairs*, 72d Congress, 1st Session (Washington, 1932). The reports on these bills, "Philippine Independence," *House Report No. 806*, 72d Congress, 1st Session (Washington, 1932) and "Philippine Independence," *Senate Report No. 354*, 72d Congress, 1st Session (Washington, 1932) also touch on the immigration issue.

CONTEMPORARY ARTICLES

Advocates of the restriction of Mexican immigration published a great many articles in popular magazines in support of their position. Kenneth Roberts wrote a series for the *Saturday Evening Post*, "Wet and Other Mexicans," *200* (February 4, 1928), "Mexicans or Ruin," *200* (February 18, 1928), and "The Docile Mexicans," *200* (March

10, 1928). Other articles of this nature include Richard Washburn Child, "Our Open Back Doors," *American Legion Monthly, 5* (1928), 18–19, 52–6; C. M. Goethe, "The Influx of Mexican Amerinds," *Eugenics, 2* (1929), 6–9; and Roy Garis, "The Mexicanization of American Business," *Saturday Evening Post, 202* (February 8, 1930).

GENERAL WORKS

Manuel Gamio, *Mexican Immigration to the United States* (Chicago, 1930) and Bruno Lasker, *Filipino Immigration* (Chicago, 1931) are excellent studies of these two migrations. The evolution of Philippine independence is fully described in Grayson Kirk, *Philippine Independence* (New York, 1936) and in Garel Grunder and William Livezey, *The Philippines and the United States* (Norman, Oklahoma, 1951).

V. *Immigration Problems of the 1930's*

MANUSCRIPT SOURCES

The Papers of the House and Senate Immigration Committees in the National Archives provide a good deal of information on immigration matters in this period, particularly on the attempts to reduce immigration during the depression. The Roosevelt Papers in the Franklin D. Roosevelt Library at Hyde Park also contain a considerable body of material relating to immigration policy in the 1930's. Consisting of correspondence between Roosevelt and private citizens, and memoranda from executive departments, these papers are most useful for information on the administration's policy toward refugees.

GOVERNMENTAL SOURCES

Most of the Congressional material for this period deals with the problem of immigration during the depression. For the abortive attempts to reduce the quotas, the two key hearings are "Suspension for Two Years of General Immigration into the United States," *Hearings before the Senate Committee on Immigration,* 71st Congress, 3d Session (Washington, 1930) and "Suspension and Restriction of General Immigration," *Hearings before the House Committee on Immigration and Naturalization,* 72d Congress, 1st Session (Washington, 1932). Further information is contained in "Immigration," *Hearings before the House Committee on Rules,* 71st Congress, 3d Session (Washington, 1931) and "Immigration," ibid., 72d Congress, 1st Session (Washington, 1932). Both the majority and minority viewpoints inside the House Immigration Committee are given in "Restriction of Immigration," *House Report No. 2405,* 71st Congress, 3d Session (Washington,

1931) and "Restriction of Immigration," *House Report No. 1016*, 72d Congress, 1st Session (Washington, 1932).

The U.S. Department of State, *The Immigration Work of the Department of State and its Consular Offices* (Washington, 1935) explains the origins and nature of the public charge policy. Further details on the administrative regulation of immigration are given in the U.S. Department of State, *Press Releases* (1929–37).

The attempts of the opponents of restriction to liberalize both the admission of relatives and the public charge policy can be traced in three sets of hearings, "To Exempt from the Quota Aged Parents of American Citizens," *Hearings before the House Committee on Immigration and Naturalization*, 72d Congress, 1st Session (Washington, 1932); "Review of the Action of Consular Officers in Refusing Immigration Visas," ibid., 72d Congress, 1st Session (Washington, 1932); and "Review of Refusals of Visas by Consular Officers," ibid., 73d Congress, 1st Session (Washington, 1933). "Exemption from the Quota of Aged Fathers and Mothers of American Citizens," *House Report No. 245*, 72d Congress, 1st Session (Washington, 1932) and "Appeal in Certain Refusals of Immigration Visas," *House Report No. 1193*, 72d Congress, 1st Session (Washington, 1932) describe the unsuccessful bills which resulted from the hearings.

On the refugee problem, "Certificates of Registry to Certain Political and Religious Refugees Living in the United States," *House Report No. 1097*, 73d Congress, 2d Session (Washington, 1934) gives the details of the Russian Refugee Act. The only Congressional materials dealing with the more significant question of German refugees are the hearings on Senator Wagner's proposal to take in 20,000 children, "Admission of German Refugee Children," *Hearings before the House Committee on Immigration and Naturalization*, 76th Congress, 1st Session (Washington, 1939) and "Admission of German Refugee Children," *Joint Hearings before a Subcommittee of the Senate Committee on Immigration and a Subcommittee of the House Committee on Immigration and Naturalization*, 76th Congress, 1st Session (Washington, 1939).

The report of the Fish committee, "Investigation of Communist Propaganda," *House Report No. 2290*, 71st Congress, 3d Session (Washington, 1931), contains the earliest recommendations on the issue of subversives. The viewpoints of various groups on this question are revealed in "Exclusion and Expulsion of Communists," *Hearings before the House Committee on Immigration and Naturalization*, 72d Congress, 1st Session (Washington, 1932) and "To Exclude and Expel

Alien Fascists and Communists," ibid., 74th Congress, 1st Session (Washington, 1935). "Exclusion and Expulsion of Alien Communists," *House Report No. 1353*, 72d Congress, 1st Session (Washington, 1932) and "Exclude and Deport Aliens Who Are Fascists and Communists," *House Report No. 1023*, 74th Congress, 1st Session (Washington, 1932) explain'the nature of the bills dealing with the problem of subversive immigrants.

OTHER PRINTED SOURCES

William Myers, ed., *The State Papers and other Public Writings of Herbert Hoover* (2 vols. New York, 1932) and *The Memoirs of Herbert Hoover: the Great Depression, 1929–1941* (New York, 1952) contain information on the evolution of the public charge policy. Samuel Rosenman, ed., *The Public Papers and Addresses of Franklin D. Roosevelt* (9 vols. New York, 1938–41) proved very useful, especially on the refugee problem. This work includes notes written by Roosevelt explaining the background of many of his statements and actions.

CONTEMPORARY ARTICLES

An issue of the *Annals of the American Academy of Political and Social Science*, "Refugees," *203* (May 1939) is devoted entirely to the refugee problem. The articles trace the historical development of the refugee situation and suggest possible solutions. Of the many popular articles written in this period in favor of admitting refugees, the most significant are Al Smith, "Can We Make Room for the Refugees?," *New Outlook, 162* (1933), 9–10, and Louis Adamic, "America and the Refugees," *Public Affairs Pamphlet No. 29* (1939). Henry Pratt Fairchild best stated the case against the entry of refugees in "Should the Jews Come In?" *New Republic, 97* (1939), 344, and "New Burdens for America," *Forum, 101* (1939), 316–18.

GENERAL WORKS

The most thorough treatment of the refugee situation from an international standpoint is Sir John Hope Simpson, *The Refugee Problem* (London, 1939). Harold Fields, *The Refugee in the United States* (New York, 1938) is an early and incomplete study of the assimilation of refugees, while Maurice Davie, *Refugees in America* (New York, 1947) is a definitive treatment of the same subject.

VI. *Displaced Persons Legislation*

GOVERNMENTAL SOURCES

The extensive set of hearings on the original Stratton bill, "Permitting Admission of 400,000 Displaced Persons into the United States," *Hearings before the Subcommittee on Immigration and Naturaliza-*

tion of the House Committee on the Judiciary, 80th Congress, 1st Session (Washington, 1947), is basic to any study of the displaced persons issue. These hearings contain a wealth of information on the evolution of the displaced persons problem as well as the differing viewpoints on how it should be solved. "Displaced Persons and the International Refugee Organization," *Report of a Special Subcommittee of the House Committee on Foreign Affairs,* 80th Congress, 1st Session (Washington, 1949) is very favorable toward the displaced persons, while the report of the Revercomb subcommittee's investigation, "Displaced Persons in Europe," *Senate Report No. 950,* 80th Congress, 2d Session (Washington, 1948), is much less sympathetic. The latter report contains an analysis of the Senate bill to admit displaced persons. The Fellows bill is described in "Emergency Displaced Persons Admission Act," *House Report No. 1854,* 80th Congress, 2d Session (Washington, 1948). The conference report, "Authorizing for a Limited Period of Time the Admission into the United States of Certain European Displaced Persons for Permanent Residence," *House Report No. 2410,* 80th Congress, 2d Session (Washington, 1948) gives a full description of the compromise bill that was enacted by Congress.

On the movement to liberalize the legislation adopted in 1948, two hearings are significant, "To Amend the Displaced Persons Act of 1948," *Hearings before Subcommittee No. 1 of the House Committee on the Judiciary,* 81st Congress, 1st Session (Washington, 1949) and "Displaced Persons," *Hearings before the Subcommittee on Amendments to the Displaced Persons Act of the Senate Committee on the Judiciary,* 81st Congress, 1st and 2d Sessions (Washington, 1950). "Amending the Displaced Persons Act of 1948," *House Report No. 581,* 81st Congress, 1st Session (Washington, 1949) and "Amending the Displaced Persons Act of 1948," *Senate Report No. 1237,* 81st Congress, 2d Session (Washington, 1950) state the viewpoints of both the majority and the minority within the Congressional Judiciary committees. An analysis of the final bill is given in the conference report, "Amending the Displaced Persons Act of 1948," *House Report No. 2187,* 81st Congress, 2d Session (Washington, 1950).

"Displaced Persons and Their Resettlement in the United States," *House Report No. 1507,* 81st Congress, 2d Session (Washington, 1950) evaluates sympathetically the results of the displaced persons program. A special investigation conducted by a subcommittee of the House Judiciary Committee, "Expellees and Refugees of German Ethnic Origin," *House Report No. 1841,* 81st Congress, 2d Session (Washington, 1950) contains a great deal of information on the *Volksdeutsche.*

The administration of the displaced persons program is described in the U.S. Displaced Persons Commission, *Semi-Annual Reports to the President and to the Congress* (Washington, 1949–51). The final report of this body, *Memo to America: the DP Story* (Washington, 1952), summarizes the entire program and contains a brief résumé of its legislative history.

GENERAL WORKS

Eugene Kulischer deals with the displaced persons issue against the broad background of long-range European demographic trends in a brilliant study, *Europe on the Move* (New York, 1948). Jacques Vernant, *The Refugee in the Post-War World* (New Haven, 1953) describes the various categories of uprooted peoples and the help extended to them by the free countries.

VII. Postwar Policy and the McCarran Act

GOVERNMENTAL SOURCES

There is a series of committee hearings and reports dealing with the reversal of the Asiatic exclusion policy. The basic sources for the extension of quotas to China and India are "Repeal of the Chinese Exclusion Acts," *Hearings before the House Committee on Immigration and Naturalization*, 78th Congress, 1st Session (Washington, 1943); "To Grant a Quota to Eastern Hemisphere Indians," ibid., 79th Congress, 1st Session (Washington, 1945); "Repealing the Chinese Exclusion Laws," *House Report No. 732*, 78th Congress, 1st Session (Washington, 1943); and "Authorizing the Admission into the United States of Persons of Races Indigenous to India," *House Report No. 854*, 79th Congress, 1st Session (Washington, 1945). The hearing on the Judd bill, "Providing for Equality under Naturalization and Immigration Laws," *Hearings before the Subcommittee on Immigration and Naturalization of the House Committee on the Judiciary*, 80th Congress, 2d Session (Washington, 1948), contains the views of various groups on the complete reversal of the exclusion policy. A full description of this measure is given in "To Make Immigration Quotas Available to Asian and Pacific Peoples," *House Report No. 65*, 81st Congress, 1st Session (Washington, 1949).

The conflicting views on immigration policy in the immediate postwar years are revealed in the hearings conducted by the Dickstein investigating subcommittee, "Study of Problems Relating to Immigration and Deportation and Other Problems," *Hearings before Subcommittee I of the House Committee on Immigration and Naturalization*, 79th Congress, 1st Session (Washington, 1945). "Immigration and

Naturalization Laws and Problems," *House Report No. 1312,* 79th Congress, 1st Session (Washington, 1945) contains the conclusions and recommendations of this subcommittee.

"To Deny Admission to the United States of Certain Aliens and to Reduce Immigration Quotas," *Hearings before the House Committee on Immigration and Naturalization,* 79th Congress, 2d Session (Washington, 1946) provides information on the restrictionist attempt both to decrease quota immigration and to exclude former Nazis. The abortive bill to accomplish the latter objective is described in "Amending the Immigration Laws to Deny Admission to the United States of Certain Aliens," *House Report No. 2041,* 79th Congress, 2d Session (Washington, 1946). On the later movement to tighten up the immigration laws in regard to subversives, the need for more stringent exclusion of Communists is discussed in "Communist Activities among Aliens and National Groups," *Hearings before the Subcommittee on Immigration and Naturalization of the Senate Judiciary Committee,* 81st Congress, 1st Session (Washington, 1949). "Exclusion and Expulsion of Subversive Aliens from the United States," *Senate Report No. 2230,* 81st Congress, 2d Session (Washington, 1950) deals with the McCarran bill to exclude Communists and Fascists which was enacted as part of the Internal Security Act of 1950, described in "Protecting the Internal Security of the United States," *Senate Report No. 2369,* 81st Congress, 2d Session (Washington, 1950).

The key source for the study of the formulation of the McCarran Act is "The Immigration and Naturalization Systems of the United States," *Senate Report No. 1515,* 81st Congress, 2d Session (Washington, 1950). This extensive report contains both a summary of the investigation conducted by the McCarran subcommittee and the recommendations of this group which formed the basis for the omnibus bill. Equally important is the set of hearings held on the McCarran and Walter bills, "Revision of Immigration, Naturalization and Nationality Laws," *Joint Hearings before the Subcommittees of the Committees on the Judiciary,* 82d Congress, 1st Session (Washington, 1951), which reveals the views of the supporters and opponents of restriction. Two committee reports, "Revising the Laws Relating to Immigration, Naturalization, and Nationality," *House Report No. 1365,* 82d Congress, 2d Session (Washington, 1952) and "Revision of Immigration and Nationality Laws," *Senate Report No. 1137,* 82d Congress, 2d Session (Washington, 1952), provide further information on the McCarran and Walter bills. Both reports include minority views by the opponents of restriction on the committees.

The most severe criticisms of the McCarran bill came after it was passed. The *Hearings before the President's Commission on Immigration and Naturalization* (Washington, 1952) contain nearly 2,000 pages of testimony by representatives of groups interested in immigration, most of which is highly critical of the McCarran Act. The report of the President's Commission on Immigration and Naturalization, *Whom We Shall Welcome* (Washington, 1953), condemns the McCarran Act as discriminatory and recommends the abolition of the national origins quota system.

CONTEMPORARY ARTICLES AND BOOKS

Many articles appeared in 1942 and 1943 urging the repeal of the Chinese exclusion laws and the extension of a quota to China. Of these, the most significant is Charles Nelson Spinks, "Repeal Chinese Exclusion," *Asia and the Americas, 42* (1942), 92–4.

A publication of the Milbank Memorial Fund, *Postwar Problems of Migration* (New York, 1947) includes two articles bearing on immigration policy: E. P. Hutchinson, "The Present Status of Our Immigration Laws," pp. 82–94, and Warren Thompson, "The Demographic and Economic Implications of Larger Immigration," pp. 95–109. "Reappraising Our Immigration Policy," *Annals of the American Academy of Political and Social Science, 262* (1949), 1–192, contains a series of articles dealing with many aspects of the immigration problem. A concise statistical analysis of the effectiveness of the quota system in reducing immigration is given in Helen Eckerson and Gertrude Krichefsky, "Immigration Restriction in the United States," *Monthly Review of the Immigration and Naturalization Service, 4* (January 1947), 82–91.

The best statement of the antirestrictionist position on immigration issued in the postwar period is the report of the National Committee on Immigration Policy, William Bernard, ed., *American Immigration Policy—a Reappraisal* (New York, 1950).

GENERAL WORKS

Fred Riggs, *Pressures on Congress* (New York, 1950) is an excellent study of the repeal of the Chinese exclusion laws. Written as an analysis of pressure group techniques, this book is especially valuable for its treatment of the Citizens Committee to Repeal Chinese Exclusion. Two books have been written on immigration policy since the passage of the McCarran Act. Milton Konvitz, *Civil Rights in Immigration* (Ithaca, New York, 1953) is a scholarly appraisal of the nature of the present laws which makes no attempt to explore the factors involved in the formulation of policy. The author's strong bias against the McCarran Act mars his presentation, and the book is chiefly valuable as a statement of the antirestrictionist position on immigration policy. J. Campbell Bruce, *The Golden Door* (New York, 1954) is a journalistic condemnation of the McCarran Act which traces the impact of the law on individual immigrants. Highly partisan, this book urges a sweeping revision of the immigration laws.

INDEX

Date Due

MAR 11 '66		
MAY 12 '66		
MAY 12 '66		
MAR 4 6		
APR 3 '68		
OCT 15 '68		
DEC 10 '69		
MAR 20 71		
Apr 1		
APR 19 7		
MAR 12 7		
OC 5 '81		
NO 2 '81		
DE 14 '81		
NOV 29 '83		
NO 0 '85		
NOV 24 '85		
APR 19 '88		
🔲	PRINTED	IN U. S. A.